The Property of

Anton Schaberle

in

Ann Arbor Business-

College (Mich)

June, 3. 1867.

Aug 8 "

THE AMERICAN COMMERCIAL ARITHMETIC,

FOR THE USE OF

COMMERCIAL COLLEGES,

Private Students, Schools and Counting-Houses,

EMBRACING

AN EXTENSIVE COURSE BOTH IN THEORY AND PRACTICE

TOGETHER WITH

THE LAWS OF THE UNITED STATES RELATING TO INTEREST. DAMAGES ON BILLS, AND THE COLLECTING OF DEBTS,

BY

T. A. BRYCE, M.A., LL.D.,

AUTHOR OF TREATISES ON ALGEBRA AND GEOMETRY.

ADOPTED AND USED IN THE

ANN ARBOR BUSINESS COLLEGE.

ANN ARBOR, MICH.:

PUBLISHED BY A. C. PARSON, A.M.,

PRESIDENT, ANN ARBOR BUSINESS COLLEGE

1867.

PREFACE.

THOUGH elementary works on Arithmetic are in abundance, yet it seems desirable that there should be added to this an extensive treatise on the commercial rules, and commercial laws and usages.

It is not enough that the school-boy should be provided with a course suited to his age. There must be supplied to him something higher as he advances in age and progress, and nears the period when he is to enter on real business life.

The Author's aim has, therefore, been to combine these two objects, and to produce a work adequate to carry the learner from the very elements up to the highest rules required by those preparing for business. As the work proceeded, it was found necessary to extend the original programme considerably, and, therefore, also the limits of the book, so as to make it useful to all classes in the community.

In carrying out this plan, much care has been taken to unfold the theory of Arithmetic as a SCIENCE in as concise a manner as seemed consistent with clearness, and at the same time to show its applications as an ART. Every effort has been made to render the business part so copious and practical as to afford the young student ample information and discipline in all the principles and usages of commercial intercourse. For the same reason some articles on Commercial Law have been introduced, as it was a prominent part of the Author's aim to produce a work which should be found useful, not only in the class-room, and the learner's study, but also on the merchant's table, and the accountant's desk. The Author begs to tender his best thanks to J. Smith Homans, Esq., New York City, Editor and Proprietor of the "Banker's Magazine and Statistical Register," for the able manner in which he supplied this part of the work.

Throughout the work particular care has been taken not to enunciate any rule without explaining the *reason* of the operation, for, without a knowledge of the principle, the operator is a mere calculating machine that can work but a certain round, and is almost sure to be at fault when any novel case arises. The explanations are, of course, more or less the result of reading, but, nevertheless, they are mainly derived from personal study and experience in teaching. The great mass of the exercises are likewise entirely new, though the Author has not scrupled to make selections from some of the most approved works on the subject; but in doing so, he has confined himself almost entirely to such questions as are to be found in nearly all popular books, and which, therefore, are to be looked upon as the common property of science.

Algebraic forms have been avoided as much as possible, as being unsuited to a large proportion of those for whom the book is intended, and to many altogether unintelligible, and besides, those who understand Algebraic modes will have all the less difficulty in understanding the Arithmetical ones. Even in the more purely mathematical parts the subject has been popularized as much as possible.

In arranging the subjects it was necessary to follow a certain logical order, but the intelligent teacher and learner will often find it necessary to depart from that order. (See suggestions to teachers.)

Every one will admit that rules and definitions should be expressed in the smallest possible number of words, consistent with perspicuity and accuracy. Great pains have been taken to carry out this principle in every case. Indeed, it might be desirable, if practicable, not to enunciate any rules, but simply to illustrate each case by a few examples, and leave the learner to take the *principle* into his mind, as his rule, without the encumbrance of words.

Copious exercises are appended to each rule, and especially to the most important, such as Fractions, Analysis, Percentage, with its applications, &c. Besides these, there have been introduced extensive collections of mixed exercises throughout the body of the work, besides a large number at the end. The utility of such miscellaneous questions will be readily admitted by all, but the *reason* why they are of so much importance seems strangely overlooked or misunderstood even by writers on the subject. They are spoken of as *review* exercises, but their great value depends on something still more important. An illustration will best serve here.

A class is working questions on a certain rule, and each member of the class has just heard the rule enunciated and explained, and therefore readily applies it. So far one important object is attained, viz., freedom of operation. But something more is necessary. The

SUGGESTIONS TO TEACHERS.

THE author would first refer to the remark made in the Preface that he does not expect that the Teacher will follow the logical order adopted in the book, and even advises that he should not do so in many cases. He knows by experience that the same order does not suit all students any more than the same medical treatment suits all patients. The coure requires to be varied according to age, ability and acquirements. The greatest difficulties generally present themselves at the earliest stages. What more serious difficulty, for example, has a child to encounter than the learning of the alphabet? Though this is perhaps the extreme case, yet others will be found to be in proportion. For beginners, therefore, we recommend the following course.

Let the elementary rules be carefully explained and illustrated by *simple examples,* and the pupil shown how to work easy exercises; this done, let the whole be reviewed; and exercises of a more difficult kind proposed. The decimal coinage should then be taken up. In explaining this part of the subject the teacher ought to notice carefully that the operations in this case differ in no way from those already gone through in reference to whole numbers, except in the preserving of the mark that separates the cents from the dollars, usually called the decinal point. The next step ought to be the whole subject of denominate numbers, and in illustration and application, the rule of practice. After a thorough review of all the ground now gone over, Simple Proportion may be entered upon, using such questions as do not involve Fractions. Then, after a course of Fractions has been gone through, Proportion should be reviewed, and questions which involve Fractions proposed. After this it will generally be found desirable to study Percentage, with its applications.

The order in which the rest of the course shall be taken is comparatively unimportant, as the student has now realized a capital on which he can draw upon for any purpose. The author would, in the strongest manner possible, impress on the minds of teachers the great utility of frequent reviews, and especiallv of constant exercise in the addition of money columns.

by that of Decimals. Barter, too, has been passed by, as questions of that class can easily be solved by the Rule of Proportion, which has been fully explained.

The subject of Analysis has been gone into at considerable length, and it is hoped that the new manner in which the explanations and solutions are presented, and the extensive collection of exercises appended, will contribute to make this a valuable part of the treatise.

The view given of Decimal Fractions seems the only true one, and calculated to give the student clear notions regarding the nature of the notation, as a simple extension of the common Arabic system, and also appropriate to show the convenience and utility of Decimals. The distinction beeween *Decimals* and *Decimal Fractions* has been ignored as being " A distinction without a difference." *Decimals* is merely a short way of writing *Decimal Fractions* ; thus, .7 is merely a convenient mode of writing $\frac{7}{10}$. These differ in form only, but otherwise are as perfectly identical as $\frac{3}{4}$ and $\frac{6}{8}$.

The contracted methods of Multiplication and Division will be found, after some practice, extremely useful and expeditious in Decimals expressed by long lines of figures.

The averaging of Accounts and Equations of Payments, Cash Balance and Partnership Settlements, have been introduced as essential parts of a commercial education, and, it is hoped, will form a most important and useful study for those preparing for business, and probably a safe guide to many in business who have not systematically studied the subject.

SUGGESTIONS TO TEACHERS.

THE author would first refer to the remark made in the Preface that he does not expect that the Teacher will follow the logical order adopted in the book, and even advises that he should not do so in many cases. He knows by experience that the same order does not suit all students any more than the same medical treatment suits all patients. The coure requires to be varied according to age, ability and acquirements. The greatest difficulties generally present themselves at the earliest stages. What more serious difficulty, for example, has a child to encounter than the learning of the alphabet? Though this is perhaps the extreme case, yet others will be found to be in proportion. For beginners, therefore, we recommend the following course.

Let the elementary rules be carefully explained and illustrated by *simple examples*, and the pupil shown how to work easy exercises; this done, let the whole be reviewed; and exercises of a more difficult kind proposed. The decimal coinage should then be taken up. In explaining this part of the subject the teacher ought to notice carefully that the operations in this case differ in no way from those already gone through in reference to whole numbers, except in the preserving of the mark that separates the cents from the dollars, usually called the decinal point. The next step ought to be the whole subject of denominate numbers, and in illustration and application, the rule of practice. After a thorough review of all the ground now gone over, Simple Proportion may be entered upon, using such questions as do not involve Fractions. Then, after a course of Fractions has been gone through, Proportion should be reviewed, and questions which involve Fractions proposed. After this it will generally be found desirable to study Percentage, with its applications.

The order in which the rest of the course shall be taken is comparatively unimportant, as the student has now realized a capital on which he can draw upon for any purpose. The author would, in the strongest manner possible, impress on the minds of teachers the great utility of frequent reviews, and especiallv of constant exercise in the addition of money columns.

To make the exercises under each rule of progressive difficulty, as far as possible, has been an object kept constantly in view, as also to give each exercise the semblance of a real question, for all persons, especially the young, take greater interest in exercises that assume the form of reality than in such as are merely abstract; and, besides, this is a preparatory exercise to the application of the rules afterwards. At every stage the greatest care should be taken that the learner thoroughly understands the meaning of each rule, and the conditions of each question and the terms in which it is expressed, before he attempts to solve it.

The Teacher should not always be talking or working on the black-board; he should require the pupils to speak a good deal in answer to questions, and also work much on their slates, and each in his turn on the board for illustration to the rest.

Finally, it is suggested to every Teacher to keep constantly before his mind both of the two chief works he has to accomplish.

First, the developement of the mental powers of his pupil; and, *secondly*, imparting to him such knowledge as he will require to use when he enters upon life, either as a professional man, or a merchant or clerk. Some seem to consider these two objects incompatible, as if taking up time in mental training left insufficient time for the imparting of actual knowledge. This is a palpable errror, for the more the mental powers are cultivated, the more readily and rapidly will any species of knowledge be apprehended, and the more surely, too, will it be retained when it has been mastered. Mental culture is at once the foundation and the means; the other is the superstructure raised on that foundation and by that means; or it may be compared to a great capital judiciously embarked in trade, and often turned, and therefore yielding good. profits. It frequently happens, however, from the peculiar circumstances of individuals and families, and even communities, that young men require to be hurried into business, so as to be able to support themselves; but even in such cases the desired object will be much more readily and securely attained by such a course than by what is usually and not inappropriately called "*Cramming*." Every effort has been made to give to this book the character here recommended, especially in the explanatory parts.

SUGGESTIONS TO COMMERCIAL STUDENTS.

THE foregoing suggestions are addressed directly to the Teacher, but a careful consideration of them by the Student will, it is hoped, be found highly profitable. A few additional hints are subjoined for the benefit of those seeking a liberal and practical commercial education.

As in all branches, so in Arithmetic, it is of the utmost consequence to digest the rules of the art thoroughly, and store them in the memory, to be reproduced when required, and applied with accuracy. But this is not enough; something more is needed by the Student. To be an eminent accountant he must acquire rapidity of operation. Accuracy, it is true, should be attained first, especially as it is the direct means of arriving at readiness and rapidity. Accuracy may be called the foundation, readiness and rapidity the two wings of the superstructure. Either of these acquirements is indeed valuable in itself, but it is the combination of them that constitutes real effective skill, and makes the possessor relied upon, and looked up to in mercantile circles. Some one may ask, "How are these to be acquired?" The answer is as simple as it is undeniably true; *only by extensive practice*, not in the counting-house or warehouse, indeed, though these will improve and mature them, but in the school and college, so that you may *take* them with you to the business office when you go to your first day's duty. *Go prepared* is a maxim that all intelligent business men will affirm. Be so prepared that you will not keep your customers waiting restlessly in your office or warehouse while you are puzzling through the account you are to render to him, but strive rather to surprise him by having your bill ready so soon.

Another important help to the attaining of this rapidity, as noticed in the note at foot of page 18, is not to use the *tongue* in calculating but the *eye* and the *mind.*

Nor should the course of self-discipline end here. To be an expert accountant even, is but one part, though an important one of a qualification for business. Study Commercial geography—commercial and international relations—political economy—tariffs, &c., &c.

Study *even politics*, not for their own sake but on account of the manner in which they affect trade and commerce.

Do not, except in the case of some serious difficulty, indulge in the indolent habit of asking your teacher or fellow student to work the question for you; work it out yourself—rely upon your self, and aim at the freedom and correctness which will give you confidence in yourself, or rather in your powers and acquirements. Another caution will not be out of place. Many students follow the practice of keeping the text book beside them to see what the answer is; this has the same effect as a *leading question* in an examination, being a guide to the *mode* by seeing the *result*. Study and use the *mode* to come at the *result*; gain that knowledge of principles and correctness of operation that will inspire the confidence that your answer is correct without knowing what answer the text book or the teacher may assign to it.

There are two things of such constant occurrence and requiring such extreme accuracy that they must be specially mentioned,—they are the addition of money columns and the making of Bills of Parcels. Too much care and practice can scarcely be bestowed on these.

TABLE OF CONTENTS.

ARITHMETIC

ARTICLE 1.—ARITHMETIC treats of numbers in theory and practice. In relation to theory it is a science, and in relation to practice it is an art.

All computations are made by fixing on a certain quantity, called a unit, or one, and repeating that unit any required number of times. Various units are selected, according to the nature and extent of the quantity or space to be measured. For example, in measuring length or distance, if the extent is small, such as the length of a pane of glass, we select a small unit, called an inch, and repeating that unit any required number of times, say twelve, we say the pane is twelve inches long,—if a more extended space is to be measured, it is convenient to adopt a larger unit,—thus, if we wish to measure the length of a desk, we should probably select a unit called a foot, equal to twelve of the preceding units,—if we wish to measure the length of a room, we should select a still larger unit, called a yard, equal to three of the last,—again, if we wish to measure the length of a field, we should adopt a unit equal to five and a-half of the last, and called a perch or rod,—if we wish to note the distance between New York and Buffalo, we have recourse to a still larger unit, called a mile, and equal to three hundred and twenty of the last,—finally, when astronomers are estimating the distance of any planet, say the earth, from the sun, they generally use a unit equal to a million of the last-mentioned, and they say that the earth is ninety-five millions of miles from the sun, but they simply note the distance as ninety-five; and in the same manner they mark the distance of Venus as sixty-nine, meaning in both cases that each unit is a million of miles. A similar illustration may be applied to every kind or measurement.

The symbols or characters now almost universally used to denote quantity or magnitude, are the Arabic figures, or digits, 1, 2, 3, 4, 5, 6, 7, 8, 9, 0. These, by various combinations, can be made to represent any quantity or magnitude whatsoever. The first nine are called significant figures, because they always denote some real quantity,—the last, called nought (often improperly ought,) or cipher, or zero, simply indicates the absence of any significant figure.

NUMERATION.

2.—NUMERATION is the mode of marking and reading off any line of figures that has been written down, so as to ascertain its value readily and express that value in words. For this purpose every such line is divided into sets or lots of three figures each, counting from right to left, and each set is called a period,—thus, 888888888 forms three periods by marking the figures in threes from right to left by a character of the same form as the comma in composition,—thus, 888,888,888. The first period is called the period of units, the second the period of thousands, the third the period of millions, and so on,—billions, trillions, quadrillions, &c., &c., to any required extent, which seldom exceeds millions.

The first figure of each period denotes units* of that period, the second tens, and the third hundreds of that period. Thus, in the example given above, the first figure denotes eight units in the period of units, or eight ones, or, as it is usually read, simply eight; so, also, the fourth denotes eight units in the period of thousands; or eight times one thousand, or eight thousands; the seventh figure again denotes eight units in the period of millions, or eight times one million, or eight millions; again, the second, fifth, and eighth figures denote tens in the period of units, thousands and millions, respectively; lastly, the third, sixth and ninth figures denote hundreds in the periods of units, thousands and millions, respectively. Such a line, then, as 888,888,888 is read eight hundred and eigety-eight millions, eight hundred and eighty-eight thousands, eight hundred and eighty-eight.

Every period but the last must have three figures. Thus, in the line 43,279,865 the first and second periods have three digits each, units, tens and hundreds, but the third has only two, units and tens, but no hundreds, and therefore is read forty-three millions, two hundred and seventy-nine thousands, eight hundred and sixty-five.

RULE FOR NUMERATION.

Beginning at the right, count off periods of three digits each till not more than three are left; then read off each period from left to

---

* It is somewhat awkward that the term units is used for two purposes, viz.: as the name of the first period and also as the name of the first figure of each period. Though we cannot well change what usage has so long established, yet the teacher may obviate the difficulty by varying the expression occasionally, if not habitually, saying, E. G., units in the *unity* period, or the *place* of units in the units period.

right by naming as many hundreds, tens and units as each contains, and adding at the end of each period its proper name. The name of the unity period is usually omitted. When a cipher occurs no mention is made of that place in the period, but the cipher is counted as a digit; thus, in the line 360,708,091 each cipher is counted a digit, but the reading is three hundred and sixty millions, seven hundred and eight thousands and ninety-one.

EXERCISES

Divide into periods and read the following lines:

1.—586729341	2.—976852734	3.—2178427385
4.—92879357485	5.—4638709120	6.—1111111111111111
7.—2822828228288	8.—10904870	9.—1010101010101

NOTATION.

3.—NOTATION is the mode of expressing any quantity or magnitude by the combination of conventional symbols or characters. Thus, by the Roman notation, the letter I. stands for *one*, II. for *two*, X. for *ten*, &c.; thus, XII. stands for *one* ten and *two* units. By the Arabic notation, any digit standing alone, as 5 in the margin, denotes simply five units, but if another digit (5) be placed to the right of it, then the new 5 denotes units and the other 5 becomes tens, so that appending a second digit makes the first one ten times its original value; again, if another digit (5) be subjoined, it takes the place of units, and the 5 next to it becomes tens and the third becomes hundreds, so that each of them has ten times the value in the third line that it had in the second; so also, if another digit (5) be added, each of the three to the left of it will have ten times the value that it had in the third line, and so on. Universally, every digit placed to the right makes every one to the left ten times its previous value.

5
55
555
5555

The use of the tenth of the Arabic characters, the cipher (0) will be made more clear by the rule of notation than by numeration. If I am counting my cash and find that I have *eight* ten-dollar bills, and *eight* one-dollar bills, it is plain from Art. 2 that if I write 8 alone this must represent the one-dollar bills, and to represent the ten-dollar bills along with the one-dollar bills I must write 88, for the figure to the left being ten times that to the right, will stand correctly for the ten-dollar bills, just as that to the right, being in the units' place, stands for the one-dollar bills.—But if I have no one-dollar bills and write 8, this would stand for only one-dollar bills, and hence the necessity for introducing a non-significant character and writing 80, for though the cipher represents no quantity, yet by being put in the place of units it throws the 8 to be in the place of tens, and therefore the 8 now stands fitly for the *eight* ten-dollar bills, and is written $80.—Again, if I find that I have *two* one-hundred-dollar bills, *six* one-dollar bills, but *no* ten-dollar bills, and I write only 26, this would be plainly incorrect, for the 2 would stand for ten-dollar bills only, but by inserting a zero mark between the figures I throw the 2 into the place of hundreds, and $206 represents correctly that I have *two* one-hundred dollar bills, and *six* one-dollar bills, but *no* ten-dollar bills. The superiority of this simple system over the cumbrous Roman one will be manifest from its simplicity and brevity by writing *eighty-eight* according to both systems—thus: LXXXVIII. and 88.

RULE FOR NOTATION.

Write the significant figures of the first period named in their proper places, filling up any places *not named* with ciphers, just as if you were writing the units period with nothing to follow; then, to indicate that something *is* to follow, place a comma to the right, and do the same for every period down to units, inclusive. For example, teacher says: "Write down one hundred and six millions;" pupil writes 106 and pauses; teacher adds, "ninety thousand;" pupil fills up thus: 106,090, and pauses; teacher concludes: "and eighteen;" pupil completes 106,090,018. If the teacher should say sixteen millions and the pupil write 016, the cipher would be manifestly superfluous, as it has no effect on figures placed to the right of it, but only on those placed to the left.

EXERCISES.

Write in figures and read the following quantities:

1. Ten millions, seven thousand and eleven.
2. Ninety billions, seven thousand and ten.
3. Eighteen millions, sixty thousand and nine hundred.
4. Forty thousand and nine hundred.

5. Eighty-seven millions and one.

6. Ninety thousand, seven hundred and eight.

7. Eleven millions, eight hundred thousand and twenty-four.

8. Six hundred and seven thousand and ninety-seven.

9. Eight hundred and seventy billions, sixty thousand and eighteen.

10. Eleven billions, eleven millions, eleven thousand and eleven.

AXIOMS.

4.—AXIOMS used in the sequel:

I. Things that are equal to the same thing, or to equals, are equal.

II. If equals be added to equals, the wholes are equal.

Corollary.—If equals be multiplied by the same, the products are equal.

III. If equals be taken from equals, the remainders are equal.

Cor.—If equals be divided by the same, the quotients are equal.

IV. The whole is greater than its part

Cor.—The whole is equal to all its parts taken together.

V. Magnitudes which coincide, or occupy the same or equal spaces, are equal.

N. B.—This axiom is modified by, but still is the principle of, all business transactions, purchases, sales, barters, exchanges, &c., &c., where the articles traded in are not *equals*, but *equivalents*.

ADDITION.

5.—ADDITION is the mode of combining two or more numbers into one. The operation depends on axiom II. The result is called the sum. Thus: $8+$9+$6=$23. The sign plus (+) indicates addition.

To illustrate the operation, let it be required to find the sum of the five numbers of dollars noted in the margin. First, the numbers are placed so that those of the same *name* are in vertical columns, *i. e.*, units under units, tens under tens, &c. Next, we find that the sum of the units' column is (Ax. IV., *Cor.*) 27, *i. e.*, *two* tens and *seven* units. Next, we find that the sum of the tens' column is 35, but, as it is the *tens'*

$287654
758287
612873
494768
836195
____

27
350
2400
27000
260000
2700000
$2989777

column, we write (Art. 3) 350; in the same manner we find the sum of the hundreds' column to be 2400; the sums of the others will be seen by inspection. Having thus obtained the sum of each column, each being *summed* as if *units*, but placed in succession towards *the left* (by Arts. 2 and 5), we now take the sum of the partial results, which (Axiom IV. *Cor.*) is the sum of the whole, viz.: $2,969,777. In practice the operation is much abbreviated in the following manner:—When the units' column has been added, and we find the sum to be 27, *i. e.*, 7 units and 2 tens, we write down the 7 units under the units' column, and add up (Art. 3) the 2 tens with the tens' column, and we find the sum is 35 *tens*, *i. e.*, 5 *tens* and 3 *hundreds*, and we place the 5 *tens* under the *tens'* column, and add up the 3 *hundreds* with the *hundreds'* column, and so on.

$287654
758287
612873
494768
836195
$2989777

The transferring of the tens, obtained by adding the *units'* column to the *tens'* column, and the *hundreds* obtained by adding the *tens'* column to the *hundreds'* column, &c., &c., is called carrying. In all such operations the learner should carefully bear in mind the principle explained in Art. 3., that every figure to the left is ten times the value that it would have if one place farther to the right.*

EXERCISES.

Find the sums of the following quantities:

(1)	(2)	(3)	(4)
895763		99876	
49176	987654231	63879	89765324
283527	123456789	54387	42356798
659845	908760504	789	56798423
7984	890705063	137568	23567989
31659	759086391	278652	79842356
968438	670998767	85945	65324897
2896392	4340661745	721096	357655787

* We would strongly recommend every one who wishes to become an expert accountant, to avoid the common practice of drawling up a column of figures in the manner that may be sufficiently illustrated by the adding of the units' column of the above example. Never say 5 and 8 are 13; 13 and 3 are 16: 16 and 7 are 23; 23 and 4 are 27; but run up your column thus: 5, 13, 16, 23,

(5)	(6)	(7)	(8)
			738
			659
			471
78563			897
47986	12345		658
5798	67890	918273	856
19843	98765	651928	789
56479	43219	374859	978
28795	87654	263748	654
897	32169	597485	999
1984	78912	986879	888
68195	65439	98765	777
3879	98765	9876	666
698	43288	987	555
5879	77877	456879	897
17985	98989	345678	978
336981	**805312**	**4705357**	**12460**

(9)	(10)	(11)	(12)
189			1298
976	98	47	764
85	89	96	5837
73	76	83	6495
338	67	59	789
793	281	74	638
49	592	82	546
75	678	97	98
218	58	68	475
365	67	75	394
113	98	49	89
279	149	76	157
67	67	54	638
76	54	78	594
84	72	69	789
1379	298	37	114
5159	**2744**	**1044**	**19715**

27, for that is the mode to secure both rapidity and accuracy. The same remark will apply equally to multiplication, and therefore to every arithmetical operation. To enforce this advice let us add a simple example to caution the student before he approaches multiplication. In multiplying 497 by 6, avoid the tediousness of saying 6 times 7 is 42—2 and carry 4—6 times 9 is 54, and 4 is 58—8 and carry 5—6 times 4 is 24, and 5 is 29 ; but practice the eye, aided by the memory, to take in at a glance 6 times 7 is 42, &c.—The quick operator uses the eye, and not the tongue.

There is no method of proving the correctness of any addition with positive certainty, but a very convenient mode of checking is to add each column both upwards and downwards. Another mode is, to add by parts and take the sum of those. This is a very secure method in the case of long columns, but not so ready as the former. If the same result is found by each method, the sum may be accounted correct.

SUBTRACTION.

6. SUBTRACTION is the converse of addition, *i. e.*, it is the mode of finding the difference between two numbers, or, in other words, the excess of one number above another. The number to be subtracted is called the subtrahend, and that from which it is to be taken the minuend, and the result is called the remainder, difference or excess. The sign used for subtraction is a line (—) called *minus*, or less. Let it be required to find the difference between $578643957 and $235412712. Having placed them in vertical columns, as in addition, it is obvious that 2 units taken from 7 units will leave 5 units, and that 1 ten taken from 5 tens will leave 4 tens, and so on. But if it is required to find the excess of $513674208 above $347895319, we find that each figure of the subtrahend, except the last, counting from right to left, is greater than the corresponding one of the minuend, and therefore, to find the correct difference, we have recourse to a simple artifice, which is deduced from the principle of the notation, and may be illustrated in the following manner:— Taking the question in the margin, we are first required to subtract 7 units from 3 units. Now, though the algebraic notation furnishes the means of noting the difference directly, the ordinary arithmetical form does not, but still it furnishes the means of doing it indirectly. By Art. 3 each figure to the left is ten times the value of the next to its right, therefore we take one of the 3 tens and call it ten units, and add it to the 3 units, and thus we have 13 units, which let us enclose in a parenthesis or bracket, thus: (13), to indicate that the whole quantity, 13, is to occupy the units' place; when *one* of the *three* tens has been thus transferred to the units'

```
578643957
235412712
---------
343231245
```

```
333,333
177,777
-------
155,556
```

```
2(12)(12)(12)(12)(13)
1  7   7   7   7   7
---------------------
1  5   5   5   5   6
```

place, only *two* tens remain in the place of tens, and we are now required to take 7 tens from 2 tens; to do this we have recourse to the same artifice, by calling one of the hundreds *tens*, which gives 10 tens and 2 tens, and so on to the end, the last 3 necessarily becoming 2. We can now subtract 7 from 13, &c., &c. This mode of resolution depends on the corollary to Axiom IV. The parts into which the whole is virtually resolved are shown in the margin. This artifice is popularly called borrowing. In practice the resolution can be effected mentally as we proceed, and as each figure from which we *borrow* is diminished by unity, it is usual to count it as it stands, and to compensate for this to increase the one below it by one, for, as in the example, 7 from 12 is the same as 8 from 13, and 2 from 3 is the same as 1 from 2. We are now prepared to answer the proposed question, as annexed, and we say 9 from 8, we cannot, and there are no tens to borrow from, we therefore take one of the hundreds and call it 10 *tens*, and one of the tens and call it 10 units, which with 8 units makes 18 units, and we take 9 from 18 and 9 remain. We have now only 9 tens left, but we reckon them as ten, and to compensate for the surplus ten, we reckon the 1 below as 2, and say 2 from 10 and 8 remain. We proceed thus to the end, and find the whole remainder to be $165778889.

```
200000
120000
 12000
  1200
   120
    13
------
333333
```

```
$513674208
$347895319
----------
$165778889
```

EXERCISES. REMAINDERS.

1.—From	847639021	take	476584359=	371054662.
2. "	1010305061	"	670685093=	339619968.
3. "	59638743	"	18796854=	40841889.
4. "	7813257	"	3745679=	4067578.
5. "	111111111	"	98657293=	12453818.

In Subtraction, as in Addition, we have no method of proof that arrives at positive certainty, but either of the two following methods may be generally relied upon.

1.—Add the remainder and subtrahend, and if the sum is equal to the minuend, it is to be presumed that the work is correct.

2.—Subtract the remainder from the minuend, and if this second remainder is the same as the subtrahend, the work may be accounted correct.

MULTIPLICATION.

7.—MULTIPLICATION may be simply defined by saying that it is a short method of performing addition, when all the quantities to be added are the same or equal. Thus: 6+6+6+6+6+6+6+6, means that eight sixes are to be added together, or that six is to be repeated as often as there are units in eight, and we say that 8 times 6 is 48, and write it thus: $8\times 6=48$. So also 8+8+8+8+8+8 gives 48. So that 6.8=8.6=48, and thus we can construct a multiplication table. The number to be repeated is called the multiplicand, and the one that shows how often it is to be repeated is called the multiplier, and the result is called the product, or what is produced, and hence the multiplier and multiplicand are also called the factors or makers, or producers, and the operation may be called *finding* a product when the factors are given. Hence also the mode of carrying is the same in multiplication as in addition.

MULTIPLICATION TABLE.

Twice	3 times	4 times	5 times	6 times	7 times
1 is 2	1 is 3	1 is 4	1 is 5	1 is 6	1 is 7
2 — 4	2 — 6	2 — 8	2 — 10	2 — 12	2 — 14
3 — 6	3 — 9	3 — 12	3 — 15	3 — 18	3 — 21
4 — 8	4 — 12	4 — 16	4 — 20	4 — 24	4 — 28
5 — 10	5 — 15	5 — 20	5 — 25	5 — 30	5 — 35
6 — 12	6 — 18	6 — 24	6 — 30	6 — 36	6 — 42
7 — 14	7 — 21	7 — 28	7 — 35	7 — 42	7 — 49
8 — 16	8 — 24	8 — 32	8 — 40	8 — 48	8 — 56
9 — 18	9 — 27	9 — 36	9 — 45	9 — 54	9 — 63
10 — 20	10 — 30	10 — 40	10 — 50	10 — 60	10 — 70
11 — 22	11 — 33	11 — 44	11 — 55	11 — 66	11 — 77
12 — 24	12 — 36	12 — 48	12 — 60	12 — 72	12 — 84

8 times	9 times	10 times	11 times	12 times
1 is 8	1 is 9	1 is 10	1 is 11	1 is 12
2 — 16	2 — 18	2 — 20	2 — 22	2 — 24
3 — 24	3 — 27	3 — 30	3 — 33	3 — 36
4 — 32	4 — 36	4 — 40	4 — 44	4 — 48
5 — 40	5 — 45	5 — 50	5 — 55	5 — 60
6 — 48	6 — 54	6 — 60	6 — 66	6 — 72
7 — 56	7 — 63	7 — 70	7 — 77	7 — 84
8 — 64	8 — 72	8 — 80	8 — 88	8 — 96
9 — 72	9 — 81	9 — 90	9 — 99	9 —108
10 — 80	10 — 90	10 —100	10 —110	10 —120
11 — 88	11 — 99	11 —110	11 —121	11 —132
12 — 96	12 —108	12 —120	12 —132	12 —144

Regarding the following part of this table, see suggestions to Teachers:

13 times	14 times	15 times	16 times	17 times	18 times	19 times
2 is 26	2 is 28	2 is 30	2 is 32	2 is 34	2 is 36	2 is 38
3 — 39	3 — 42	3 — 45	3 — 48	3 — 51	3 — 54	3 — 57
4 — 52	4 — 56	4 — 60	4 — 64	4 — 68	4 — 72	4 — 76
5 — 65	5 — 70	5 — 75	5 — 80	5 — 85	5 — 90	5 — 95
6 — 78	6 — 84	6 — 90	6 — 96	6 — 102	6 — 108	6 — 114
7 — 91	7 — 98	7 — 105	7 — 112	7 — 119	7 — 126	7 — 133
8 — 104	8 — 112	8 — 120	8 — 128	8 — 136	8 — 144	8 — 152
9 — 117	9 — 126	9 — 135	9 — 144	9 — 153	9 — 162	9 — 171

We have in the above table corrected the gross grammatical blunder so common of saying eight times two ARE sixteen.

When more than two factors are given, the operation is called continued multiplication, as $6 \times 3 \times 2 \times 5 = 180$.

When the factors consist of more figures than one, the most convenient mode of operation is that shown by the annexed example, where the multiplicand is first repeated 8 times, then 60 times, or which is the same thing 6 times when the first figure of the second line is placed under the second figure of the first line, *i. e.* (art. 2,) in the place of tens, and then the partial products are added, which (Ax. IV. Cor.) gives the full product. Hence we deduce the

```
 345186
    268
-------
2761488
2070916
690372
--------
92507848
```

RULE FOR MULTIPLICATION.

Place the multiplier under the multiplicand, units under units, tens under tens, &c., &c.,—commencing at the right, multiply each figure of the multiplicand by each figure of the multiplier in succession, placing the results in parallel lines, and units, tens, &c., in vertical columns,—add all the lines, and the sum of all the partial products will (Ax. IV. Cor.) be the whole product required.

As far as the learner has committed a multiplication table to memory, say to 12 times 12, the work can be done by a single operation.

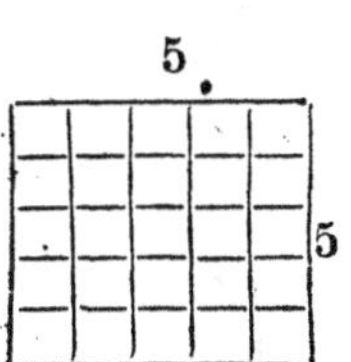

When any number is multiplied by itself, the product is called the square or second power of that number, and the product of three equal factors is called a cube or third power, the product of four equal factors the fourth power, &c., &c. The terms *square* and *cube* are derived from superficial and solid measurement. The annexed square has each of its sides divided into 5 equal parts, and it will be found on inspection that the whole figure contains

25 (=5×5) small squares, all equal in area, and having all their sides equal.—Hence because 5×5 represents the whole area, 25 is called the square of 5, or the second power of 5, because it is the product of the two equal factors 5 and 5. A cube is a solid body, the length, breadth and thickness of which are all equal, and hence, if these dimensions be each represented by 5, the whole solid will be represented by 5×5×5=125, which is therefore called the cube or third power of 5. The terms square and cube are often used without any reference to superficial and solid measure. For example, in lineal measure an expression for distance in a straight line is often called the square and cube of a certain number, thus: 81 is called the square, and 729 the cube of 9, although these are only used to show that the distance is not 9 in either case, but in the one 9×9, and in the other 9×9×9. In such cases the terms second and third power are therefore to be preferred, and since no solid can have more than three dimensions, we have no term corresponding to square and cube for the product of four or more equal factors, and therefore we are obliged to use the words fourth power, fifth power, &c., &c.

CONTRACTIONS AND PROOF.

There are many cases in which multiplication may be performed by contracted methods, but the utility of these, for the purposes of accuracy, is, at least, doubtful. The most secure method in the great majority of cases, is to follow the general rule. Multiplication by 10, 100, &c., is effected at once by adding a cipher for ten, two for 100, &c., &c. The following is, next to the above, the most safe and useful contraction that can be adopted. It is exhibited in the subjoined examples, but purposely without explanation, as an exercise for the learner's reflection:

ORDINARY METHOD.	CONTRACTED METHOD.	ORDINARY METHOD.	CONTRACTED METHOD.
35697×17	35697×17	35697×71	35697×71
17	249879	71	249879
249879	606849	35697	2534487
35697		249879	
606849		2534487	

The only practically useful proof of the correctness of the product, is the one subjoined, but even it, though it seldom fails, does not secure positive certainty:

Add together all the figures of each factor separately, rejecting 9 from all sums that contain it, and multiply the remainders together, rejecting every 9 from the result,—add the figures of the product in the same manner, and if the two remainders are equal, the work *may* be accounted as correct, but if they are not equal, the work *must* be wrong. The reason of this proof depends on the property of the number 9, that if any number be divided by 9, the remainder will be the same as if the sum of its digits were divided by 9.—Thus; 7422153÷9=824683+6, and the sum of the digits is 24, and 24÷9=2+6, *i. e.* 9 is contained in 24 twice with a remainder 6. Every 9 is rejected because 9 is contained in itself once evenly, and therefore cannot affect the remainder. Let it now be required to multiply 122 by 24. Now, 122=9×13+5, and 24=9×2+6, and if we multiply together the two factors thus resolved, we get 9×13×9×2+9×2×5+9×13×6+6×5, and since 9 is a factor of all but the last, the last only will give a remainder when divided by 9, and therefore the whole product will give the same remainder when divided by 9, as 6×5÷9, which gives the remiainder 3, for 6×5=30 and 30÷9 gives 3 with a remainder 3. To test this by trial, we find 122÷9=13 with a remainder 5, and 24÷9=2 with a remainder 6, and the product of these remainders is 6×5=30, and 30÷9=3 with a remainder 3. Again, 122×24=2928, and 2928÷9=325 with a remainder 3, as in the case of the factors.

EXERCISES.

1. 7896×5=39480.
2. 581967×8=4655736.
3. 938746×4=3754984.
4. 193784×7=1356488.
5. 391876×9=3526884.
6. 987456×6=5924736.
7. 496783×52=25832716.
8. 719864×43=30954152.
9. 375967×64=24061888.
10. 27859×29=807911.
11. 679854×83=56427882.
12. 759684×187=142060908.
13. 5372×1634=8777848

14. Find the second power of 389? Ans. 151321.

15. Find the third power of 538? Ans. 155720872.

16. Find the fourth power of 144? Ans. 429981696.

17. Find the cube of 99? Ans. 970299.

18. 5796 seamen have to be paid 169 dollars each; what is the amount of the treasury order for that purpose? Ans. $979,524.

19. A block of buildings is 87 feet long; 38 feet deep, and 29 feet high; how many cubic yards does it contain? Ans. $3550\frac{8}{9}$ cubic yards:

20. If 29 oil wells yield 19 gallons an hour each; how much will they all yield in a year? Ans. 201115 gals.

21. If the rate on each of 1597 houses be $19; what is the whole assessment? Ans. $30343.

22. If 1297 persons have paid up 9 shares each in a railway company, and each share is $15; what is the working capital of the company? Ans. $172095

DIVISION.

8.—DIVISION is the converse operation to multiplication. It is the mode of finding a required factor when a product and another factor are given. It bears the same relation to subtraction that multiplication does to addition, as will be seen below. By Ax. IV. Cor. we may resolve any complex quantity into its component parts; so division is resolving a certain quantity called the dividend into the number of parts indicated by another quantity called the divisor, (divider,) and the result is called the quotient (how often.) Let it be required to find how often 8 is contained in 279,856. We can resolve 279,856 as in the margin; then dividing the lines separately by 8, we obtain the partial quotients, the sum of which is the whole quotient. But this resolution may be done mentally as we proceed. We first see that 8 is not contained in 2, therefore we take 27, and find that 8 is contained in it 3 times, with a remainder 3; next combining this 3 with the next figure 9, we get 39, in which 8 is contained 4 times, with a remainder 7; combining this 7 with the next figure 8, we have 78, in which 8 is contained 9 times, with a remainder 6; combining this with the 5 following, we obtain 65, and 8 is contained in it 8 times, with a remainder 1, which combined with the 6 makes 16, and 8 is contained twice in 16. The correctness of the result may be tested by multiplying the quotient by the divisor. When the divisor consists of more than one figure, the learner must have recourse to a trial quotient, but after some practice he will have little difficulty in finding each figure by inspection.

8	240000	30000
	32000	4000
	7200	900
	640	80
	16	2
8	279856	34982

Let it be required to find how often 298 is contained in 431766.—The numbers being arranged in the convenient order indicated in the margin, we mark off to the right of the dividend blank spaces for the trial and true quotients. We readily see that 2 is contained *twice* in 4, but cannot so easily see whether the whole divisor 298 is contained twice in the same number of figures of the dividend, (viz. 431,) we therefore make trial, and place the 2 in the trial quotient, and multiply the divisor by 2 to find how much we shall have to subtract from 431. We find 298×2=596, larger than 431, and therefore we reject 2 and try 1. Now 298×1=298, less than 431, so we subtract and find a remainder of 133, and as this proves correct, we place the 1 obtained in the true quotient. We find our next partial divdend by writing 7, the next figure of the dividend after the remainder 133. Our experience of the first case suggests to us that though 2 is contained 6 times in 13, yet on multiplying something will have to be carried from the 98 which we expect will make the result too large, and therefore we at once try 5, but we find that 298×5=1490, which is larger than 1337, and so we try 4, and find 298×4=1192, which being less than 1337, we subtract and find a remainder of 145; and having placed the 4 in the true quotient, we bring down the next figure of the dividend, giving a partial dividend 1456. By inspection, as before, we see that 6 would be too large, owing to the carrying from 98, we try 5 and find 298×5=1490, which is larger than 1456; we try 4, and find 298×4=1192, which is less than 1456, so we subtract and find a remainder of 264. Having placed this 4 after the other 4 in the true quotient, we bring down 6, the last figure of the dividend, we try 9, and find 298×9=2682, which is greater than our last partial dividend, 2646; we try 8, and find 298×8=2384, and this being less than 2646, we subtract it from

```
298)431766(2.1.5.4.5.4.9.8 trials.
    298    1448 true quotient.
    ----
    1337
    1192
    ----
     1456
     1192
     ----
      2646
      2384
      ----
       262
      ----
       298
```

that number, and find a final remainder of 262, and close the question by entering 8 in the true quotient. The mode adopted to indicate that the remainder 262 still remains to be divided, which cannot be actually done, as it is less than the divisor, is to write the 298 below the 262, and draw a line between them, thus $\frac{262}{298}$, as also is seen in the margin. The resolution into partial dividends is also shown in the margin, where it will be seen that the partial dividends, including the remainder, make up the whole original dividend. So also the partial quotients are exhibited, making up the whole true quotient.

298	298000	=1000
	119200	= 400
	11920	= 40
	2384	= 8
Remainder	262	
		1448
Dividend	431766	

That the trial quotient is not a single number, like the true quotient, but merely a succession of detached numbers, used as separate trials, is indicated by placing a full point between each pair. When we have multiplied the divisor by any figure in the trial quotient, and subtracted the product from the partial dividend, should the remainder be greater than the divisor, we perceive that the trial figure is too small, and we must try a larger.

From these illustrations we can deduce a

RULE FOR DIVISION.

(1.) Place the given numbers in the same horizontal line, putting the divisor to the left of the dividend, with a vertical line between them, draw another vertical line to the right of the dividend, and enter the quotient, figure by figure as obtained, to the right of that line. (2.) Find by the principles of multiplication, how often the divisor is contained in the same number of figures of the dividend; place the number thus obtained in the quotient, and multiply the divisor by it, and subtract the product from the corresponding partial dividend. (3.) To the remainder annex the next figure of the dividend, and proceed as before, and so on till all the figures of the dividend are exhausted. (4.) Should there be a remainder, write it and the divisor after the quotient, thus: $\frac{\text{remainder,}}{\text{divisor,}}$

The divisor is often written to the right of the dividend, and the quotient written below it, a horizontal line separating the two.

EXAMPLE OF FORM 1

476)8593504(18053$\frac{276}{476}$.
476
———
3833
3808
———
2550
2380
———
1704
1428
———
276

EXAMPLE OF FORM 2.

1860904	87
174	21389$\frac{61}{87}$
120	
87	
339	
261	
780	
696	
844	
783	
61	

EXERCISES.

1. 1554768÷216=7198.
2. 31884470÷779=40930.
3. 57380625÷7575=7575.
4. I2810098÷732=17500$\frac{98}{732}$.
5. 9313702859÷4687319=1987$\frac{9}{4687319}$.
6. 449148410476÷73885246=6079$\frac{32}{73885246}$.
7. 109588282929÷1386=7902468$\frac{279}{1386}$.
8. 35676210832÷79094451=764095$\frac{1673087}{79094451}$.
9. 536818834÷907=591862.
10. 170064915561÷759=2240644479.
I1. 554270297961÷7584=73084163$\frac{5769}{7584}$.
12. 60435674634529÷764095=79094451$\frac{97684}{764095}$.

13. How many bags, each containing 87 pounds, will 24,853,464 pounds of flour fill? Ans. 285,672.

14. 857 houses pay annually a tax of $41136; what is the average on each per quarter? Ans. $12.

15. $9297175 of prize money are to be divided among 97,865 sailors; what is the share of each? Ans. $95.

16. 120,815,231 pounds of cotton are made up in 233,879 bales; how many pounds in each bale? Ans 89.

DIVISION.

1. 49687532÷2=24843766.
2. 57986327÷3=19328775$\frac{2}{3}$.

3. 87965328÷4=21991332.
4. 7963821÷5=1592764$\frac{1}{5}$.
5. 6875324÷6=1145887$\frac{1}{3}$.
6. 3987654÷7=569664$\frac{6}{7}$.
7. 19876532÷8=2484566$\frac{1}{2}$.
8. 2976854÷9=330761$\frac{5}{9}$.
9. 4967532÷10=496753$\frac{1}{5}$.
10. 46879352÷11=4261759$\frac{3}{11}$.
11. 18765314÷12=1563777$\frac{1}{6}$.
12. 78654246÷18=4369680$\frac{1}{3}$.
13. 75088÷52=1444.
14. 1674918÷189=8862.
15. 31884470÷779=40930.
16. 57380628÷7575=7575$\frac{3}{7575}$.
17. 554270292198÷7584=73084163$\frac{1}{1266}$.
18. 88789980979÷9584=9264397$\frac{131}{9584}$.
19. 102030429729÷123456=826452$\frac{95073}{12345}$.
20. 267817946000÷36500=10077204.

21. 497 men fell 163798 trees; how many does each fell on an average? Ans. 329.

22. If 148 houses pay a tax of $7844; what is the rate on each on an average? Ans. $53.

23. If $415143630 are levied from 4455 townships; what is the portion of each on an average? Ans. $93186.

24. How many lots of 6754 each are contained in 396809151372? Ans. 58763718.

25. What quotient will be obtained by dividing 961504803 twice by 987? Ans. 987.

9.—TABLES of MONEY, WEIGHTS & MEASURES.

BRITISH OR STERLING MONEY.

4 farthings, or 2 half pennies, are	1 penny (d.)
12 pence	1 shilling (s.)
20 shillings	1 pound (£)

DECIMAL COINAGE.

10 mills (M) are	1 cent (ct.)
10 cents	1 dime (d.)
10 dimes, or 100 cents	1 dollar ($)

AVOIRDUPOIS WEIGHT.

TABLE.

16 drams make	1 ounce,	marked	oz.
16 ounces	1 pound,	"	lb.
25 pounds	1 quarter,	"	qr.
4 quarters	1 hundredweight,	"	cwt.
20 cwt	1 ton,	"	t.

NOTE.—This weight is used in weighing heavy articles, as meat, groceries, vegetables, grain, etc.

TROY WEIGHT.

TABLE.

24 grains (grs.) make	1 pennyweight,	marked	dwt.
20 pennyweights	1 ounce,	"	oz.
12 ounces	1 pound,	"	lb.

NOTE.—Troy weight is used in weighing the precious metals and stones.

APOTHECARIES' WEIGHT.

TABLE.

20 grains (grs.) make	1 scruple,	marked	scr.
3 scruples	1 dram,	"	dr.
8 drams	1 ounce,	"	oz.
12 ounces	1 pound,	"	lb.

NOTE.—Apothecaries and Physicians mix their medicines by this weight, but they buy and sell by Avoirdupois.

PRODUCE WEIGHT-TABLE.

GRAIN.			SEEDS.		
Wheat	60	pounds to the bushel.	Clover	60	pounds to the bushel.
Oats	34	" " "	Flax	50	" " "
Corn	56	" " "	Timothy	48	" " "
Corn in cob	80	" " "	Hemp	54	" " "
Barley	48	" " "	Blue grass	14	" " "
Rye	56	" " "	Red Top	8	" " "
Buckwheat	48	" " "	Hungarian grass	48	" " "
Peas	60	" " "	Millet	48	" " "
Beans	60	" " "	Rape	50	" " "
Tares	60	" " "			

VEGETABLES.			VEGETABLES.		
Potatoes	60	pounds to the bushel.	Castor Beans	40	pounds to the bushel.
Parsnips	60	" " "	Malt	36	" " "
Carrots	60	" " "	DriedPeaches	33	" " "
Turnips	60	" " "	Dried Apples	22	" " "
Beets	60	" " "	Salt	56	" " "
Onions	60	" " "	Bran	20	" " "

LINEAR (OR LONG) AND SQUARE MEASURE.

LINEAR.		SQUARE.	
12 inches (in.) make	1 foot (ft.)	144 inches make	1 foot (ft.)
3 feet	1 yard (yd.)	9 feet	1 yard (yd.)
$5\frac{1}{2}$ yards	1 rod or perch.	$30\frac{1}{4}$ yards	1 rod (rd.)
40 rods	1 furlong (fur.)	40 rods	1 rood (r.)
8 furlongs	1 mile (m.)	4 roods	1 acre (a.)

LAND MEASURE.

LENGTH.		AREA.	
$7\frac{92}{100}$ inches make	1 link.	10,000 square links make	1 sq. chain
25 links	1 rod.	10 square chains	1 acre.
4 rods or 100 links	1 chain.		
80 chains	1 mile.		

In solid measure, *i. e.*, the measurement of solids, 1728 (the third power or cube of 12,) inches make 1 cubic foot, and 27 cubic feet (*i. e.* 3×3×3,) make 1 cubic yard. In measuring timber, 40 cubic feet of round timber make what is called a ton, and the same name is given to 50 feet of hewn timber. A cord of firewood is 8 feet long, 4 feet wide, and 4 feet high, and therefore its solid content is 8×4×4=128 feet.

Dry goods are measured by the yard, and fractions of a yard, the fractions used being one-quarter, one-eighth, and one-sixteenth.

MEASURES OF CAPACITY.

DRY.		LIQUID.	
2 pints make......	1 quart (qt.)	4 gills make.....	1 pint (pt.)
4 quarts	1 gallon (gal.)	2 pints.........	1 quart (qt.)
2 gallons..........	1 peck (pk.)	4 quarts	1 gallon (gal.)
4 pecks	1 bushel (bu.)	63 gallons........	1 hogshead (hhd.)
36 bushels	1 chaldron (ch.)	2 hogsheads	1 pipe (pi.)
The last is seldom used.		2 pipes	1 tun (tun.)

MEASURE OF TIME.		ANGULAR OR CIRCULAR MEASURE.	
60 seconds make.........	1 minute.	60 seconds make.	1 minute (1'.)
60 minutes..............	1 hour.	60 minutes	1 degree (1°.)
24 hours................	1 day.	360 degrees	1 complete circle.
365¼ days	1 year.		

There are other units applied to certain articles, e. g., 12 articles, one dozen; 20 articles, one score; 144 articles, one gross; 24 sheets of paper, one quire; 20 quires, one ream.—14lbs., one stone. This last weight is varied in many places, 15lbs. and 16lbs., according to the nature of the article sold, e. g.,—potatoes, as an allowance for earth adhering.

THE CALENDAR MONTHS OF THE YEAR.

January	has	31	days.	July..................	has	31	days
February	"	28	"	August	"	31	"
March	"	31	"	September............	"	30	"
April................	"	30	"	October..............	"	31	"
May	"	31	"	November............	"	30	"
June	"	30	"	December	"	31	"

Every fourth year is called Leap-year, in which February has 29 days.—If the last two figures denoting the year can be divided evenly by 4, it is Leap-year.

DECIMAL COINAGE.

10. THE principle of the decimal coinage is generally understood to depend on the rules of decimal fractions; but as it is merely a separate and co-ordinate result of the common system of notation, we may explain it here, independently of the theory of decimal fractions.

We have already explained, that according to the Arabic notation, each digit has one-tenth the value that it would have if situated one place farther to the left. Thus, in the number 88, the digit to the right expresses 8 units, while that to the left expresses 8 tens. Now we cannot have any integer less than unity, but we may have to make calculations respecting quantities less than the unit under consideration, *e. g.*, in calculating by dollars, we may have to take cents into account, and as the cent is a sub-division of the unit, a dollar, some new character must be introduced to indicate this transition from the integral unit to a part of it. This is done very simply by interposing a mark like the period or full point (.) in printing.—This is usually called the decimal point, though it sometimes gets the vague and awkward name of the separatrix. This simple but admirable contrivance is ascribed to one Stevinus or Stevens, of the Netherlands, who gave his suggestion to the public about the year 1585. Its excellence consists in its being simply an extension of the common notation. The original system marks only the repetition of the unit of measure,—this applies the same principle to the sub-division of the unit into parts. To explain this, we have only to carry out the illustration already given regarding integers. We saw that the extreme right hand figure, 8 in our example, stood for 8 units, and was *one-tenth* of the preceding one; just in the same manner another figure, 8, placed to the right of the units' figure, will express *one-tenth* of those units, and the decimal point is used to mark this descending from integers to parts of the integral unit, and is written thus: 8.8, and means eight units, and eighth-tenths of that unit. If another 8 be added, thus: 8.88, it will express eight-tenths of the preceding unit, *i. e.*, eight-tenths of one-tenth, which is the same as eight one-hundredths of unity, and thus we have the descending scale by tenths towards the right of the decimal point, in the same manner as we had the ascending scale by tens towards the left. As a farther illustration, we may begin at the extreme right, as in 888.888, and we find throughout that each figure to the left is ten times that immediately to its right.

The decimal coinage adopts a certain unit called a dollar—the dollar is then sub-divided into ten equal parts, and each part is called a dime; the dime, in like manner, is divided into ten equal parts, and each part is called a cent; and the cent is divided into ten equal parts, and each part is called a mill. The mill enters into many calculations, though no coin of its value has ever been issued. It is from this sub-division by ten, that the name *decimal*, derived from the latin *decem*, ten, is applied to this coinage. In the example 8.888, the first 8 means 8 dollars; the second, 8-tenths of a dollar, or 8 dimes, or 80 cents; the third, 8-tenths of a dime, or 8 one-hundredths of a dollar, or 8 cents; and the fourth 8-tenths of a cent, or 8 one-hundredths of a dime, or 8 one-thousandths of a dollar, or a mill, (from the latin *mille*, a thousand.) In naming any sum, it is not usual to mention either dimes or mills, but only dollars and cents. Thus: $\overset{\$}{12}.\overset{d.c.m.}{875}$ is written \$12.875, or \$12.87½ and is read twelve dollars eighty-seven and-a-half cents, which is perfectly correct, as 8 dimes make 80 cents, and 5 mills make half a cent. We noted, in treating of simple division, that when the terms in which a question is expressed require us to divide a less number by a greater, or in the case of remainders, the division is indicated by writing the dividend above the divisor, and separating them by a line,—thus: 7÷8 is written $\frac{7}{8}$. So to indicate that 1 dollar is divided into 100 cents, we write $\$_{\frac{1}{100}}$, which means the one-hundredth part of a dollar, and therefore dollars and cents are sometimes written, especially in bills and drafts, in this manner, $\$12.\frac{25}{100}$, but the form \$12.25 is generally preferable. To show the reason of the form \$1.05, for one dollar and five cents, we have only to notice that the form \$1.5, would mean one dollar and five dimes, or fifty cents; whereas \$1.05 means one dollar, no dimes, and five cents.

From the foregoing explanations, it is plain that the rules for the addition, subtraction, multiplication and division of abstract numbers, or applicate numbers of only one denomination, apply also to dollars and cents, because they increase from right to left, and decrease from left to right, according to the same law, that is, in the former case by tens, and in the latter by tenths.

It would be of great benefit to the whole commercial community, and perhaps still greater to the farmer, if the decimal scale were adopted in weights and measures, as well as in money, as it would materially simplify and expedite all calculations. Every one must feel and admit the very great ease and rapidity with which every operation is effected, accounts made up, and books kept in dollars and cents, in comparison with the sub-division into pounds, shillings and pence, and the difference would be at least as great regarding weights and measures. It would also very much accelerate the learner's progress, for it would save him the heavy labour of committing to memory the formidable host of tables, through which he has now to cut his way—the whole processes of reduction would be compressed into "nut-shell" dimensions, and the memory would not be over-taxed in after years to keep up the recollection of the tables conned in youth. Besides, by the plan we have suggested, the pupil could pass at once from the elementary rules to the higher ones, such as proportion and interest, and could either get into business in a much shorter time than is possible at present, or devote his time to higher and more important studies.

EXERCISES.

Addition of dollars and cents.

(1.)	(2.)	(3.)	(4.)
		$85.50	$116.20
	$13.19	49.63	291.45
$125.75	14.16	92.18	89.75
98.50	85.92	37.09	365.84
25.15	64.15	8.92	91.50
76.05	37.25	76.45	76.15
91.11½	91.20	25.75	485.00
43.87½	18.75	64.16	157.92
84.20	29.10	18.60	263.75
67.62½	47.85	59.11	188.25
39.80	55.55	148.17	39.48
17.37½	72.63	265.90	136.13
669.44	529.75	931.46	2301 42

(5.)	(6.)	(7.)	(8.)
$11.27			$55.63
45.15	$44.50	$296.75	17.75
54.72	67.23	176.84	84.18
31.30	89.75	518.50	29.88
49.50	27.63	369.63	45.13
16.75	95.13	627.45	38.81
84.28	38.88	258.13	67.25
14.85	17.45	591.18	96.20
9.44	56.64	179.25	77.63
28.09	73.85	567.42	68.75
345.35	511.06	3585.15	521.21

(9.)

Sold to J. JONES,

20 yards cloth	$75.25
14 mats	21.56
16 hats	33.50
5 pairs of blankets	28.75
15 yards sealskin	40.25
15 yards of serge	9.63
28 yards fine cloth	112.88
	321.82

(10.)

$157.29
268.73
985.45
197.06
385.18
876.75
795.85
567.13
659.63
4893.07

(11.)

Sold to S. FULTON, Aurora,

12 pairs of worsted stockings	$13.50
18 " " flannel drawers	22.75
24 " " kid gloves	8.63
56 school books	49.72
29 yards of satin	83.23
96 school copy books	1.84
180 yards of ribbon	29.76
84 yards of ticking	22.68
122 yards of sheeting	23.18
	255.29

12. The shares in an oil-well speculation are $5 each; A. takes 15 shares; B. 25; C. 20; D. 1; E. 11; F. 37; G. 16; H. 18; I. 8; K. 21; L. 14; and 14 other persons take 10 shares each; what is the capital of the company, and how many shares are there?

Ans. $1,630 and 326 shares.

13. If 17 vessels bring to the port of Boston cargoes of the following values; what does the whole amount to? $2365.75, $1793.87, $3815.25, $2718.63, $4186.50, $3179.13, $1623.88, $4311.75, $1987.38, $2975.75, and the other 7 average $2689.13.

Ans. $47781.80.

Subtraction of dollars and cents.

(1.)	(2.)	(3.)
$567819.83	$83756.17	$17423 37½
278956.89	76489.71	9654.63½
288862.94	7266.46	7768.74

4. What is the difference between 2769 dollars and 50 cents, and 987 dollars 87½ cents? Ans. $1781.62½.

5. The debit side of a ledger is $1770.80, and the credit side $876.50; what is the balance? Ans. $894.30.

6. The credit side of a cash book is $8795.88, and the debit side is $10358.18; what is the balance? Ans. $1562.30.

7. A firm owes $227968.25, and the estate is worth $98764.75; what is the state of the affairs of the firm? Ans.—The firm is unable to pay $129,203.50 over and above the assets.

8. A ship and cargo were worth $27509.50,—the ship was lost. nd only $6784.60 worth of the cargo saved; what was the loss? Ans. $20724.90.

Multiplication of dollars and cents. *

(1.)	(2.)	(3.)	(4.)
$365.75	$1873.47	$865.63	$24786.38
87	69	93	45
256025	1686123	259689	12393190
292600	1124082	779067	9914552
31820.25	129269.43	80503.59	1115387.10

Division of dollars and cents.

1. $28642.14÷29=$987.66.
2. $37133.34÷87=$426.82.
3. $60509.68÷76=$796.18.
4. $43009.75÷98=$438.87½.
5. $1943243.55÷983=$1976.85
6. $31421.25÷63=$498.75.
7. $28479.75÷78=365.12½.
8. $2595.37½÷769=$3.37½.

9. $2927.30 a year; how much per day? Ans. $8.02.

10. $3953.19 a year; how much for every working day? Ans. $12.63.

11. 269 persons have to pay a tax of $1312.72; what is the average tax on each? Ans. $4.88.

12. A collection of $544.04 is made by 1876 persons; how much did each give on an average? Ans. 29 cents.

* We must here caution the tyro against such modes of expression as this,—"multiply $85 by $12." Such an expression is simply absurd, for to say $12 times $85, might as well mean 1200 times $85, or 12000 times $85, which would all give widely different results. We may indeed have to multiply a denominate number representing $85, by another denominate number representing $12, as often happens in questions involving proportion, *e. g.*, in interest; but so soon as we use the number 12, or any denominate number as a multiplier it ceases to be denominate, and becomes abstract, and no longer represents any denomination, but merely the number of times the other is to be repeated. We object even to the putting of such questions as "catch questions,"

DECIMAL AND DUODECIMAL CURRENCIES.

As there is frequent intercourse between the United States and the Lower British American Provinces, it has been thought desirable to show the method of changing Decimal or Federal currency into Duodecimal or Halifax currency, and *vice versa.* The traffic between the coast line of the States and that of the Lower British Provinces is very considerable. The trader, therefore, of either requires to be perfectly familiar not only with the comparative value of the currencies of both countries, but also with the coins and paper money used by both. Besides there is constant personal intercourse by travelling and migration, and this makes an intimate acquaintance with all the details of both currencies a most important acquirement. This applies more or less, though in different degrees, to all the British Provinces, except to Canada, where the decimal system has been adopted, though, unfortunately, not universally followed; but it is highly probable that, if the proposed confederation of the British Provinces should be carried, the decimal coinage will be universally adopted, and universally adhered to by the next generation at least, if not by the present.

For the same reasons the mode of changing Federal into Sterling money, and *vice versa,* has been explained under the head of Sterling Exchange. This seems quite as necessary as the preceding, because the traffic between the States and Britain is on an extensive scale, and the coming and going of passengers may now be reckoned by thousands, all of whom require to understand thoroughly both currencies and the circulating media of both countries. The increasing facilities of communication are progressively and rapidly extending the trade, including the passenger traffic, between the two countries, and hence the greater necessity that all persons engaged in business, or in any way exchanging operations, should intimately understand how to change the money of each country into that of the other.

---

for the learner is but too apt to look at the question just as it stands, without ever thinking of the principle on which it is intended to try him. The absurdity of the expression may be shown by the different lights in which the long discussed question, to multiply 2s. 6d. by 2s. 6d. may be viewed. (1.) As 2s. 6d, is $\frac{1}{8}$ of a pound, the question may be taken as meaning that 2s. 6d. is to be divided into 8 equal parts, and 1 of them taken, which would be $3\frac{3}{4}$d. (2.) As 2s. 6d. is $2\frac{1}{2}$ shillings, the question might be taken as meaning that 2s. 6d. was to be

The origin of the mark ($) for dollars is somewhat uncertain. Some suppose it to be a contraction for U. S., the initials of the United States, but it seems to have been in use in continental Europe before the discovery of America, and therefore must be an importation. The following explanation of its origin seems more probable, for if the other were correct, we should surely have some record of it. According to an ancient fable or fancy, the pillars of Hercules marked the limits of the world towards the west and were said to support the world. From their position at the entrance to the Mediterranean Sea they were objects of interest to the Spaniards and were represented on one side of their coin called the *real*, and in the coin for 8 reals the 8 was warped around them, thus forming the mark.

To reduce currency money to the denominations of the decimal coinage. Since 100 cents make 1 dollar, and 4 dollars make 1 pound, 400 cents make 1 pound currency, and therefore to find the number of cents in any given number of pounds, we must multiply the pounds by 400. Again, since 20 cents make 1 shilling or 12 pence, to find the number of cents in any given number of shillings, we must multiply the shillings by 20. Lastly, 5 cents are equal to 3 pence, and 12 farthings are also equal to 3 pence, and (Ax. I.) things that are equal to the same thing, are equal to one another; therefore, 5 cents are equal to 12 farthings, and 1 farthing is the $\frac{1}{12}$ of 5 cents, or $\frac{5}{12}$ of 1 cent. Hence to find the number of cents in any number of pence and farthings, we multiply the number of farthings in the given pence and farthings by 5, and divide the product by 12. Having obtained the three results, we add them all together. Thus to change £48 ·18s. 9¾d. to dollars and cents, we multiply 48 by 400, 18 by 20, and take $\frac{5}{12}$ of 9¾, or 39 farthings, and add the three together, which gives us 19576¼ cents, or $195.76¼.

$$
\begin{aligned}
48\times 400 &= 19200\\
18\times 20 &= 360\\
9\tfrac{3}{4} = 39\text{f.}\times \tfrac{5}{12} &= 16\tfrac{1}{4}\\
\hline
&\ 19576\tfrac{1}{4}
\end{aligned}
$$

repeated 2½ times, which would make 6s. 3d. (3.) The interpretation might be, that as 2s. 6d. is 30 pence, that the other 2s. 6d. is to be repeated 30 times, which would give £3 15s. 0d. (4.) The phrase may also be interpreted as meaning that 30d. was to be repeated 30 times, which would also give £3 15s. 0d. The last two interpretations are the same in two different forms, and give the same result. This is the only view in which the expression has any sense, and proves our statement, that whenever a denominate number is used as a multiplier, it ceases to be denominate, and becomes abstract. The same principle will apply to division.

EXERCISES.

(1.)

$£79 \times 400 = 31600$
$16 \times 20 = 320$
$6\frac{1}{2}d \times \frac{5}{12} = 10\frac{5}{6}$

$\$319.30\frac{5}{6}$

(2.)

$£117 \times 400 = 46800$
$17 \times 20 = 340$
$8\frac{3}{4}d \times \frac{5}{12} = 14\frac{7}{12}$

$\$471.54\frac{7}{12}$

3. $£87.14.10\frac{3}{4} = \$350.97\frac{11}{12}$.
4. $£29.19.9 = \$119.95$.
5. $£67.13.4\frac{3}{4} = \$270.67\frac{11}{12}$.
6. $£279.15.10\frac{1}{2} = \$1119.17\frac{1}{2}$.
7. $£118.11.4\frac{1}{2} = \$474.27\frac{1}{2}$.
8. $£79.8.4 = \$317.66\frac{2}{3}$.
9. $£37.18.8 = \$151.73\frac{1}{3}$.
10. $£57.8.11\frac{3}{4} = \$229.79\frac{7}{12}$.
11. $£49.7.6 = \$197.50$.
12. $£137.16.8 = \$551.33\frac{1}{3}$.
13. $£236.19.2\frac{1}{2} = \$947.84\frac{1}{6}$.
14. $£19.16.8 = \$79.33\frac{1}{3}$.
15. $£98.1.1\frac{1}{2} = \$392.22\frac{1}{2}$.
16. $£87.11.8 = \$350.33\frac{1}{3}$.
17. $£457.12.6 = \$1830.50$.
18. $£219.4.7\frac{3}{4} = \$876.92\frac{11}{12}$.
19. $£49.9.4\frac{3}{4} = \$197.87\frac{11}{12}$.
20. $£287.18.10\frac{1}{2} = \$1151.77\frac{1}{2}$.

To change dollars and cents to Halifax currency, we must reverse the above operation. Thus, to reduce $\$195.76\frac{1}{4}$ to £. s. d.—

```
400)19576¼(48
    400
    ----
    3576¼
    3200
    ----
 20)376¼(18
    20
    ---
    176
    160
    ---
     16¼
     12
    ---
  5)195 (39
```

First, reduce the dollars and cents to cents, then divide by 400, which gives 48, the even number of pounds, with a remainder of $376\frac{1}{4}$ cents; then divide this remainder by 20, which gives 18, the number of shillings, with a remainder of $16\frac{1}{4}$ cents, as in the converse operation, we multiplied by 5, and divided by 12, so now we multiply by 12, and divide by 5; thus, $16\frac{1}{4} \times 12 = 195$, and $195 \div 5 = 39$, the number of farthings, and this being reduced to pence and farthings, gives $9\frac{3}{4}$, so that $\$195.76\frac{1}{4} = £48.18.9\frac{3}{4}$.

Or the work may be shortened by the following method. As \$4 make £1, the number of £'s in $\$195.76\frac{1}{4}$, will be the same as the number of times that 4 is contained in the 195 dollars, which gives £48, and \$3 remain-

$\$195—76\frac{1}{4}$

4)195

£48—300

20)376$\frac{1}{4}$

s18—16$\frac{1}{4}$

3

5)48$\frac{3}{4}$

9$\frac{3}{4}$d.

ing. Now, these three dollars are equivalent to 300 cents, which added to the remaining 76$\frac{1}{4}$ cents, gives 376$\frac{1}{4}$ cents; this divided by 20, will give the shillings, because 20 cents are equal to one shilling, and it is self-evident that the number of shillings in 376$\frac{1}{4}$ cents, will be the same as the number of times 20 is contained in that number, which gives 18 shillings, and 16$\frac{1}{4}$ cents remaining. Lastly, as 5 cents are equal to 3 pence, one cent will be equal to $\frac{1}{5}$ of 3 pence, which is $\frac{3}{5}$ of a penny; therefore, if one cent is equal to $\frac{3}{5}$ of a penny, the remaining 16$\frac{1}{4}$ cents will be equal to 16$\frac{1}{4}$ times $\frac{3}{5}$ of a penny, which is 9$\frac{3}{4}$d.; hence we have \$195.76$\frac{1}{4}$ equal to £48.18.9$\frac{3}{4}$.

EXERCISES.

1.	Reduce \$119.95 to Halifax currency.	Ans. £29.19.9.
2.	Reduce \$270.67$\frac{1}{12}$ " "	Ans. £67.13.4$\frac{3}{4}$.
3.	Reduce \$474.27$\frac{1}{2}$ " "	Ans. £118.11.4$\frac{1}{2}$
4.	Reduce \$197.50 " "	Ans. £49.7.6.
5.	Reduce \$1119.17$\frac{1}{2}$ " "	Ans. £279.15.10$\frac{1}{2}$.
6.	Reduce \$551.33$\frac{1}{3}$ " "	Ans. £137.16.8.
7.	Reduce \$1830.50 " "	Ans. £457.12.6.
8.	Reduce \$1151.77$\frac{1}{2}$ " "	Ans. £287.18.10$\frac{1}{2}$.

MIXED EXERCISES.

1.	Reduce £436.7.8$\frac{1}{2}$ to dollars and cents.	Ans. \$1745.54$\frac{1}{6}$.
2.	Reduce \$547.87 to Halifax currency.	Ans. £136.19.4$\frac{1}{5}$.
3.	Reduce £783.13.5$\frac{1}{4}$ to dollars and cents.	Ans. \$3134.68$\frac{3}{4}$.
4.	Reduce \$576.85 to Halifax currency.	Ans. 144.4.3.
5.	Reduce £606.19.8$\frac{3}{4}$ to dollars and cents.	Ans. \$2427.94$\frac{7}{12}$.
6.	Reduce \$375.99 to Halifax currency.	Ans. £93.19.11$\frac{2}{5}$.
7.	Reduce 3s. 8$\frac{1}{4}$d. to dollars and cents.	Ans. 73$\frac{3}{4}$ cents.
8.	Reduce 17 cents to Halifax currency.	Ans. 10$\frac{1}{5}$ pence.
9.	Reduce 10$\frac{3}{4}$ pence to dollars and cents.	Ans. 17$\frac{11}{12}$ cents.
10.	Reduce 23 cents to old Canadian currency.	Ans. 13$\frac{4}{5}$ pence

REDUCTION.

11.—Reduction is the mode of expressing any given quantity in terms of a higher or lower denomination, *e. g.*, expressing any given number of dollars as cents, and *vice versa*, any number of cents as dollars.

When a higher denomination is changed to a lower (as dollars to cents), the process is called reduction *de*scending, and when a lower is changed to a higher (cents to dollars), it is called reduction *as*cending.

Beginners are generally puzzled by the word *reduction*, which in its ordinary acceptation means *making less*, whereas the learner finds that when dollars are changed to cents, the number denoting the amount is increased a hundred fold. The explanation lies in the original use of the word redue, *to bring back*, which would suggest that the dollars were originally cents and are *brought back* to cents, or that the cents were originally dollars and are *brought back* to dollars. Thus, by a transition common in all languages, the idea of *bringing back* was gradually lost, and the idea of *changing* from one denomination to another alone retained. Again, since one dollar is equal to one hundred cents, it is plain that the number representing any amount in cents will be one hundred times greater, *taken abstractly*, than that representing the same in dollars, and so in all denominate numbers. Some explain the term reduction as taken originally from the changing of a higher to a lower denomination, and afterwards applied to the converse operation. This seems satisfactory enough as regards the present meaning of the word but does not accord with its derivation. Either explanation will clear up the young learner's conception of the term.

```
cwt. qrs. lbs.
17.3.20
 4
 —
 71
 25
 ——
 375
142
 ——
1795
```

If we wish to express 17 cwt. 3 qrs. 20 lbs., in terms of the lowest denomination, viz. lbs., we must first find how many quarters are equivalent to 17 cwt. 3 qrs. which we find by multiplying the 17 cwt. by 4 and adding in the 3 qrs. for 4 qrs. make 1 cwt,—and then since 25 lbs. make 1 qr. we multiply the 71 qrs. by 25 to find the number of lbs. which, with the 20 odd lbs. added in, is 1795 lbs., and thus we see that 1795 lbs. are equivalent to 17 cwt. 3 qrs. 20 lbs.

```
25)1795
   ————
4) 71 qrs. 20.
  ————————
  17 cwt. 3 qrs. 20 lbs.
```

The proof depends on the converse operation, as in the margin, for, since the number denoting the pounds is, abstractly, 25 times the number denoting the quarters, we must divide the number denoting the pounds by 25 to obtain that denoting the quarters, and, in like manner, we must divide the number representing the quarters by 4 to find that denoting the hundreds weight, the remainders in each case being written as sub-denominations.

```
26 acres, 2 roods, 36 rods.
 4
----
 106
  40
----
4276 rods.—Ans.
```

In the same manner 26 acres, 2 roods, 36 rods will be reduced to rods by multiplying the acres by by 4 and adding the odd roods, which gives 106 roods, and this multiplied by 40 with the odd rods added in gives the rods, for 4 roods make one acre and 40 rods 1 rood. Conversely the rods *divided* by 40 will give 106 roods and 36 rods over, and 106 roods divided by 4 will give 26 acres and 2 roods over, the same as the original qnestion—26 acres, 2 rods, 36 roods.

EXERCISES.

1. How many dollars are there in 47986 cents? Ans. $479.86.
2. How many cents are there in 187 dollars? Ans. 18700.
3. How many pounds are there in 2 tons 16 cwt. 2 qrs. and 21 lbs? Ans. 5671.
4. How many pounds are there in 18 cwt. and 22 lbs.? Ans. 1822.
5. Reduce 14796 lbs. to tons, &c.? Ans. 7 tons, 7 cwt., 3 qrs., 21 lbs.
6. Reduce 7643 quarters to tons, &c.? Ans. 95 tons, 10 cwt., 3 qrs.
7. How many drams are there in 18 lbs. 13 oz. and 15 drs.? Ans. 4831.
8. How many pounds are there in 2785 drams? Ans. 10 lbs., 14 oz., 1 dr.
9. How many grains are there in 17 lbs., 11 oz., 18 dwt. and 22 grains? Ans. 103654.
10. How many lbs. in 16891 grs.? Ans. 8 lbs., 1 oz., 13 dwt., 19 grs.
11. How many gills in 4 tuns, 1 pipe, 1 hdd, and 52 gals.?
12. How many tuns, &c. in 198462 drams?
13. How many bushels in 8964 lbs. of wheat?
14. How many bushels in 14382 lbs. of barley?
15. How many bushels in 48628 lbs. of peas?
16. How many bushels in 4683 lbs. of timothy seed?

17. Reduce 98 miles, 5 furlongs and 30 rods to rods?

Ans. 31590 rods.

18. How many inches from Albany to New York (150 miles).

19. How many miles are there in 527168 feet?

Ans. 99 miles, 6 fur., 29 pr., 2 yds., 3 ft., 6 in.

20. Reduce 57 acres, 3 roods and 24 rods to rods?

Ans. 9264 rods.

21. How many square yards are there in 17 acres, 2 roods and 18 rods? Ans. $85244\frac{1}{2}$ yards.

22. Find the number of acres, &c., in 479685971 square inches.

Ans. a. 76.1.35.19.2.119.

23. How many acres do 176984 square yards make?

Ans. a. $36.2.10.21\frac{1}{2}$.

24. How many square links are there in 37 acres?

Ans. 3,700,000 links.

25. How many acres, &c., in 479,863,201 square links?

Ans. 4798 a., 6 ch., 3201.

26. 7,864,391 cubic inches; how many cubic yards?

Ans. yds. 168.15.263.

27. 9 cubic yards, 7 cubic feet, 821 cubic inches; how many cubic inches? Ans. 432821 cubic inches.

28. How many gills does a tun contain? Ans. 8064 gills.

29. How many gallons, &c., do 479865 gills make?

Ans. gals. 14995.3.0.1.

30. How many pints are there in 28 bu., 3 pecks and 1 gal.?—

Ans. 1848 pints.

31. 27 yards, 3 qrs., 3 nails; how many nails? Ans. 447 nails.

32. 286 nails; how many yards, &c.?

Ans. 17 yards, 3 qrs., 2 nls.

33. 36° 40' 25"; how many seconds? Ans. 132025".

34. How many degrees, &c., in 49786"? Ans. 13° 49'.46".

35. The area of New York State is 29.440,000 acres; how many square miles?

36. How long would it take a railway train to move a distance equal to that of the earth from the sun (95 millions of miles), at a speed of 52 miles an hour? Ans. 208 years, 201 days, $19\frac{1}{13}$ hours.

37. The area of Pennsylvania is 47000 square miles; how many square feet?

38. Sound moves about 1130 feet in a second of time; how long would it be in moving from the earth to the sun?

Ans. 14years, 27 days, 15 hours, 50 min., $5\frac{350}{1130}$ sec.

39. How many seconds of this century had elapsed at the end of 1864, counting the day at 24 hours? Ans. 2,019,686,400″.

40. The great bell of Moscow weighs 127,836 lbs.; how many tons, &c., does it weigh, the quarter being 28 lbs.?

Ans. 57t. 1c. 1q. 16lbs.

41. How many days from the 11th July, 1861, to the 1st of April, 1864? Ans. 995 days.

42. A congregation of 569 persons made a collection of £40.6.1; how many pence did each give on an average? Ans. 17d.

43. The British mint can strike off 20,000 coins in an hour; what is the value of all the pennies coined in one day of 12 hours' work? Ans. £1,000.

44. 417 tons of fish were caught at Newfoundland in one season, and sold by the stone of 14 lbs., at an average price of 42 cents a stone; what did they bring? Ans. $25020.

45. How many feet from pole to pole, the earth's diameter being 7945 miles? Ans. 41949600 feet.

DENOMINATE NUMBERS.

12.—WHEN numbers are spoken of in general, without reference to any particular articles, such as money or merchandise, they are called abstract, but when they are applied to such articles they are sometimes called *applicate*, as being *applied* to some particular articles to express their quantity; sometimes they are called *concrete*, (growing together,) as attached to some particular substances, and sometimes they are called *denominate*, as denoting quantities that consist of different denominations, as dollars and cents,—pounds, ounces, &c. The elementary rules of addition, subtraction, multiplication and division, are performed on denominate numbers, exactly in the same way as on abstract numbers, with this single difference, that when a lower denomination is added, and gives a sum equal to one or more units of the next higher denomination, we carry that unit, or those units, to the next higher denomination. Thus: if the sum were 24 inches, we should call that two feet. In abstract and decimal numbers we always reduce, or carry, by tens.

Here we find the sum of the inches to be 34, and as 12 inches make one foot, the number of feet in 34 inches will be the same as the number of times that 12 is contained in 34, which is twice, with a remainder of 10, therefore we write the 10 under the column of inches, and add up the 2 feet with the column of feet, and obtain 11 feet, and as 3 feet make 1 yard, the number of yards will be the same as the number of times that 3 is contained in 11, which is 3 times with a remainder of 2; we therefore write the 2 odd feet under the column of feet, and add up the 3 yards with the column of yards, and the whole amounts to 94 yds., 2 ft., 10 in. The same operation would be carried out if we had rods, &c., given, and is applicable to all operations in denominate numbers of any kind. In the exercises on the addition of denominate numbers, one question in abstract numbers is given to contrast with the denominate.

yds. ft. in.
12.2. 9
16.1.11
27.3. 8
36.3. 4
94.2.10

EXERCISES.

(1.)	(2.)	(3.)	(4.)
		£76.18. 4	$1967.87½
	$857.63	17.11. 4½	2075.75
7865437	189.50	99.19. 9	3194.62½
198675	684.87½	11.11.11	7658.50
8476154	498.75	67.15.10½	8976.37½
1869538	867.12½	79.19. 9	2873.12½
4187643	365.37½	28.12. 1	1769.25
5768299	917.25	63. 8. 4½	2481.92
28365746	4380.50½	445.17. 5½	30997.42

(5.)	(6.)	(7.)	(8.)
lbs. oz. drs.	t. cwt. qrs. lbs.	lbs. oz. dwt. grs.	lbs. oz. drs. scr. grs.
13.14.10	26.17.3.21	3.11.16.21	5.11.7.2.19
15.11.10	18 11.0.19	5. 8. 7.11	4.10.4.1. 7
11. 4. 9	25.15.1.16	7. 9.18.23	3.11.6.2.14
8.12.13	13.17.2.20	11.10.15.17	1. 9.3.1.12
15. 7. 8	39. 4.1.23	12. 7. 9. 8	2. 4.5.0.10
10.13.11	28.16.3.14	16.10.11.22	6. 7.2.2. 9
8. 9. 6		18. 8.19.18	2. 8.1.1.13
4.15.15			
89.10. 2	153. 3.2.13	77. 8. 0. 0	28. 4.0.1. 4

(9.)	(10.)	(11.)	(12.)
m. fur. rods. yds.	yds. ft. in. l.	ac. roods, rd.	rods. yds. ft. in.
176.7.39.5	18.2.11.11	29.3.39	39.30.8.143
85.4.20.1	14.2. 7. 9	57.2.18	18.11.4. 68
79.6.29.3	8.1.10. 7	118.0.26	24. 4.7.118
42.3. 8.2	11.0. 7. 6	75.3.11	11.21.2. 96
67.1.11.2	7.2. 8. 5	51.1. 8	15.27.0.124
118.3.10.3	16.2. 9.10	94.1.19	27. 6.3. 87
81.2.31.1	8.1. 7. 6	63.2.21	19.25.2. 38
79.0.21.2		78.1.15	
18.3.33.3		19.3.33	
749.2. 6.0	87.0. 3. 6	589.0.30	157. 6.3. 98

(13.)	(14.)	(15.)	(16.)
a. ch. links.	ch. b. p. g. qt. pt.	tu. pi. hhd. gal. qt. pt. gl.	yds. qrs. nls.
79.9.9999	5.35.3.1.3.1	6.1.1.1.3.1.3	36.3.2
117.4.3650	7.18.2.0.1.1	4.0.1.1.2.0.2	19.1.3
47.5. 941	8. 7.1.1.0.1	5.1.0.0.1.1.1	87.2.1
56.2.1182	3.26.0.0.1.0	1.1.0.1.0	63.0.2
27.7.2813	4.18.0.1.0.1		74.2.2
36.1. 771			93.3.3
84.8.1160			
449.8. 516	29.34.0.0.3.0	16.1.1.5.0.0.2	375.2.1

(17.)	(18.)	(19.)	(20.)
cwt. qrs. lbs.		yrs. days. hrs. min. sec.	cwt. qrs. lbs.
87.3.11	359°.59′.59″	33.364.23.59.59	18.1.18
49.1.18	153 .40 .45	28.113.11.48.48	22.3.11
28.3.15	270 . 0 . 0	17. 97.12. 0. 0	9.2.18
36.1. 8	179 .45 .30	1.307.23.48.49	12.1.15
88.1.16	81 .30 .10	12.114. 0. 0. 0	8.3.24
57.3.14	89 .59 .59		31.2. 0
348.3.7	1134 .56 .23	93.267.23.37.36	103.3.11

LEDGER ACCOUNTS.

The debit and credit sides of four folios of a ledger are as below, what are the balances?

(21.) Dr.	(21.) Cr.	(22.) Dr.	(22.) Cr.
$1214.75	$2763.80	$198.75	$118.50
863.09	471.38	47.63	9.05
291.45	365.50	18.11	16.25
318.25	297.11	97.38	37.08
1789.87	584.88	85.88	19.13
947.63	963.15	76.20	47.75
2000.00	1257.75	4.50	65.92
798.38	189.60	181.60	32.40
2018.50	98.13	19.25	76.50
164.30	756.25	76.38	7.75
277.15	87.50	219.50	197.25
1165.20	163.63	48.75	15.75
367.40	1291.00	93.15	8.38
984.70	784.25	25.50	93.15
273.60	79.75	81.05	67.45
584.10	81.18	28.30	5.45
1200.00	318.50	69.08	18.09
68.75	1819.20	157.11	4.12
79.15	58.50	278.00	57.60
56.18	176.25	59.50	28.88
2860.14		11.25	
		941.12	

(23.) Dr.	(23.) Cr.	(24.) Dr.	(24.) Cr.
$81.19	$80.10	$177.88	$156.92
17.11	15.65	291.16	285.15
45.38	39.88	356.13	356.12
19.63	10.13	189.38	178.25
187.13	176.15	471.63	469.10
87.63	89.92	785.88	698.80
87.88	77.81	911.50	930.75
111.11	99.88	583.15	496.20
134.56	16.97	432.61	547.60
179.51	87.63	355.55	478.99
340.25	75.75	638.27	546.54
224.12	56.51	436.15	372.25
156.12	37.23	325.36	252.12
$	$	$	$

(25.) Dr.	(25.) Cr.	(26.) Dr.	(26.) Cr.
$176.93	$1237.75	$1087.63	4786.87
27.85	2763.18	457.88	183.05
79.37	194.25	190.37	97.75
98.11	39.37	87.12	149.15
35.40	8.25	94.25	13.25
83.50	11.87	47.20	41.18
1127.25	29.05	39.15	8.50
48.18	63.20	8.75	9.75
250.00	71.80	367.40	11.12
779.63	13.10	18.93	183.62
154.20	45.50	67.45	79.10
59.75	25.20	21.63	814.00
68.87	43.15	298.50	95.50
18.75	7.50	78.60	218.00
28.63	50.00	189.00	59.87
71.38	87.75	47.15	18.05
293.63	5.00	68.10	77.40
185.10	31.60	54.30	38.87
9.05	13.40	12.12	15.62
64.20	90.75	89.75	9.87
38.75	15.15	118.00	14.12
45.45	67.63	69.50	89.50
215.87	58.50	48.75	4.20
7.75	67.05	36.12	67.37
93.92	49.35	91.20	81.09
81.88	21.25	87.63	7.05
68.25	35.15	90.00	57.20
99.99	20.13	100.75	114.25
18.12	92.87	49.15	297.00
27.13	35.28	87.63	78.75
168.00	81.18	43.25	564.87
75.75	10.80	81.37	961.34
738.38	51.25	92.65	268.34
18.24	67.54	37.49	567.84
136.25	91.12	46.87	987.69
126.72	18.35	91.13	356.78
834.15	42.54	54.12	978.65
128.71	16.21	64.54	546.37
136.78	25.51	57.62	786.42
178.16	53.99	38.94	428.97
284.77	62.87	61.87	642.85
326.54	91.54	93.89	509.64
412.13	32.21	89.78	428.04
391.15	54.12	21.46	106.70
267.18	77.99	64.98	500.00
125.13	42.51	73.75	250.09

SUBTRACTION.

(1.)	(2.)	(3.)
$147985.87½	£1573.11. 4½	$810731.37½
86997.75	976.15.10½	341876.62½

4. I have taken this month in trade $1796.18, and paid $673.10 for Fall goods, and expended for private purposes $36.80 and lodged the rest in the Bank, how much have I banked? Ans. $986.28

5. I bought 47 tons, 17 cwt., 1 qr., 18 lbs. of grain, and have sold 29 tons, 18 cwt., 3 qrs.; 22 lbs. of it; how much have I in store? Ans. 17 tons, 18 cwt., 1 qr. 21 lbs.

6. If the distance from Washington to Dover be 161 miles, 1 furlong and 20 rods, and that of Baton Rouge 1407 miles, 1 furlong, 36 rods, how much farther is Baton Rouge from Washington than Dover? Ans. 1245 m. 7 f. 36r.

7. A farmer possessed 1279 acres, 2 roods, 21 rods, and by his will left 789 acres, 3 roods, 36 rods to his eldest son, and the rest to the second; how much had the younger?

Ans. 489 acres, 2 roods, 25 rods.

8. The latitude of London (England,) is 51° .30'.49"N., and that of Gibraltar 36°.6'.30" N.; how many degrees is Gibraltar south of London? Ans. 15°.24'.19"

9. The earth performs a revolution round the sun in about 365 days, 5 hours, 48 minutes and 48 seconds, and the planet Jupiter in about 4332 days, 14 hours, 26 minutes and 55 seconds; how much longer dees it take Jupiter to perform one revolution than the earth?

Ans. 3967 days, 8 h., 38 min., 7 sec.

10. I bought 54 tbs,, 10 oz. of tobacco, and 11 oz. of it were lost by drying; and I sold 36 lbs., 12 oz. of it to A.; and 11 lbs., 9 oz. to B.; and used 3 lbs., 14 oz. myself; how much have I remaining, and how much did I get for what I sold, at 6 cents an ounce, and how much did my own consumption and loss by drying come to at the cost price, which was 5 cents an ounce?

Ans. (1.) 1 lb. 12 oz. (2.) $46.38. (3.) $3. 65.

MULTIPLICATION.

1. $1796×47=$84412.
2. £2.19.2¼×144=£426.3.0.
3. $168.87½×64=$10808.
4. £1.2.9×225=£255.18.9.

5. Find the duty on 97 consignments of merchandise at $86.62½ each? Ans. $8402.62½

It is often convenient to multiply denominate numbers by the *factors* of the multiplier. Thus: to multiply by 84 is the same as to multiply by 7 and 12. Thus, in the annexed examples, since 12×7=84, 18 tons, 12 cwt., 2 qrs., 11 lbs.×84, is the same as 18 tons, 12 cwt., 2 qrs., 11 lbs.×12×7, &c.

(6.)	(7.)	(8.)
tons. cwt. qrs. lbs.	ac. roods. rds.	yds. ft. in.
18.12.2.11×84	27.2.29.×72	11.3. 7×150
12	8	5
223.11.1. 7	221.1.32	60.2.11
7	9	5
1564.19.0.24	1993.0. 8	304.2.76
		1829.0. 6

(9.)	[10.)
cwt. qrs. lbs.	lbs. oz. drs.
23.3.22×49	49.11.12×63
7	7
167.3. 4	348. 2. 4
7	9
1174.2. 3	3133. 4. 4

yds.	ft.	in.
11 ..	3 ..	7
		150
		1050
	87 ..	6
	450 ..	0
	537 ..	0
179 ..	0 ..	6
1650 ..	0 ..	0
1829 ..	0 ..	6

Thus: 11 yds., 3 ft., 7 in., multiplied by 150, will give (1) 150 times 7, which is 1050 in., and divided by 12, is 87 ft., 6 in.,—(2) 150 times 3, which is 450 ft., and added to the 87 already found, gives 537 ft., and divided by 3, gives 179 ft. without remainder,—(3) 150 times 11 is 1650 yards, which, added to the 179 already found, gives 1829 ft., so that the final result is 1829 yds., 0 ft., 6 in., as already obtained by the method of factors.

cwt. qrs. lbs		cwt. qrs. lbs.
9.3.22+86	£2.13.1¼	1.2.17+27
86	125	27
857.1.17	£331.18.0¼	45.0. 9

6. How many seconds has a person lived who has completed his twentieth year, the year consisting of 365 days, 5 hours, 48 minutes, and 48 seconds? Ans. 631138560.

7. Bought 7 loads of hay, each weighing 1 ton, 3 cwt., 3 qrs., 12 lbs; what did the whole weigh?

8. If a man can reap 3 acres and 35 rods per day, how much will he reap in 30 days? Ans. 96 acres, 90 rods.

9. If a steamboat ply across a channel, the breadth of which is equal to 2°, $25'$, $10''$, what angular space has she traversed at the end of 20 trips? Ans. 48°, $23'$.

10. Hamilton, Ross & Co., of Boston, have charged me on an invoice of 60 tons, 17 cwt., 1 qr., and 20 lbs. of iron, at $55 per ton, and 1 pipe, 1 hhd., 34 gals. and 3 qts. of wine, at $3.60 per gal. $4213.57, how much is this amount astray?

11. If a man saves 45 cents a day, how much will he save in the year, omitting the Sabbaths?

12. If 12 gallons, 3 quarts, 1 pint of molasses be nsed in a hotel in a week, how much would be used in a year at that rate?

Ans. 10 hhds., 39 gals., 2 qts.

13. If a man can saw one cord of wood in 8 hours, 45 minutes, 50 seconds, in what time will he saw 11 cords?

Ans. 4 days, 24 minutes, 10 seconds.

14. If 13 waggons carry 3 tons, 15 cwt., 1 qr., 15 lbs. each how much do they all carry? Ans. 49 tons, 0 cwt., 0 qr., 20 lbs.

15. If a man travel 20 miles, 5 furlongs, and 20 rods a day, how much would he travel at that rate in a year?

Ans. 7550 m., 7 fur., 20 rods.

16. There are 24 piles of wood, each containing 3 cords, 42 cubic feet; what is the whole quantity? Ans. 79 cords, 120 ft.

17. If 17 hhds. of sugar weigh 12 cwt., 1 qr., 20 lbs. each, how much will the whole weigh? Ans. 211 cwt., 2 qrs., 15 lbs.

18. Allowing 75 yards, 18 feet, for the surface of 9 rooms, how much paper would be required to cover the wall?

Ans. 693 sq. yards.

19. Purchased from R. Bell 498 cwt., 3 qrs., 21 lbs. of iron at 7 cents per lb.; what does it amount to?

20. What must I receive for 2 lbs., 5 ozs., 14 dwts., 21 grs. of gold, at $18.50 per oz.?

21. Delivered James Grant 7 tuns, 1 pipe, 49 gals. of Port Wine at $2.75 per gal.; what is the amount of the invoice?

DIVISION.

In Division, all remainders are to be reduced to the next lower denomination, and in that form divided, to get the units of that denomination.

EXERCISES.

1. A silversmith made half-a-dozen spoons weighing 2 lbs., 8 ozs., 10 dwts.; what was the weight of each? Ans. 5 ozs., 8 dwts., 8 grs.

2. If 45 waggons carry 685 bushels, 2 pecks, 4 quarts, how much does each carry on equal distribution? Ans. 15 bushels, $7\frac{5}{9}$ quarts.

3. If a labourer receives 149 lbs., 13 ozs. of meat as payment for 26 days' work, how much is that per day, on an average?
Ans. 5 lbs., $12\frac{5}{26}$ ozs.

4. If a steamer occupies 48 days, 17 hours, and 40 minutes, in making 121 trips; what is the average time? Ans. 9 h. 40 min.

5. If 98 bushels, 3 pecks, and 2 quarts of grain, can be packed in 37 equal-sized barrels; how much will there be in each?
Ans. 2 bush., 2 pecks, $5\frac{17}{37}$ qts

6. If a man has an income of $75000 a year; how much has he an hour, allowing the year to consist of just 365 days?

7. An English nobleman has £124,685 a year; how much has he per minute, the pound being worth $4.84, and the year to consist of 365 days, 5 hours, 48 minutes, and 48 seconds? Ans. $1.14+

8. In a coal mine, 97 tons, 13 cwt., 2 qrs. were raised in 97 days; how much was that per day, on an average?

9. If $15.50 be the value of 1 lb. of silver, what will be the weight of $500,000 worth?
Ans. 32258 lbs., 8 oz., 15 dwts., $11\frac{19}{31}$ grs.

11. If 1246 bushels of wheat are produced in a field of 16 acres what is the yield per acre? Ans. 77 bush., 3 pecks, 5 qts., $1\frac{3}{4}$ pts.

12. A gardener pulled 13500 bushels of apples off 60 trees; how many, on an average, were in each bushel? Ans. 230.

13. If 13 hogsheads of sugar weigh 6 tons, 8 cwts., 2 qrs., 7 lbs., what is the weight of each? Ans. 9 cwt., 3 qrs., 14 lbs.

14. What is the twenty-third part of 137 lbs., 9 oz., 18 dwts., 22 grs.? Ans. 5 lbs., 11 oz., 18 dwts., $5\frac{3}{23}$ grs.

15. A shipment of sugar consisted of 8003 tons, 17 cwt., 1 qr., 12 lbs., 10 oz., net weight; it was to be shared equally by 451 grocers; how much did each get?

Ans. 17 tons, 14 cwt., 3 qrs., 18 lbs. 14 oz.

16. If a horse runs 174 miles, 26 rods, in 14 hours, what is his speed per hour? Ans. 12 miles, 3 fur., 19 rods.

17. A farmer divided his farm, containing 322 acres, 2 roods, 10 rods, equally among his seven sons and 6 sons-in-law; what was the share of each? Ans. 24 acres, 3 roods, 10 rods.

18. If 132 bushels, 3 pecks, 7 quarts of corn be distributed equally among 23 poor persons; how much does each get?

Ans. 5 bushels, 3 pecks, 1 quart.

19. A man having purchased 119 cwt., 3 qrs., 23 lbs of hay, and drew home in 6 waggons; how much was on each waggon?

Ans. 19 cwt., 3 qrs., 23 lbs.

MIXED EXERCISES ON DENOMINATE NUMBERS.

20. A gentleman, by his will, left an estate worth $2490, to be divided among his two sons and 3 daughters in the following proportions:—The widow was to receive *one-third* of the whole, less $346; the younger son $212 more than his mother; the older son as much as his mother and brother, lacking $335.50, and the three daughters were to have the remainder, share and share alike; what was the share of each?

Ans. The widow got $484; the older son got $$844\frac{1}{2}$; the younger son got $696; each daughter got $$155\frac{1}{6}$.

21. A gentleman left a property in land, consisting of 448 acres, 3 roods, 24 rods, to be divided among his four children in the following proportions:—The youngest was to get 4 acres, 3 roods, 6 rods more than the eighth part; the second youngest was to get one-fifth of the remainder; the oldest but one was to get one-third of the remainder, and the oldest the residue; what was the share of each?

Ans. The youngest got 60 acres, 3 roods, 24 rods; the next got 77 acres, 2 roods, 16 rods; the next got 103 acres, 1 rood, $34\frac{2}{3}$ rods; the oldest got 206 acres, 3 roods, $29\frac{1}{3}$ rods.

22. A ship made the following headway on six successive days: On Monday, 3°, 8′, 45″ south, and 1°, 51′ east; on Tuesday, 2°, 36′ south, and 2°, 1′, 15″ east; on Wednesday, 4°, 0′, 52″ south, and 1° east; on Thursday, 1°, 48′, 52″ south, and 3°, 16′, 22″ east; on Friday, 1°, 19′ south, and 48′, 29″ east; and on Saturday, 59′, 30″ south, and 3°, 52′, 11″ east; find her distances south and east from the port of departure.

Ans. South 13°, 52′, 59″; East 12°, 49′, 17″.

23. A vintner sold in one week, 51 hogsheads, 53 gallons, 1 quart, 1 pint; in the next week, 27 hogsheads, 39 gallons, 3 quarts; in the next week, 19 hogsheads, 13 gallons, 3 quarts; how much did he sell in the three weeks?

Ans. 88 hogsheads, 43 gallons, 3 quarts, 1 pint.

24. In a pile of wood there are 37 cords, 119 cubic feet, 76 cubic inches; in another there are 9 cords, 104 cubic feet; in a third there are 48 cords, 7 cubic feet, 127 cubic inches, and in a fourth there are 61 cords, 139 cubic inches. Find the whole amount. Ans. 156 cords, 102 feet, 342 inches.

25. The following cargo was landed at Portland from Liverpool: 78 tons, 3 cwt., 2 qrs., 26 lbs. of Irish pork; 125 tons, 15 cwt., 1 qr., 9 lbs. of iron; 90 tons, 12 cwt., 2 qrs., 20 lbs. of West of England cloth goods; 225 tons, 9 cwt., 12 lbs. of Scotch coal, and 106 tons, 1 qr. of Staffordshire pottery; what is the whole amount of the consignment? Ans. 636 tons, 1 cwt., 16 lbs.

26. If a man can count 100 one-dollar bills in a minute, and keep working 10 hours a day; how long will it take him to count a million? Ans. $16\frac{2}{3}$ days.

27. The earth's equatorial diameter is 41847426 feet; how many miles? Ans. 7925 and 3426 feet.

28. The earth's polar diameter is 7899 miles, 900 feet; how many feet? Ans. 41707620 feet.

29. Sound is calculated to move 1130 feet per second; how far off is a cannon, the report of which is heard in 1′ 9″?

Ans. 77970 feet.

30. If the circumference of a waggon wheel be $14\frac{2}{3}$ feet; how often will it turn round in a mile, (5280 feet)? Ans. 360 times.

GREATEST COMMON MEASURE.

13.—When any quantity is contained an even number of times in a greater, the greater is called a multiple of the less, and the less a submultiple, measure or aliquot part of the greater. Thus: 48 is a multiple of 2, 3, 4, 6, 8, 12, 16 and 24, and each of these is a submultiple of 48.

When one quantity divides two or more others evenly it is called a common measure of those quantities, and the greatest number that will divide them all is called the greatest common measure. Thus: 7 is a common measure of 63 and 49, and it is also the greatest common measure, for no larger number will divide both evenly.

When any quantity is measured evenly by two or more others, it is called a common multiple of them. Thus: 24 is a common multiple of 2, 3, 4, 6, 8 and 12.

A number which can be divided into two equal integral parts is called an *even number*, and one which cannot be so divided is called an *odd number*. Hence all numbers of the series 2, 4, 6, 8, 10, 12, &c., are even, while those of the series 1, 3, 5, 7, 9, 11, &c., are odd. Hence the sum of any number of even quantities is even; also, the sum of any even number of odd quantities is even; but the sum of any odd number of odd quantities is odd. This principle is of great use in checking additions.

A prime number is one which has no integral factors except itself and unity; a composite number is one that has integral factors greater than unity, and numbers which have no common factor greater than unity are said to be *prime to each other*. Of the first kind are 1, 2, 3, 5, 7, 11, &c., of the second, 4, 6, 8, 9, 10, 12, &c.; also, 2 and 7 are prime to each other, and so are 6 and 7.

If one quantity measure another it will measure any multiple of it. Thus: since 3 measures 6, it will also measure 12, 18, 24, &c., because it is a factor of all these.

If one quantity measure two or more others, it will also measure their sum and difference, and also the sum and difference of any multiples of them, because it measures them when they are taken separately.

Hence, if one number divide the whole of another number, and also one part of it, it will divide the other part too. Thus: 6 divides 24 and 18, and so the other part, 6; 9 divides 45 and 27, and also the remainder, 18. Also, if a number be composed of several parts, each of which has a common factor, that factor will also measure their sum. Thus: 9 measures 18, 27, and 36, and their sum, 81.

From these principles we can deduce a rule for finding the greatest common measure of two or more quantities.

RULE.

Divide the greater by the less, and then the less by the remainder, until nothing is left, and the last divisor will be the greatest common measure.

EXAMPLE.

2145	3471
1326	2145
819	1326
507	819
312	507
195	312
117	195
78	117
39	78
	78

A concise form of the work is exhibited in the margin. The quotients are omitted as unnecessary. The last divisor, 39, is the G. C. M., as may be proved by trial. If it is required to find the G. C. M. of more than two numbers, first find the G. C. M. of two of them, and then the G. C. M. of that and another, and so on.

EXERCISES.

Find the G. C. M. of the following quantities:

1. 247 and 323. Ans. 19.
2. 532 and 1274. Ans. 14.
3. 741 and 1273. Ans. 19.
4. 10416 and 25761 Ans. 93.
5. 408 and 1266. Ans. 6.
6. 285714 and 999999. Ans. 142857.
7. 15863 and 21489. Ans. 29.
8. 8280 and 11385. Ans. 1035.
9. 17222 and 32943. Ans. 79.
10. 19752 and 69132. Ans. 9876.

We may often find the G. C. M. by inspection. For example, in exercise 5, we see that 2 will measure both quantities (Art. 13), for both are even, and also that 3 will measure both, because it measures the sum of the digits (Art. 16.)

The least common multiple of two or more numbers is the smallest number that is divisible by all of them. Thus: 48 is a common multiple of 2, 3, 4, 6, 8 and 12, but 24 is the *least* common multiple of them.

It is plain that the least common multiple of quantities that have no common factor is their product. Thus: the L. C. M. of 5, 7, 6 is 210. But if the quantities have a common factor, that factor is to be taken only once. Thus: 96, 48, 24, are all common multiples of 2, 3, 4, 6, 8, 12, but the least of these, 24, contains only the factors 3 and 8, which are prime to each other, for 2, 3, 4, 6 are all contained in 12, and 8 and 12 have a common factor, 4, which being left out of one of them, 8, gives $2\times12=24$, or, being left out of the other, 12, gives $8\times3=24$. From this we derive the

RULE:

Expunge all common factors and take the continued product of all the results and divisors. Thus, to find the L. C. M. of 2, 3, 4, 6, 9, 18, 27, 30, arrange them in a horizontal line, and as 2, 3, 6, 9 are all contained in 18, they may be omitted, as in the second line, then, as 2 is contained in 4, 18 and 30, it may be divided out, and as 9 in the third line is contained in 27, it may be omitted, as in the fourth line; and 27 and 15 being both divisible by 3, we obtain in the fifth line 2, 9, 5, all prime to each other, and the products of these and the divisors 3 and 2 is the L. C. M., 540

```
2...3...4...6...9...18...27...30
--------------------------------
             2|4...18...27...30
              ------------------
               2... 9...27...15
               ----------------
                  3|2...27...15
                   ------------
                     2... 9... 5
                               9
                             ---
                              45
                               2
                             ---
                              90
                               3
                             ---
                             270
                               2
                             ---
                             540
```

EXERCISES

Find the L. C. M. of the following quantities:

1. 8, 12, 16, 24, 33. Ans. 528.
2. 35, 42, 45, 81, 100. Ans. 56700.
3. 2, 4, 8, 16, 32, 64, 128 Ans. 128.
4. 2, 3, 5, 7, 11. Ans. 2310.
5. 3, 9, 27, 81, 243, 729. Ans. 729.
6. 12, 16, 18, 30, 48. Ans. 720.
7. 3, 4, 5, 6, 7. Ans. 420.
8. 2, 3, 4, 5, 6, 7, 8, 9. Ans. 2520.
9. 2, 4, 7, 12, 16, 21, 56. Ans. 336.
10. 2, 9, 11, 33. Ans. 198.

EXAMPLES FOR PRACTICE.

1. What will 320 caps cost at $7.50 each? Ans. $2400.

2. If you can purchase slates at 20 cents each; how many can you buy for $7.40? Ans. 37.

3. If you can walk 4 miles an hour; how far can you go in 24 hours? Ans. 96.

4. What will be the cost of 216 barrels of pork at $7.50 per barrel? Ans. $1620.

5. How many sheep can be bought for $560 at $3.50 per head? Ans. 160.

6. If 825 pounds of beef are consumed by a garrison in one day; what will be the cost for 6 days at 11 cents per pound for beef? Ans. $544.50.

7. A farmer sold 185 acres of land at $25 per acre, and received in payment 17 horses at $70 each, and 12 cows at $20 each; how much remains due? Ans. $3195.

8. A merchant bought 120 yards of American tweed at $1.15 a yard; 60 yards of flannel at 95 cents per yard, and 13 dozen pairs of gloves at 35 cents per pair; what was the amount of his bill? Ans. $249.60.

9. At $2 per gallon; how much wine can be bought for $84? Ans. 42 gals.

10. A boy had $5.50, and he paid one dollar and five cents for a book; how much had he left? Ans. $4.45.

11. What will 18 cords of wood cost at $4.75 per cord? Ans. $85.50.

12. How many pounds of sugar can be bought for $9.35, at 11 cents per pound? Ans. 85 lbs.

13. What will a jury of 12 men receive for coming from Kingston to Albany at 10 cents a mile each; the distance being 60 miles?

14. A grocer bought a hogshead of molasses at 32 cents per gallon; but 18 gallons leaked out, and he sold the remainder at 55 cents per gallon; did he make or lose, and how much?

Ans. He gained $4.59.

15. If a clerk's salary is $600 a year, and his personal expenses $320; how many years before he will be worth $6600, if he has $1000 at the present time? Ans. 20 years.

16. A speculator bought 200 bushels of apples for $90, and sold the same for $120; how much did he make per bushel?

Ans. 15 cents.

17. A person sells 15 tons of hay at $22 per ton, and receives in payment a carriage worth $125, a cow worth $45, a colt worth $40, and the balance in cash; how much money ought he to receive?

Ans. $120.

18. How many pounds of butter, at 20 cents per pound, must be given for 18 pounds of tea worth 75 cents per pound?

Ans. 67½ lbs.

19. A grocer bought 7 barrels of fish at $18 per barrel; but one barrel proved to be bad, which he sold for $5 less than cost, and the remainder at an advance of $3 per barrel; did he gain or lose, and how much? Ans. Lost $13.

20. A man bought a drove of cattle for $18130, and after selling 84 of them at $51 each, the rest stood him in $43 each; how many did he buy? Ans. 406.

21. What will 2 cwt. of cheese cost at 9½ cents per pound?

Ans. $19 00.

22. A. is worth $960, B. is worth five times as much as A., less $600, and C. is worth three times as much as A. and B. and $300 more; what are B. and C. worth each, and how much are they all worth? Ans. B. $4200; C. $15780; all $20940.

23. A boy bought a dozen knives at 15 cents each, and after selling half of them at the rate of $2.22 per dozen, he lost three, and sold the balance at 25 cents each; did he make or lose, and how much? Ans. Gained 6 cents.

24. A labourer bought a coat worth $16, a vest worth $3, and a

pair of pants worth $5.50; how many days had he to work to pay for his suit; his services being worth 50 cents per day?

Ans. 49 days.

25. What will 14 bushels of clover seed cost at 12½ cents per pound? Ans. $105.

26. A farmer sold a load of oats weighing 1836 pounds, at 30 cents per bushel; how much did he receive for the same?

Ans. $16.20.

27. A produce dealer bought at one time, one load of wheat weighing 3240 pounds, at $1.05 per bushel; one load of barley weighing 2400 pounds, at 85 cents per bushel; one load of rye weighing 2800 pounds, at 65 cents per bushel; two loads of pease, each 2400 pounds, at 68 cents per bushel; three loads of buckwheat, each weighing 1400, at 55½ cents per bushel; and a quantity of oats weighing 578 pounds, at 33 cents per bushel; what had he to pay for the whole? Ans. $250.15½.

28. A farmer has 12 sheep worth $3.50 each; 9 pigs worth $4.65 each; one cow worth $35, and a fine horse valued at $150. He exchanges them with his neighbour for a yoke of oxen worth $75; two lambs worth $1.925 each; a carriage worth $100, and takes the balance in calves at $4.50; how many calves does he receive?

Ans. 20.

29. A and B sat down to count their money, and found that they had together $225, but A had $15 more than B; how much had each? Ans. A $120, B $105.

30. A miller bought 250 bushels of oats for $85 and sold 225 bushels for $70; what did the remainder cost him per bushel?

Ans. 60c.

31. A widow lady has a farm valued at $6720; also three houses, worth $12530, $11324, and $9875. She has a daughter and two sons. To the daughter she gives one-fourth the value of the farm, and one-third the value of the houses, and then divides the remainder equally among the boys, how much did each receive?

Ans. daughter $12923, each son, $13763.

32. A man went into business with a capital of $1500; the first year he gained $800, the second year $950, the third year $700, and the fourth year 625, when he invested the whole in a cargo of tea and doubled his money; what was he then worth. Ans. $9150.

33. A boy paid out 30 cents for apples, at the rate of 6 for 3 cents; how many apples did he purchase? Ans. 60.

34. A schoolboy bought 12 oranges at 3 cents each, and sold them for 12 cents more than he paid for them; how much did he sell them at each? Ans. 4c.

35. A clerk's income is $2698 a year, and his expenses $4.50 per day; how much will he save in two years? Ans. $2111.

36. A speculator bought 200 acres of land at $45 per acre, and afterwards sold 150 acres of it for $11550; the balance he sold at a gain of $5 per acre, and received in payment $250 cash, and the balance in sheep at $5 each; how many sheep did he receive? Ans. 450 sheep.

37. A butcher bought 9 calves for $54, and 9 lambs for $31.50; how much more did he pay for a calf than a lamb? Ans. $2.50.

38. A farmer sold to a grocer 380 pounds of pork, at 7 cents per pound; 150 pounds of butter, at 17 cents per pound, and one cheese weighing 53 pounds, at 9 cents per pound; and received in payment 22 pounds of sugar, at the rate of 11 pounds for a dollar; 150 pounds of nails, at 6 cents per pound; 15 pounds of tea, at 65 cents per pound; one half-barrel of fish, at $18 per barrel, and one suit of clothes worth $27; did the farmer owe the grocer, or the grocer the farmer, and how much? Ans. the grocer owed the farmer 12 cents.

39. A milkman sold 120 quarts of milk, at 5 cents per quart, and took in payment, one pig worth $1.50, and the balance in sheeting, at 10 cents per yard; how many yards did he receive? Ans. 45 yards.

40. How many pounds of cheese, at 9 cents per pound, must be given for 27 pounds of tea worth 80 cents per pound? Ans. 240

FRACTIONS.

14.—Vulgar or Common Fractions.—When we have divided any number by a less, and find no remainder, the quotient is called an integer, or whole number. When we have divided any number by a less as far as possible, and find a remainder still to be divided, but less than the divisor, and therefore not actually divisible by it, we must have recourse to some method of indicating this. We have seen already that the conventional sign of division is this mark (÷); thus, 3÷4 means that 3 is to be divided by 4, and this being impossible, we indicate the operation either as above or by writing the three in the place of the upper dot, and the 4 in the place of the lower, thus, $\frac{3}{4}$.

The nature of a fraction may be viewed in two ways. *First*, we may consider that a unit is divided into a certain number of equal parts and a certain number of these parts taken; or, *secondly*, that a number greater than unity is divided into certain equal parts, and *one* of these parts taken; thus, $\frac{3}{4}$ means either that a unit is divided into 4 equal parts and three of them taken, or that three is divided into 4 equal parts and one of them taken. For example, if a foot be divided into 4 equal parts, each of these parts will be 3 inches, and three of them will be nine inches; and since 3 feet make 36 inches, if we divide 3 feet into 4 equal parts, each of these parts will be 9 inches, and hence $\frac{3}{4}$ of $1=\frac{1}{4}$ of 3. The lower figure is called the denominator, because it shows the denomination or number of parts into which the unit is supposed to be divided, and the upper one is called the numerator, because it shows the number of those parts considered in any given question. When both are spoken of together they are called the *terms* of the fraction.

What may be considered the fundamental principle on which all the operations in fractions depend is this: that the form, but not the value of a fraction, is altered, if both the terms are either multiplied or divided by the same quantity. If we take the fraction $\frac{3}{4}$ and multiply its terms by 2, we get $\frac{6}{8}$. Now, the $\frac{1}{8}$ of a foot is an inch and-a-half, and therefore $\frac{6}{8}$ is 6 inches and 6 half-inches, or 9 inches; but we have seen that $\frac{3}{4}$ of a foot is 9 inches, therefore $\frac{3}{4}$ of a foot is the same as $\frac{6}{8}$ of a foot. So also $\frac{3}{4}$ of £1 and $\frac{6}{8}$ of £1 are both 15s. The same will hold good whatever the unit of measure may be, or whatever the fraction of that unit. Hence, universally the *form* of a fraction is altered if its terms be either multiplied or divided by the same number, but its *value* remains the same.

Again, if we multiply the numerator 3 by 2, but leave the denominator 4 unchanged, we obtain $\frac{6}{4}$, and, keeping to our first illustration, $\frac{6}{4}$ of a foot is 6 times three inches, or 18 inches, which is double of 9 inches, the value of $\frac{3}{4}$. We should have obtained the same result by taking $\frac{6}{8}$ and dividing its denominator by 2, without dividing its numerator. Hence, a fraction is multiplied by either multiplying its numerator or dividing its denominator. In like manner, if we take the fraction $\frac{6}{8}$ and divide its numerator by 2, we obtain $\frac{3}{8}$, and if we multiply the denominator of its equal $\frac{3}{4}$ by 2, we obtain the same rusult, $\frac{3}{8}$. Hence, $\frac{3}{8}$ is $\frac{1}{2}$ of $\frac{3}{4}$, and therefore a fraction is divided by either dividing its numerator or multiplying its denominator. These principles may also be referred to the obvious fact that in dividing any quantity the greater the divisor the less the quotient, and the less the divisor the greater the quotient. As it is always desirable to have the smallest numbers possible to handle, let the operator observe this as a universal rule—*divide when you can.*

Fractions are classified in four different ways, according to four different circumstances.

I. They are divided into Proper and Improper Fractions.

A proper fraction is one whose numerator is less than its denominator. In strictness such alone is a fraction. An improper fraction is one whose numerator is greater than its denominator. Strictly this is not really a fraction, but only a certain quantity expressed in the fractional form.

II. Simple and Compound Fractions.

The term simple fraction, as opposed to compound fraction, expresses that the fraction is multiplied by unity alone, as $\frac{5}{8}$, which means either $\frac{5}{8}$ of 1 or $\frac{1}{8}$ of 5, or $\frac{5}{8}\times1=\frac{1}{8}\times5$.

A compound fraction is one that is multiplied by some other quantity. A fraction is called compound if either multiplier or multiplicand, or both, be fractional. Thus: $\frac{3}{4}$ of $\frac{5}{6}$ and $\frac{7}{8}$ of 11 are both compound, and are written $\frac{3}{4}\times\frac{5}{6}$ and $\frac{7}{8}\times11$.

III. Simple and Complex Fractions.

The term simple fraction, as opposed to complex fraction, means that there is only one division. Thus: $\frac{15}{16}$ means that a single number, 15, is divided by a single number, 16.

A complex fraction is one of which either the numerator or denominator, or both, are fractional, that is, it indicates a division, when either the given product or given factor, or both, are fractional. Thus: $\frac{3}{4}\div\frac{7}{11}$, or $\dfrac{\frac{3}{4}}{\frac{7}{11}}$ and $\dfrac{8}{\frac{5}{9}}$ and $\dfrac{\frac{11}{12}}{7}$ are complex fractions and exhibit the only three posssible forms.

IV. Vulgar, or Common, and Decimal Fractions.

Decimal fractions are those expressed with a denominator, 10, or a power of 10, *e. g.*, $\frac{7}{10}$, $\frac{19}{100}$, $\frac{21}{1000}$.

Any fraction not so expressed is called vulgar or common. Thus: $\frac{3}{4}$ would be called a common fraction, but its equivalent, $\frac{75}{100}$, would be called a decimal fraction, and is written ·75, the denominator being omitted, but its existence being indicated by the mark (·), called the decimal point.

A mixed quantity is one expressed partly by a whole number and partly by a fraction, as $4\frac{7}{8}$, $12\frac{1}{2}$. This is not another kind of fraction, but simply another mode of writing an improper fraction, when the division indicated has been performed as far as possible Thus: $\frac{39}{8}=4\frac{7}{8}$, and $\frac{25}{2}=12\frac{1}{2}$.

It is often said that there are six kinds of fractions—proper, improper, simple, compound, complex, and mixed. This is logically incorrect, for a proper fraction is simple, and a mixed quantity is an improper fraction in another form.

15.—Operations in Common Fractions.—From the principles laid down (Art. 21,) we can deduce rules for all the operations in fractions.

I. An improper fraction is reduced to a mixed quantity by performing the division indicated, as $\frac{217}{9}=24\frac{1}{9}$.

II. A mixed quantity is reduced to an improper fraction by multiplying the integral part by the denominator and adding in the numerator, as $12\frac{7}{8}=\frac{103}{8}$.

So also an integer may be expressed in the fractional form by writing 1 as a denominator, and multiplying the terms by whatever number will bring it to any required denomination. Thus: to reduce 7 to the same denomination as $\frac{5}{6}$, write $\frac{7}{1}$ and multiply the terms by 6, and the result, $\frac{42}{6}$, will be equivalent to the integer 7, and of the same form as $\frac{5}{6}$.

EXERCISES.

1. Express $\frac{441}{9}$ as a whole or mixed number. Ans. 49.
2. Express $\frac{87}{16}$ as a whole or mixed number. Ans. $5\frac{7}{16}$.
3. Express $\frac{781}{11}$ as a whole or mixed number. Ans. 71.
4. Express $\frac{129}{22}$ as a whole or mixed number. Ans. $5\frac{19}{22}$.
5. Express $\frac{19876}{3579}$ as a whole or mixed number Ans. $5\frac{1981}{3579}$.
6. Express $\frac{859}{78}$ as a whole or mixed number. Ans. $11\frac{1}{78}$.
7. Express $\frac{365}{52}$ as a whole or mixed number. Ans. $7\frac{1}{52}$.
8. Express $\frac{89}{12}$ as a whole or mixed number. Ans. $7\frac{5}{12}$.
9. Express $\frac{1157}{13}$ as a whole or mixed number. Ans. 89.
10. Express $\frac{117}{11}$ as a whole or mixed number. Ans. $10\frac{7}{11}$.
11. Express $\frac{149}{63}$ as a whole or mixed number. Ans. $2\frac{23}{63}$.
12. Express $\frac{176}{9}$ as a whole or mixed number. Ans. $19\frac{5}{9}$.
13. Express $\frac{211}{17}$ as a whole or mixed number. Ans. $12\frac{7}{17}$.
14. Express $\frac{29}{7}$ as a whole or mixed number. Ans. $4\frac{1}{7}$.

15. Express $\frac{97}{4}$ as a whole or mixed number. Ans. $24\frac{1}{4}$.
16. Express $\frac{118}{21}$ as a whole or mixed number. Ans. $5\frac{13}{21}$.
17. Express $\frac{99}{31}$ as a whole or mixed number. Ans. $3\frac{6}{31}$.
18. Express $\frac{11}{2}$ as a whole or mixed number. Ans. $5\frac{1}{2}$.
19. Express $\frac{121}{4}$ as a whole or mixed number. Ans. $30\frac{1}{4}$.
20. Express $\frac{1331}{16}$ as a whole or mixed number. Ans. $83\frac{3}{16}$.
21. Express $\frac{181}{20}$ as a whole or mixed number. Ans. $9\frac{1}{20}$.
22. Express $27\frac{1}{2}$ as an improper fraction. Ans. $\frac{55}{2}$.
23. Express $66\frac{1}{9}$ as an improper fraction. Ans. $\frac{595}{9}$.
24. Express $15\frac{17}{19}$ as an improper fraction. Ans. $\frac{302}{19}$.
25. Express $7\frac{3}{4}$ as an improper fraction. Ans. $\frac{31}{4}$.
26. Express 49 as a fraction with the same denominator as $\frac{12}{13}$. Ans. $\frac{637}{13}$.
27. Express 19s. as a fraction of £1. Ans. $\frac{19}{20}$.
28. Express 11 inches as a fraction of a foot. Ans. $\frac{11}{12}$.
29. Bring $\frac{1}{2}$, $\frac{1}{3}$, $\frac{1}{4}$, $\frac{1}{6}$, $\frac{1}{12}$ to the same denomination. Ans. $\frac{6}{12}$, $\frac{4}{12}$, $\frac{3}{12}$, $\frac{2}{12}$, $\frac{1}{12}$.
30. Express 11 as a fraction having the same denominator as $\frac{17}{701}$. Ans. $\frac{7711}{701}$.

III. To reduce a fraction to its lowest terms or simplest form, divide the terms by their greatest common measure. This is often readily done by inspection, as $\frac{48}{72}=\frac{4}{6}=\frac{2}{3}$, but in such questions as $\frac{1092}{6552}$, the most secure and speedy method is to find the G. C. M. of the terms and divide them by it. Thus: the G. C. M. of the fraction $\frac{1092}{6552}$ is 1092, and the terms of the fraction divided by this give $\frac{1}{6}$, the simplest form.

EXERCISES.

1. Reduce $\frac{4536}{13608}$ to its lowest terms or simplest form. Ans. $\frac{1}{3}$.
2. Reduce $\frac{5971}{9383}$ to its lowest terms or simplest form. Ans. $\frac{7}{11}$.
3. Reduce $\frac{2920}{3285}$ to its lowest terms or simplest form. Ans. $\frac{8}{9}$.
4. Reduce $\frac{72000}{960000}$ to its lowest terms or simplest form. Ans. $\frac{3}{40}$.
5. Reduce $\frac{3580}{4296}$ to its lowest terms or simplest form. Ans. $\frac{5}{6}$.
6. Reduce $\frac{87615}{175230}$ to its lowest terms or simplest form. Ans. $\frac{1}{2}$.
7. Reduce $\frac{987}{12831}$ to its lowest terms or simplest form. Ans. $\frac{1}{13}$.
8. Reduce $\frac{3333}{4444}$ to its lowest terms or simplest form. Ans. $\frac{3}{4}$.
9. Reduce $\frac{5034}{6712}$ to its lowest terms or simplest form. Ans. $\frac{3}{4}$.

10. Reduce $\frac{135}{20391}$ to its lowest terms or simplest form. Ans. $\frac{2}{3}$.

11. Reduce $\frac{33595}{114223}$ to its lowest terms or simplest form. Ans. $\frac{5}{17}$.

12. Reduce $\frac{6935}{7300}$ to its lowest terms or simplest form. Ans. $\frac{19}{20}$.

13. Reduce $\frac{571428}{1999998}$ to its lowest terms or simplest form. Ans. $\frac{2}{7}$.

14. Reduce $\frac{31185}{50457}$ to its lowest terms or simplest form. Ans. $\frac{945}{1529}$.

15. Reduce $\frac{1638}{2106}$ to its lowest terms or simplest form. Ans. $\frac{7}{9}$.

16. Reduce $\frac{1827}{3045}$ to its lowest terms or simplest form. Ans. $\frac{3}{5}$.

17. Reduce $\frac{272}{425}$ to its lowest terms or simplest form. Ans. $\frac{16}{25}$.

18. Reduce $\frac{873}{3395}$ to its lowest terms or simplest form. Ans. $\frac{9}{35}$.

19. Reduce $\frac{41472}{96768}$ to its lowest terms or simplest form. Ans. $\frac{3}{7}$.

20. Reduce $\frac{63624}{69408}$ to its lowest terms or simplest form. Ans. $\frac{11}{12}$.

21. Reduce $\frac{7890570100000}{15781140200000}$ to its lowest terms or simplest form. Ans. $\frac{1}{2}$.

IV. To multiply one fraction by another, multiply numerator by numerator and denominator by denominator.

```
      1
1 ... 1 ... 1
111...111...111
```

Thus: $\frac{1}{3}\times\frac{1}{3}=\frac{1}{9}$. To illustrate that $\frac{1}{3}$ of $\frac{1}{3}$ is $\frac{1}{9}$, take a line and let it be divided into 3 parts, and each of those again into 3 parts, as in the margin, we find that the result is 9 parts, each, of course, being $\frac{1}{9}$ of the unit.

We have seen that a fraction is multiplied by multiplying the numerator or dividing the denominator. Now, if it were required to multiply $\frac{3}{4}$ by $\frac{5}{7}$, we could not divide the denominator, as 5 is not contained in 4, and therefore we multiply the numerator and obtain $\frac{15}{4}$, but we have multiplied by a quantity equal to 7 times the given one, and therefore we must divide the product by 7, *i. e.* (Art. 21,) we must multiply the denominator 4 by 7, which gives $\frac{15}{28}$ for the correct product.

EXERCISES.

1. Multiply $\frac{5}{12}$ by $\frac{13}{17}$? Ans. $\frac{65}{204}$.
2. What is the product of $\frac{3}{4}$ by $\frac{11}{13}$? Ans. $\frac{33}{52}$.
3. What is the product of $\frac{7}{12}$ by $\frac{5}{6}$? Ans. $\frac{35}{72}$.
4. What is the product of $\frac{5}{6}$ by $\frac{13}{14}$? Ans. $\frac{65}{84}$.
5. What is the product of $\frac{1}{2}$ by $\frac{19}{20}$? Ans. $\frac{19}{40}$.

6. What is the product of $\frac{7}{8}$ by $\frac{9}{10}$? Ans. $\frac{63}{80}$.
7. What is the product of $\frac{99}{100}$ by $\frac{7}{10}$? Ans. $\frac{693}{1000}$.
8. What is the product of $\frac{36}{55}$ by $\frac{7}{11}$? Ans. $\frac{252}{605}$.
9. What is the product of $\frac{8}{9}$ by $\frac{4}{5}$? Ans. $\frac{32}{45}$.
10. What is the product of $\frac{12}{13}$ by $\frac{7}{11}$? Ans. $\frac{84}{143}$.

When the product has been obtained it should be reduced to its lowest terms. Thus: the product of $\frac{7}{11}$ by $\frac{11}{13}$ is $\frac{77}{143}$, the terms of which are both divisible by 11, and so we get the equivalent fraction $\frac{7}{13}$. But we might as well have divided by 11 before multiplying, for by this method we should at once have found the fraction in its simplest form, viz., $\frac{7}{13}$. In the same manner any number or numbers which are factors of both numerator and denominator, may be omitted in the operation. This we call cancelling in preference to the excessively awkward term "cancellation." This method will be clearly seen in exercise 11.

If either the multiplier or multiplicand be a mixed quantity, it must be reduced to an improper fraction before the multiplication is performed. Thus: $8\frac{3}{4}\times5\frac{5}{6}=\frac{35}{4}\times\frac{35}{6}=\frac{1225}{24}=51\frac{1}{24}$.

11. What fraction is equal to $\frac{1}{2}$ of $\frac{2}{3}$ of $\frac{3}{4}$ of $\frac{4}{5}$ of $\frac{5}{6}$ of $\frac{6}{7}$ of $\frac{7}{8}$ of $\frac{8}{9}$? Ans. $\frac{1}{9}$.
12. What quantity is equal to $12\frac{1}{2}$ multiplied by $7\frac{5}{6}$? Ans. $97\frac{11}{12}$.
13. What quantity is equal to $19\frac{1}{8}$ multiplied by $1\frac{15}{17}$? Ans. 36.
14. What is the value of $\frac{5}{6}$ of $\frac{4}{5}$ of $\frac{18}{23}$ of $\frac{1}{8}$?
15. What is the value of $\frac{1}{3}$ of $\frac{5}{7}$ of $\frac{8}{9}$ of $\frac{11}{13}$? Ans. $\frac{440}{2457}$.
16. What is the product of $27\frac{5}{8}$ by $3\frac{8}{9}$? Ans. $107\frac{31}{72}$.
17. What is the product of $\frac{18}{19}$ by $\frac{19}{20}$? Ans. $\frac{9}{10}$.
18. What is the product of $5\frac{1}{2}$ by $5\frac{1}{2}$? Ans. $30\frac{1}{4}$.
19. Find the square and cube of $\frac{17}{22}$? Ans. $\frac{289}{484}$ and $\frac{4913}{10648}$.
20. What is the cube of $\frac{39}{40}$? Ans. $\frac{59319}{64000}$.
21. Multiply 27 by $\frac{1}{27}$? Ans. 1.

V.—DIVISION OF FRACTIONS.

To divide one fraction by another, multiply by the reciprocal of the divisor; or, in other words, invert the divisor and multiply. In the language of science, the reciprocal of a fraction is the fraction with its terms inverted. Thus: $\frac{8}{7}$ is the reciprocal of $\frac{7}{8}$; $\frac{4}{3}$ of $\frac{3}{4}$. To find the reciprocal of a whole number, we must first represent it as having a denominator 1,—thus $4=\frac{4}{1}$; $6=\frac{6}{1}$, and therefore the reciprocals are $\frac{1}{4}$ and $\frac{1}{6}$. The rule for division may be proved in two ways:

FIRST PROOF.—Let it be required to divide $\frac{7}{11}$ by $\frac{5}{6}$. If we had been required to divide by the whole number 5, we should either have divided (Art. 14,) the numerator, or multiplied the denominator,—as the numerator is not divisible by 5, we multiply the denominator, and obtain $\frac{7}{55}$; but we have divided by a quantity equal to six times the given one, and therefore, to compensate, we must multiply the result by 6, which gives $\frac{42}{55}$.

SECOND PROOF.—Write the question in the complex form— $\frac{\frac{7}{11}}{\frac{5}{6}}$, then (Art. 14,) multiply both terms by 11, and $\frac{7}{\frac{55}{6}}$ is obtained; and again multiply the terms by 6, and $\frac{42}{55}$ is the result as before.—The two operations are virtually the same, though exhibited in different forms, and both are equivalent to the technical rule, "Invert the divisor and multiply."

Mixed quantities must be reduced to improper fractions as in multiplication. The expressions *multiplication* and *division*, as applied to fractions, are extensions of the ordinary meanings of those terms, for in their original meaning, the former implies increase, and the latter decrease; but when two proper fractions are multiplied together, the product is less than either of the factors, and when one proper fraction is divided by another, the quotient is greater than either the divisor or dividend. This will be seen by the annexed examples:

$\frac{3}{4}\times\frac{7}{8}=\frac{21}{32}$. But $\frac{3}{4}=\frac{24}{32}$ and $\frac{7}{8}=\frac{28}{32}$, both greater than $\frac{21}{32}$.

Also, $\frac{7}{8}\div\frac{3}{4}=\frac{7}{8}\times\frac{4}{3}=\frac{28}{24}$. But $\frac{7}{8}=\frac{21}{24}$ and $\frac{3}{4}=\frac{18}{24}$, both less than $\frac{28}{24}$.

If two fractions have a common denominator, their quotient is the quotient of their numerators. We have placed multiplication and division of fractions before addition and subtraction, because, as in whole numbers, multiplication and division are deduced from addition and subtraction, so conversely in fractions, addition and subtraction are to be deduced from multiplication and division, for a fraction is produced by division, and the multiplication of a fraction is merely the repeating of the divided unit a certain number of times. Thus: $\frac{1}{8}$ is a unit divided into 8 equal parts, and $\frac{7}{8}$ is that fraction repeated 7 times.

EXERCISES.

1. Divide $\frac{3}{11}$ by $\frac{2}{3}$; $\frac{3}{11}\div\frac{2}{3}=\frac{3}{11}\times\frac{3}{2}$. Ans. $\frac{9}{22}$
2. What is the quotient of $\frac{13}{14}$ divided by $\frac{13}{15}$? Ans. $\frac{15}{14}=1\frac{1}{14}$.
3. What is the quotient of $\frac{7}{22}$ divided by $\frac{113}{355}$? Ans. $\frac{2485}{2486}$.
4. What is the quotient of $\frac{29}{45}$ divided by $\frac{29}{33}$? Ans. $\frac{11}{15}$.
5. What is the quotient of $\frac{115}{246}$ divided by $\frac{23}{27}$? Ans. $\frac{45}{82}$.
6. What is the quotient of 36 divided by $19\frac{1}{8}$? Ans. $1\frac{15}{17}$.
7. What is the quotient of $3\frac{5}{9}$ divided by $2\frac{5}{8}$? Ans. $1\frac{67}{189}$.
8. What is the quotient of $4\frac{1}{2}$ divided by 15? Ans. $\frac{3}{10}$.
9. What is the quotient of $\frac{50}{17}$ divided by $2\frac{17}{18}$? Ans. $\frac{900}{901}$.
10. What is the quotient of $75\frac{7}{10}$ divided by 9? Ans. $8\frac{37}{90}$.
11. What is the quotient of $6\frac{19}{21}$ divided by $9\frac{2}{3}$? Ans. $\frac{5}{7}$.
12. What is the quotient of $5\frac{4}{7}$ divided by $8\frac{7}{12}$? Ans. $\frac{468}{721}$.
13. Divide the product of $\frac{3}{4}$, $\frac{4}{5}$ and $\frac{5}{9}$ by the product of $\frac{1}{2}$, $\frac{3}{4}$ and $\frac{8}{11}$? Ans. $\frac{11}{9}=1\frac{2}{9}$.
14. What is the quotient of $\frac{7}{11}$ of $\frac{11}{13}\div\frac{3}{8}$ of $\frac{11}{13}$ of $\frac{7}{11}\div\frac{9}{10}$ of $\frac{5}{8}$? Ans. $4\frac{20}{27}$.
15. How many $\frac{1}{54}$ are there in $\frac{3}{19}$? Ans. $8\frac{10}{19}$.
16. What is the value of $\frac{5}{6}$ of $\frac{7}{8}\div\frac{3}{4}$ of $\frac{11}{12}$? Ans. $1\frac{2}{33}$.
17. Divide 27 by $\frac{1}{27}$? Ans. 729.

Hence, any quantity divided by its reciprocal gives the square of that number, and exercise 21, of multiplication, shows that any quantity multiplied by its own reciprocal gives unity.

18. Divide $\frac{80}{561}$ by $\frac{4}{9}$, and the quotient by $\frac{3}{17}$? Ans. $1\frac{9}{11}$.
19. Divide $\frac{4}{7}$ by $\frac{7}{11}$, and the quotient by $\frac{22}{23}$? Ans. $\frac{46}{49}$.
20. Divide $\frac{76}{79}$ by $\frac{13}{47}$? Ans. $3\frac{491}{1027}$.
21. Divide $\frac{11}{18}$ by $\frac{44}{36}$? Ans. $\frac{1}{2}$.

VI.—ADDITION OF FRACTIONS.

We have seen that no quantities can be added together except they are in the same denomination. We can add $\frac{4}{7}$, $\frac{3}{7}$, $\frac{5}{7}$ and $\frac{11}{7}$, as they are all of the same denomination, *sevenths*, and we find $\frac{23}{7}$. We can easily see that to add $\frac{3}{4}$ and $\frac{7}{8}$, we have only to alter the form of $\frac{3}{4}$ to $\frac{6}{8}$, and we have both fractions of the same denomination, and therefore can add them,—$\frac{6}{8}+\frac{7}{8}=\frac{13}{8}$. So, also, $\frac{1}{2}+\frac{2}{3}+\frac{3}{4}+\frac{5}{6}+\frac{7}{12}=\frac{6}{12}+\frac{8}{12}+\frac{9}{12}+\frac{10}{12}+\frac{7}{12}=\frac{40}{12}=\frac{10}{3}$. But we cannot always tell thus by inspection, and therefore must be guided by some rule. To find the value of $\frac{3}{4}+\frac{5}{6}+\frac{7}{8}+\frac{2}{9}+\frac{7}{12}$.

By Art. 13 we find the L. C. M. of 4, 6, 8, 9, 12 to be 72, and the rest of the common operation is equivalent to multiplying the terms of each fraction by 72. Thus: if the terms of $\frac{3}{4}$ be both multiplied by 72, we get $\frac{216}{288}=\frac{54\times4}{72\times4}=\frac{54}{72}$, but we might as well have divided 72 by 4 before multiplying, and, to balance that, have multiplied the numerator 3, not by 72, but by the fourth part of 72, viz., 18, giving $\frac{54}{72}$, as the following scheme will show:— $\frac{3\times72}{4\times72}=\frac{3\times18\times4}{4\times18\times4}=\frac{3\times18}{4\times18}=\frac{54}{72}$. The other fractions being altered in the same manner, we get $\frac{54}{72}+\frac{60}{72}+\frac{63}{72}+\frac{16}{72}+\frac{42}{72}$, and as these are now all of the same denomination, though not altered in value, we can add them, and we find $\frac{3}{4}+\frac{5}{6}+\frac{7}{8}+\frac{2}{9}+\frac{7}{12}=\frac{54}{72}+\frac{60}{72}+\frac{63}{72}+\frac{16}{72}+\frac{42}{72}=\frac{235}{72}$. Hence the

RULE.

Find the L. C. M. of all the denominators, which will be the common denominator; divide this common multiple by each denominator, and multiply the quotient by each numerator in succession for new numerators; add all these new numerators together, and place the common denominator below the sum, and the fraction thus obtained will be the sum of the given fractions. If the numerator, thus obtained, be greater than the denominator, the resulting fraction may be reduced to a whole or a mixed number by division.

EXERCISES.

1. Express $\frac{1}{15}+\frac{2}{15}+\frac{4}{15}+\frac{7}{15}$ as a single fraction? Ans. $\frac{14}{15}$.
2. Find the sum of $\frac{1}{2}$, $\frac{2}{3}$, $\frac{3}{4}$ and $\frac{5}{6}$? Ans. $2\frac{3}{4}$.
3. Add together $4\frac{7}{8}$, $1\frac{17}{18}$, $2\frac{23}{24}$, $3\frac{20}{27}$ and $5\frac{1}{12}$? Ans. $18\frac{65}{108}$.
4. What fraction is equal to $\frac{1}{2}+\frac{1}{4}+\frac{1}{8}+\frac{1}{16}+\frac{1}{32}+\frac{1}{64}$? Ans. $\frac{63}{64}$.
5. What fraction is equal to $1\frac{1}{2}+2\frac{2}{3}+3\frac{3}{4}+4\frac{4}{5}+5\frac{5}{6}+6\frac{6}{7}$? Ans. $25\frac{171}{420}$.
6. Express $\frac{1}{2}$ of $\frac{3}{4}+\frac{2}{3}$ of $\frac{5}{6}+\frac{3}{4}$ of $\frac{1}{2}$ as a single fraction? Ans. $\frac{47}{36}=1\frac{11}{36}$.
7. Find the sum of $1\frac{14}{15}$, $8\frac{2}{5}$, $3\frac{9}{22}$ and $4\frac{3}{8}$? Ans. $18\frac{31}{264}$.
8. Find the sum of $\frac{1}{8}$ of $\frac{4}{5}+\frac{1}{12}$ of $\frac{4}{7}+\frac{3}{8}$ of $\frac{8}{9}$? Ans. $\frac{101}{210}$.
9. What single fraction is equivalent to $\frac{1}{2}$ of $\frac{1}{3}+\frac{1}{3}$ of $\frac{1}{4}+\frac{1}{4}$ of $\frac{1}{5}$? Ans. $\frac{3}{10}$.
10. What single fraction is equivalent to $\frac{3}{4}$ of $\frac{5}{6}$ of $\frac{1}{5}+\frac{1}{8}$ of $\frac{2}{3}$ of $\frac{1}{4}+\frac{7}{8}$ of $\frac{1}{3}$ of $\frac{1}{7}$? Ans. $\frac{3}{16}$.
11. What single fraction is equivalent to $\frac{3}{5}$ of $\frac{5}{6}$ of $\frac{7}{8}+\frac{2}{3}$ of $\frac{6}{8}$ of $\frac{5}{7}$? Ans. $\frac{89}{112}$.

12. Simplify $\frac{4\frac{1}{20}+8\frac{2}{15}}{4\frac{1}{15}+8\frac{1}{10}}$? Ans. $1\frac{1}{730}$.

13. Find a single fraction equivalent to $\frac{1}{2}$ of $\frac{5}{6}$ of $\frac{2}{3}+\frac{3}{5}$ of $\frac{7}{8}$? Ans. $\frac{289}{360}$.

14. Divide the sum of $\frac{5}{11}$ and $\frac{3}{7}$ by the sum of $\frac{4}{5}$ and $\frac{3}{7}$? Ans. $\frac{340}{473}$.

15. Simplify $\frac{\frac{1}{2}+\frac{1}{4}+\frac{1}{8}+\frac{1}{16}+\frac{1}{32}+\frac{1}{64}+\frac{1}{128}}{\frac{1}{2}+\frac{3}{4}+\frac{7}{8}+\frac{15}{16}+\frac{31}{32}+\frac{63}{64}+\frac{127}{128}}$? Ans. $\frac{127}{769}$.

16. Simplify $\frac{\frac{1}{3}+\frac{4}{7}+\frac{21}{32}}{\frac{2}{5}+\frac{23}{36}+\frac{3}{5}}$? Ans. $\frac{3147}{3304}$.

VII.—SUBTRACTION OF FRACTIONS.

What we have said of addition enables us to give at once the

RULE FOR SUBTRACTION.

Reduce the given fractions, if necessary, to new ones having a common denominator, as in addition, and subtract the numerator of the less from that of the greater, and place the common denominator below the remainder, and the resulting fraction will be the difference between the given fractions.

EXAMPLES.—(1.) To subtract $\frac{5}{11}$ from $\frac{7}{11}$. Here the denominations being the same, we can subtract at once, and find the difference to be $\frac{2}{11}$. (2.) To find the value of $\frac{8}{9}-\frac{6}{7}$. These fractions brought to a common denominator, as in addition, become $\frac{56}{63}$ and $\frac{54}{63}$, and therefore the difference is $\frac{2}{63}$. (3.) To find the excess of $12\frac{1}{3}$ above $7\frac{5}{8}$, we find new fractions with a common denominator, viz., $\frac{8}{24}$ and $\frac{15}{24}$, and we write $12\frac{8}{24}-7\frac{15}{24}$. Now we are required first to subtract $\frac{15}{24}$ from $\frac{8}{24}$, but as we cannot do this directly, we take one of the 12 preceding units, and call it $\frac{24}{24}$, (for $\frac{24}{24}=1$,) then $\frac{24}{24}+\frac{8}{24}=\frac{32}{24}$, and $\frac{32}{24}-\frac{15}{24}=\frac{17}{24}$, then we subtract the 7 from the remaining 11; or, as in simple subtraction, 8 from 12, and we find the total excess to be $4\frac{17}{24}$. In practice it is most convenient to subtract 15 from 24, and add 8; thus $24-15=9$, and $9+8=17$, and the answer is $4\frac{17}{24}$.

EXERCISES.

1. $\frac{5}{6}-\frac{3}{6}=\frac{2}{6}=\frac{1}{3}$. 2. $\frac{9}{11}-\frac{5}{11}=\frac{4}{11}$. 3. $\frac{10}{13}-\frac{3}{13}=\frac{7}{13}$. 4. $\frac{7}{8}-\frac{19}{24}=\frac{1}{12}$.

5. What is the difference between $\frac{3}{8}$ and $\frac{29}{32}$? Ans. $\frac{17}{32}$.

6. What is the difference between $\frac{449}{756}$ and $\frac{65}{189}$? Ans. $\frac{1}{4}$.

7. What is the difference between $\frac{59}{60}$ and $\frac{8}{15}$? Ans. $\frac{9}{20}$.

8. What is the excess of $20\frac{4}{9}$ above $9\frac{19}{22}$? Ans. $10\frac{115}{198}$.

9. From $5\frac{23}{32}$ take $3\frac{2}{7}$? Ans. $2\frac{97}{224}$.

10. What is the difference between $5\frac{7}{12}$ and $6\frac{431}{2520}$? Ans. $\frac{1481}{2520}$.

11. What is the value of $\frac{3}{4}+\frac{5}{6}-\frac{7}{8}+\frac{7}{12}-\frac{1}{2}$? Ans. $\frac{19}{24}$.

12. What is the difference between $100\frac{3}{19}$ and $50\frac{40}{41}$?
Ans. $49\frac{142}{779}$.

13. What is the difference between $\frac{1}{2}$ of $\frac{1}{3}$ and $\frac{1}{3}$ of $\frac{1}{2}$? Ans. 0

14. What is the difference between $\frac{3}{8}$ of $\frac{7}{10}$ and $\frac{5}{6}$ of $\frac{4}{9}$?
Ans. $\frac{233}{2160}$.

15. What is the value of $\frac{1}{2}+\frac{2}{3}-\frac{3}{4}-\frac{5}{6}+\frac{11}{12}$? Ans. $\frac{1}{2}$.

VIII.—DENOMINATE FRACTIONS.

Hitherto we have treated of fractions abstractly, and we must now apply the principles laid down to denominate numbers, and show how a fraction may be transformed from one denomination to another of the same kind, *e. g.*, how a fraction of a shilling may be expressed as a fraction of a pound, and *vice versa.*

RULE.

(1.) *Reduce the given quantity to the lowest denomination which it expresses.* (2.) *Reduce the unit in the terms of which it is to be expressed to the same denomination, and* (3,) *make the former the numerator and the latter the denominator, and the fraction will be expressed in the required terms.*

EXAMPLES.

1. To express 2 ft. 9 in. as a fraction of a yard. Reducing 2 ft. 9 in. to inches, we get 33 inches, and one yard is 36 inches,—the fraction therefore is $\frac{33}{36}$ or $\frac{11}{12}$.

2. In like manner to express 2 qrs., 24 lbs. as the decimal of a cwt. we have 2 qrs., 24 lbs=74 lbs., and 1 cwt., is 100 lbs., so that the fraction is $\frac{74}{100}=\frac{37}{50}$.

3. So also 3 roods, 32 rods, expressed as a fraction of an acre is $\frac{152}{160}$ or $\frac{19}{20}$ of an acre.

4. To express 17 cwt., 2 qrs., 10 lbs. as a fraction of a ton we have $\frac{360}{2000}=\frac{36}{200}=\frac{18}{100}=\frac{9}{50}$.

5. Express 48 minutes, 48 seconds as a fraction of an hour.

6. Express 13s. 4d. as a fraction of £1. Ans. £$\frac{2}{3}$.

7. Express 36 rods as a fraction of a mile. Ans. $\frac{36}{320}=\frac{9}{80}$.

8. Express 4s. 4d. as a fraction of £1. Ans. £$\frac{13}{60}$.

9. Express $4\frac{1}{2}$d. as a fraction of 1s. Ans. $\frac{3}{8}$s.

10. Express 1 oz. troy as a fraction of 1 lb. Ans. $\frac{1}{12}$.

11. Express 40 lbs. as a fraction of 1 cwt. Ans. $\frac{2}{5}$ cwt.

12. Express 50 lbs. as a fraction of 1 ton. Ans. $\frac{1}{40}$ ton.

13. Express 72 lbs. as a fraction of 1 cwt. Ans. $\frac{18}{25}$ cwt.

14. A day is 23 hours, 56 minutes, 48 seconds, nearly; what fraction of this will 7 hours be? Ans. $\frac{525}{1796}$.

15. Express 95 square yards as a fraction of an acre. Ans. $\frac{19}{968}$.

16. Express 14 yards as a fraction of a mile. Ans. $\frac{7}{880}$.

17. What fraction of a year ($365\frac{1}{4}$ days) is one month (30 days)? Ans. $\frac{40}{487}$.

18. Express 100 yards as a fraction of a mile. Ans. $\frac{5}{88}$.

19. Express 45 cents as a fraction of a dollar. Ans. $\frac{9}{20}$.

20. Express 60 lbs. as a fraction of a cwt. Ans. $\frac{3}{5}$.

21. A man has an income of $3610 a year, and saves $\frac{3}{7}$ of it; how much does he spend? Ans. $\$2062\frac{6}{7}$.

To find the value of a fraction in the denominations which the integer contains, reduce the numerator to the next lower denomination, and divide the result by the denominator; if there be a remainder, reduce to the next denomination, and divide again, and continue the same operation till there is either no remainder, or down to the lowest denomination by which the integer is counted. Thus, since a ton is 20 cwt., $\frac{1}{7}$ of 6 tons is 120 tons divided by 7, which gives 17 cwt., with a remainder of 1, which, reduced to qrs., will give 4, in which 7 is not contained, and the 4 qrs. reduced to lbs., will give 100, and this divided by 7 produces $14\frac{2}{7}$; so that $\frac{6}{7}$ of a ton is 17 cwt., 0 qrs., $14\frac{2}{7}$ lbs.

EXERCISES.

1. What is the value of $\frac{7}{12}$ of a ton? Ans. 11 cwt., 2 qrs., $16\frac{2}{3}$ lbs.
2. What is the value of $\frac{4}{10}$ of a yard? Ans. 2 feet., $8\frac{2}{5}$ in.
3. What is the value of $\frac{13}{24}$ of a mile?
4. What is the value of $\frac{19}{20}$ of a shilling Stg.? Ans. $11\frac{2}{5}$d.
5. What is the value of $\frac{4}{7}$ of a ton? Ans. 11 cwt., 1 qr., $17\frac{6}{7}$ lbs.
6. What is the value of $\frac{2}{3}$ lb. troy? Ans. 8 oz.
7. What is the value of $\frac{6}{13}$ of a shilling? Ans. $5\frac{7}{13}$d.
8. What is the value of $\$\frac{8}{9}$? Ans. $88\frac{8}{9}$ cts.
9. What is the value of $\frac{4}{5}$ of $6? Ans. $4.80.
10. What is the value of $\frac{17}{20}$ of $8? Ans. $6.80.

To change a fraction to one of a lower denomination, reduce the numerator to that denomination, and divide by the denominator. Thus: $\frac{7}{145}$ of a dollar is 700 cts. divided by 145, which gives $4\frac{24}{29}$.

EXERCISES.

1. Express $\frac{7}{100}$ of a foot as a fraction of an inch. Ans. $\frac{21}{25}$.
2. Express $\frac{1}{120}$ of a cwt. as a fraction of a lb. Ans. $\frac{5}{6}$.
3. Express $\frac{1}{20}$ of a lb. as a fraction of an oz. Ans. $\frac{4}{5}$.
4. Express $\frac{3}{4}$ of $\frac{5}{12}$ of a yard as a fraction of a foot. Ans. $\frac{15}{16}$.
5. Express $\frac{4}{27}$ of a rod as a fraction of a yard. Ans. $\frac{22}{27}$.
6. Express $\frac{1}{2}$ of $\frac{1}{8}$ of an acre as a fraction of a rood. Ans. $\frac{1}{4}$.
7. Reduce $\frac{3}{26}$ cwt. to the fraction of a pound. Ans. $11\frac{7}{13}$ lb.
8. Reduce $\frac{1}{21}$ of a day to the fraction of a minute. Ans. $68\frac{4}{7}$ min.
9. What part of a second is the *one-millionth* part of a day? Ans. $\frac{54}{625}$ sec.
10. Reduce £$\frac{1}{36}$ to the fraction of a penny. Ans. $6\frac{2}{3}$d.
11. Reduce $\frac{1}{24}$ of a pound avoirdupois to the fraction of an oz. Ans. $\frac{2}{3}$ oz.

The reducing of a denominate fraction from one of a lower to one of a higher denomination being the converse of the last rule, we must perform the same operation on the denominator as was there performed on the numerator.

Thus, $\frac{5}{8}$d. is £$\frac{1}{384}$, for £$\frac{5}{8\times12\times20}$ = £$\frac{5}{1920}$ = £$\frac{1}{384}$.

EXERCISES.

1. What part of 1 lb. troy is $\frac{3}{5}$ of a grain? Ans. $\frac{1}{9600}$.
2. What part of 4 days is $\frac{3}{4}$ of a minute? Ans. $\frac{1}{7680}$.
3. What part of 5 bushels is $\frac{2}{3}$ of $\frac{3}{4}$ of a pint? Ans. $\frac{1}{640}$.
4. What part of a rod is $2\frac{3}{4}$ of $\frac{7}{12}$ of an inch? Ans. $\frac{7}{864}$.
5. What part of 2 weeks is $\frac{5}{14}$ of a day? Ans. $\frac{5}{196}$.

DECIMAL FRACTIONS.

16.—We have seen already (Art. 3,) that every figure to the right is *one-tenth* the value it would have if removed one place to the left. Thus, resuming our former example, 8 standing alone means 8 *units*, but if we place another 8 after it, thus 88, it now means 8 *tens*, so that the last 8 is *one-tenth* of the first. Now, since the 8 to the right expresses units, another 8 placed to the right will express *eight-tenths* of the same unit, and another subjoined will express $\frac{8}{100}$ of the unit. Thus we see that the decimal notation is directly an extension of the Arabic. Hence arose the convenient mode of writing $8\frac{7}{10}$ in the form 8.7, by which is indicated that all the figures before the decimal point (.) represent integers, and all after it fractions, each being *one-tenth* of what it would be if *one* place further to the left. Therefore 888.888 is *eight hundreds, eight tens, eight units,—eight-tenths, eight one-hundredths,* and *eight one-thousandths;* or, $\frac{8}{10}+\frac{8}{100}+\frac{8}{1000}$. These added will give $\frac{800}{1000}+\frac{80}{1000}+\frac{8}{1000}$, or $\frac{888}{1000}$, which, for brevity, is written .888, and may be read eight hundred and eighty-eight one-thousandths; or, as is usual, *point* 888, or *decimal* 888, but never properly eight hundred and eighty-eight. In the same manner as 80 means 8 tens and no units, so .08 means no tenths, but 8 hundredths, and .008 means no tenths, no hundredths, but eight one-thousandths, &c.—Hence we see that for every cipher in the denominator, which is always 10 or a power of 10, there must be a figure in the numerator when expressed decimally. Thus: $\frac{8}{1000}$ must be written decimally .008. From this we see that removing the decimal point one place to the right is the same as multiplying by 10, and removing it one place to the left is the same as dividing by 10; so, also, removing the point two places to the right is the same as multiplying by 100, and removing it two places to the left is the same as dividing by 100. This is the principle already laid down for the reduction of dollars to cents, and cents to dollars.

I.—Reduction of Common Fractions to Decimals.—Let it now be required to express the common fraction $\frac{7}{8}$ as a decimal. We have seen (Art. 14,) that we may multiply the terms of any fraction by the same number without changing the value of the fraction. Let us then multiply the terms of $\frac{5}{8}$ by 1000, and we get $\frac{5000}{8000}$. On the same principle we can divide the terms by the same number without altering the value. Let us then divide by 8, and we get $\frac{625}{1000}$, where the denominator is a power of 10, and therefore the fraction is in the decimal form, and may be written .625, the denominator being omitted. But as it is not always apparent by what power of 10 we must multiply, so that when the terms are divided by the given denominator, that denominator may be transformed into 10 or a power of 10, *i. e.*, into 1 followed by a certain number of ciphers, we may as well add ciphers, one by one, as we proceed. This is exhibited in the annexed example. From these principles we can deduce a rule for reducing a common fraction to a decimal.

```
8)50(0.625
  48
  ——
   20
   16
   ——
    40
    40
```

RULE.

Divide the numerator, with a cipher or ciphers annexed, by the denominator. Thus $\frac{11}{16}$ *will give, as in the margin,* .6875. In the examples given we find that the addition of three ciphers to the first, and four to the second, makes the numerator divisible by the denominator without remainder. Such fractions are called terminating decimals. From this we see that there are common fractions whose terms can be multiplied by such powers of 10 as will make the numerator divisible by the denominator without remainder, but it often happens that no power of ten will effect this, and that remainders occur which cannot be made divisible evenly by the denominator, by the addition of any number of ciphers. Such fractions will never terminate, and therefore are called interminate, and the common fraction can never be expressed exactly in the decimal form, and all we can do is to make an approximation more or less close, according to the number of decimal places to which we carry it. Let us take the fraction $\frac{1}{9}$.—First, 9 is not contained in 1, and therefore we place the decimal point in the quotient, and add a cipher to the numerator, and we find that 9 is contained *once* in 10, with a remainder 1,—annexing another cipher, we again obtain 1 in the quotient, and this will obviously continue *ad infinitum*.—This recurrence is marked by a dot or dash over the figure, thus: $.\dot{1}$ or .1′. If we express $\frac{1}{7}$ as a decimal, we find that after we have got six figures in the quotient, we have a remainder 1, the same as the original numerator, and therefore we should again obtain the same quotient .142857, and hence this is called a circulating or periodic decimal, and the first and last of the recurring figures are marked with a point or trait. Thus: $.\dot{1}4285\dot{7}$ or .1′42857′. Again, it often happens that some figures do not recur whilst others following them do, as in the annexed example, after we have got

```
16)110(.6875
   96
   ---
   140
   128
   ---
    120
    112
    ---
     80
     80
```

```
7)10(.i42857
  7
  --
  30
  28
  --
   20
   14
   --
    60
    56
    --
     40
     35
     --
      50
      49
      --
       1
```

(In the second working the first figure 1 and the last figure 7 of the quotient .142857 are marked with a dot.)

five figures the 11500 which gave us the third figure 3, in the quotient recurs, and by pursuing the division we should find 345 recurring without end. When all the figures recur, the fraction is called a pure periodic decimal; when only some of them recur, it is called mixed, and the term rapeater is applied when only one figure recurs, as $\frac{1}{9}$=.1111, &c.=$.\dot{1}$ or $\frac{7}{12}$=.58333, &c.=$.58\dot{3}$. Since the denominator is always 10, or a power of 10, and since 10 has no factors but 2 and 5, and therefore powers of 10 no factors but 2 and 5, or powers of these, it follows that no decimal will terminate except the denominator be expressed by either or both of these, or some power or product of them. Hence all terminating decimals are derived from common fractions having for denominator some figure of the series 2, 4, 8, 16, 32, &c., or 5, 25, 125, &c., or, 10, 20, 40, 50, 60, 80, 100, &c.

```
 4111
33300)41110(.12345.
      33300
      -----
       78100
       66600
       ------
       115000
        99900
       ------
        151000
        133200
        ------
         178000
         165500
         ------
          11500
```

EXERCISES.

1. Reduce the common fraction $\frac{1}{4}$ to a decimal. Ans. .25.
2. Reduce the common fraction $\frac{1}{2}$ to a decimal. Ans. .5.
3. Reduce the common fraction $\frac{3}{4}$ to a decimal. Ans. .75.
4. Reduce the common fraction $\frac{1}{3}$ to a decimal. Ans. $.\dot{3}$.
5. Reduce the common fraction $\frac{1}{9}$ to a decimal. Ans. $.\dot{1}$.
6. Reduce the common fraction $\frac{1}{8}$ to a decimal. Ans. .125.
7. Reduce the common fraction $\frac{1}{6}$ to a decimal. Ans. $.1\dot{6}$.
8. Reduce the common fraction $\frac{1}{7}$ to a decimal. Ans. $.\dot{1}4285\dot{7}$.
9. Reduce the common fraction $\frac{1}{5}$ to a decimal. Ans. .2.
10. Reduce the common fraction $\frac{1}{10}$ to a decimal. Ans. .1.
11. Reduce the common fraction $\frac{1}{11}$ to a decimal. Ans. $.\dot{0}\dot{9}$.
12. Reduce the common fraction $\frac{1}{12}$ to a decimal. Ans. $.08\dot{3}$.
13. Reduce the common fraction $\frac{2}{3}$ to a decimal. Ans. $.\dot{6}$.
14. Reduce the common fraction $\frac{4}{5}$ to a decimal. Ans. .8.

15. Reduce the common fraction $\frac{5}{6}$ to a decimal. Ans. $.8\dot{3}$.

16. Reduce the common fraction $\frac{3}{8}$ to a decimal. Ans. .375.

17. Reduce the common fraction $\frac{5}{8}$ to a decimal. Ans. .625.

18. Reduce the common fraction $\frac{7}{8}$ to a decimal. Ans. .875.

19. Reduce the common fraction $\frac{4}{9}$ to a decimal. Ans. $.\dot{4}$.

20. Reduce the common fraction $\frac{5}{7}$ to a decimal. Ans. $.\dot{7}1428\dot{5}$.

21. Reduce the common fraction $\frac{10}{11}$ to a decimal. Ans. $.\dot{9}\dot{0}$.

22. Reduce the common fraction $\frac{11}{12}$ to a decimal. Ans. $.91\dot{6}$.

23. Reduce the common fraction $\frac{12}{13}$ to a decimal. Ans. $.\dot{9}2307\dot{6}$.

24. Reduce the common fraction $\frac{11}{14}$ to a decimal.

25. Reduce the common fraction $\frac{11}{16}$ to a decimal. Ans. .6875.

26. Reduce the common fraction $\frac{5}{66}$ to a decimal.

27. Reduce the common fraction $\frac{11}{32}$ to a decimal. Ans. .34375.

28. Reduce the common fraction $\frac{5}{1025}$ to a decimal.

29. Reduce the common fraction $\frac{37}{79}$ to a decimal.

Ans. $.\dot{4}68354430379\dot{7}$.

30. Reduce the common fraction $\frac{4}{909}$ to a decimal. Ans. $.\dot{0}04\dot{4}$.

31. Reduce the common fraction $\frac{1}{49}$ to a decimal.

Ans. $.\dot{0}20408163265306122448979591836734693877555\dot{1}$.

32. Express $\frac{1}{99}$ decimally. Ans. $.\dot{0}\dot{1}$.

33. Express $\frac{1}{999}$ decimally. Ans. $.\dot{0}0\dot{1}$.

34. Express $\frac{1}{999}$ decimally.

35. Express $\frac{6}{10001}$ decimally. Ans. .00059994.

To reduce a denominate numbei to the form of a decimal fracion, *reduce it to the lowest denomination which it contains ; reduce he integral unit to the same denomination, and divide the former y the latter.*

Thus, to express 18s. 4d. as a decimal of £1, we must reduce it o pence, the lowest denomination given, and divide it by 240, the ıumber of pence in £1, which gives the fraction $\frac{220}{240}=\frac{22}{24}=\frac{11}{12}$, and his reduced to a decimal, gives .916 or £.916. In like manner .5s. 10½d. is reduced to half-pence, viz., 381, and the half-pence in £1 are 480, and $\frac{381}{480}=\frac{127}{160}$, which expressed decimally is .79375.

EXERCISES.

1. What decimal of £1 is 11s. $4\frac{1}{2}$d.? Ans. .56875.

2. Express 15s. $9\frac{3}{4}$d. as a decimal of £1. Ans. .790625.

3. What decimal of a square mile is an acre? Ans. .0015625.

4. Express 1 pound troy as a decimal of 1 pound, avoirdupois.* Ans. $.8\dot{2}28571\dot{4}$.

5. Reduce 17 cwt. to the decimal of a ton. Ans. .85.

6. Express $\frac{15}{16}$ of a cwt. as a decimal of a ton. Ans. .046875.

oz.
11÷16=.6875
lbs.
22.6875÷25=.9075
qrs.
2.9075÷4=.726875
cwt.
11.726875÷20=.58634375

16)11
25)22.6875
4)2.9075
20)11.726875
.58634375

The operation annexed is often convenient in practice. To reduce 11 cwt., 2 qrs., 22 lbs., 11 oz., to the decimal of a ton. First, we divide the 11 oz. by 16, the number of oz. in 1 lb., and then annex the 22 lbs., and divide by 25, the lbs in a qr., and so on. The first form of the work is best suited for illustration, the second is neater in practice. The principle is the same as that implied in the general rule given above.

ADDITIONAL EXERCISES.

7. Reduce 10 drams to the decimal of 1 lb. Ans. .0390625.

8. Reduce 11 dwt. to the decimal of 1 lb. Ans. $.0458\dot{3}$.

9. Express 1 oz., avoirdupois, as a fraction of 1 oz., troy, (see note.) Ans. $.911\dot{4}58\dot{3}$.

10. Reduce 5 hours, 48 minutes, 49.7 seconds to the decimal of a day.

---

* A caution seems necessary here, for since the pound (troy,) contains 12 ounces, and the pound (avoirdupois,) 16, the natural conclusion would be that the pound (troy) is $\frac{12}{16}$ or $\frac{3}{4}$ of the pound avoirdupois. This is not correct, for the ounce troy exceeds the ounce avoirdupois by $42\frac{1}{2}$ grains, though the pound avoirdupois (7000 grs.) exceeds the pound Troy (5760 grs.) by 1240 grains. This will be manifest from the operation on the margin, where the standard weights are given.

5760÷12=480
7000÷16=$437\frac{1}{2}$
difference.. $42\frac{1}{2}$

II.—Reduction of Decimals to Common Fractions.—To find the common fraction corresponding to any given decimal.—This involves three cases according as the fraction is a terminating decimal, a pure circulating decimal, or a mixed circulating decimal. The first case scarcely requires proof. We give it, however, in order to assist those unaccustomed to the algebraic notation, to understand more clearly the form of illustration used in the other cases.

Let us take the fraction .9375, and use d for decimal. We now write d=.9375, and multiplying both terms by 10000, we obtain 10000 d=9375, and therefore $d=\frac{9375}{10000}$, which reduced to its lowest terms is $\frac{15}{16}$, the common fraction required. This is simply putting for denominator 1, followed by a cipher for each figure in the decimal.

$$\begin{array}{r} d=.666+ \\ \hline 9\ d=6 \end{array}$$

To find the value of a pure circulator, suppose $.\dot{6}$. Put $d=.\dot{6}$, or d=.666, and multiply by 10, which gives 10 d=6.66, and writing the former expression beneath, and subtracting, we get 9 d=6, and consequently $d=\frac{6}{9}$ or $\frac{2}{3}$, the common fraction sought.

$$\begin{array}{r} d=.\dot{7}\dot{2} \\ 100\ d=72.\dot{7}\dot{2} \\ \hline 99\ d=72 \end{array}$$

Let us now seek the vulgar fraction corresponding to $.\dot{7}\dot{2}$. Put $d=.\dot{7}\dot{2}$, multiply by 100, and subtract as before, and there results a remainmainder of 99 d=72, or $d=\frac{72}{99}=\frac{8}{11}$.

$$\begin{array}{r} d=.56\dot{8}\dot{1} \\ 10000\ d=5681.\dot{8}\dot{1} \\ 100\ d=\quad 56.\dot{8}\dot{1} \\ \hline 9900\ d=5625 \end{array}$$

Again, to find the vulgar fraction corresponding to $.56\dot{8}\dot{1}$. Multiply first by 10000, and then by 100, and subtract the latter from the former, and you obtain 9900 d= 5625, and hence $d=\frac{5625}{9900}$, which reduced to its lowest terms is $\frac{25}{44}$.

From these investigations the three following rules for the three cases mentioned are derived:

I. *If the fraction be a terminating decimal make it the numerator, and for denominator write* 1, *followed by as many ciphers as there are figures in the decimal.*

II. *If the decimal be a pure circulator, make the digits of the decimal the numerator, and for denominator write as many nines as there are figures in the period*

III. *If the decimal be a mixed circulator, subtract the non-circulating part from the whole decimal to the end of the first period, both being treated as whole numbers; make the remainder the numerator, and for denominator write as many nines as there are circulating figures, and after them as many ciphers as there are non-circulating figures. In all cases reduce to the lowest terms.*

EXERCISES.

1. Find the vulgar fraction corresponding to $.\dot{0}\dot{4}$. Ans. $\frac{4}{99}$.
2. Find the vulgar fraction corresponding to $.\dot{5}\dot{4}$. Ans. $\frac{6}{11}$.
3. Find the vulgar fraction corresponding to $.24\dot{5}\dot{7}$. Ans. $\frac{811}{3300}$.
4. Find the vulgar fraction corresponding to $.\dot{1}$. Ans. $\frac{1}{9}$.
5. Find the vulgar fraction corresponding to $.\dot{3}$. Ans. $\frac{1}{3}$.
6. Find the vulgar fraction corresponding to $.\dot{7}$. Ans. $\frac{7}{9}$.
7. Find the vulgar fraction corresponding to .75. Ans. $\frac{3}{4}$.
8. Find the vulgar fraction corresponding to $.47\dot{5}4\dot{3}$. Ans. $\frac{3958}{8325}$.
9. Find the vulgar fraction corresponding to $.\dot{4}68354430379\dot{7}$. Ans. $\frac{37}{79}$.
10. Find the vulgar fraction corresponding to $.4\dot{9}$. Ans. $\frac{1}{2}$.
11. Find the vulgar fraction corresponding to $.\dot{1}6\dot{2}$. Ans. $\frac{18}{111}$.
12. Find the vulgar fraction corresponding to $.1\dot{4}$. Ans. $\frac{13}{90}$.
13. Find the vulgar fraction corresponding to $.013\dot{8}$. Ans. $\frac{1}{72}$.
14. Find the vulgar fraction corresponding to $.56\dot{8}\dot{1}$. Ans. $\frac{25}{44}$.
15. Find the vulgar fraction corresponding to $.\dot{5}9\dot{2}$. Ans. $\frac{16}{27}$.

The last rule may be deduced from the other two in the following manner:—Let us take the mixed circulator $.4\dot{1}\dot{8}$, and this being multiplied by 10, the four becomes a whole number, and to preserve the same value, 10 is put as a divisor, which gives $\frac{4.\dot{1}\dot{8}}{10}$ or $\frac{4+.\dot{1}\dot{8}}{10}$, but by rule II. we have $.\dot{1}\dot{8}=\frac{18}{99}$, and hence the whole may be written $\frac{4+\frac{18}{99}}{10}=\frac{396+18}{990}=\frac{414}{990}=\frac{23}{55}$, and this result corresponds to rule III.

IV.—ADDITION & SUBTRACTION OF DECIMALS.

From what has been said, it is plain that decimals can be added and subtracted just as whole numbers, care being taken to keep the decimal points in the same vertical line. In all operations into which repetends enter, it should be observed that in order to have a result true to any given number of places, it is generally desirable to carry out the repetend to one or two places more than the required number. It is often sufficient, however, to allow for what would be carried, which can usually be done by inspection. In all cases, respect should be had to the degree of exactness which the nature of the calculation requires. The figures beyond those required can be estimated and added in. Thus, if only five places are required, and the calculation be carried to six places, and the seventh figure is a large *one*, it should be added to the sixth figure.

This may be stated in the form of a

RULE.

Add and subtract as in whole numbers, keeping the decimal points in the same vertical line.

EXERCISES.

(1.)	(2.)	(3.)
1.78645	8.58333333+	51.250000000
3.97863	17.74747474+	3.444444444+
7.84396	112.08080808+	7.637373737+
4.32782	6.12500000	.885555555+
9.54179	15.66666667	11.875000000
11.69857	.76969697	7.875875875+
5.48491	11.00000000	7.111111111+
44.66213	171.97297979	90.079360724

In exercise 2, the eighth figure of each of the fifth and sixth lines is made 7 instead of 6, which renders it unnecessary to make any allowance for the repetends that would follow, but this change is not made on any of the last figures of exercise 3, and therefore we add 2 for what would be carried from the tenth decimal place to the ninth.

4. Find in the decimal form the sum of $\frac{1}{2}$, $\frac{2}{3}$, $\frac{3}{4}$, $\frac{2}{5}$. Ans. $2.31\dot{6}$.

5. Find in the decimal form the sum of $\frac{1}{2}$, $\frac{3}{4}$, $\frac{7}{8}$, $\frac{15}{16}$, $\frac{31}{32}$, $\frac{63}{64}$, $\frac{127}{128}$. Ans. 6.0078125.

6. Find in the decimal form the sum of $\frac{23}{25}$, $\frac{2}{5}$, $\frac{7}{24}$, $\frac{11}{15}$.

Ans. 2.345.

7. Find in the decimal form the sum of $2\frac{3}{5}$, $4\frac{7}{8}$, $5\frac{3}{10}$.

Ans. 12.775.

8. What is the sum of .786425, .975324, .176009, .32, .62519375, .4? Ans. 3.28295175.

9. Add to 6 places $18.1\dot{2}7\dot{6}$, $11.\dot{3}4\dot{9}$, $12.1\dot{4}\dot{5}$, $8.\dot{6}4\dot{8}$, $15.2\dot{3}$.

Ans. 65.504414.

10. Find to 6 places the sum of $15.\dot{7}$, $12.\dot{4}$, $18.\dot{3}8\dot{7}$, $.41\dot{6}$, $.74\dot{6}8\dot{7}$, $.\dot{9}$, $.\dot{4}\dot{5}$, $10.\dot{4}\dot{5}$, $.12\dot{3}4\dot{5}$. Ans. 59.351152.

11. What is the sum of $.\dot{7}\dot{6}$, $.41\dot{6}$, $.\dot{4}\dot{5}$, $.\dot{6}4\dot{8}$, $.2\dot{3}$ to five places of decimals? Ans. 2.52087.

12. Reduce to decimals, and find the sum of $\frac{3}{8}$, $\frac{1}{22}$, $\frac{7}{24}$, $\frac{22}{88}$.

Ans. $1.41\dot{6}$.

13. Find the sum of $.4\dot{2}\dot{7}$, $.41\dot{6}$, $1.\dot{3}2\dot{8}$, $3.0\dot{2}\dot{9}$, 5.476 to six places of decimals. Ans. 10.678037.

14. Required the sum of 1.25, $1.\dot{4}$, $1.6\dot{3}\dot{7}$, $1.88\dot{5}$, 1.684, 1.937, 1.148 and 1.764085. Ans. 12.750458.

15. Find the sum of $.4\dot{6}32\dot{1}$, $.81\dot{5}3\dot{2}$, $.1549\dot{2}\dot{6}$, $.75\dot{3}\dot{2}$ to true to four places. Ans. 2.1867.

16. From 3.468 substract 1.2591, and you find the excess 2.2089.

17. What is the excess of 10.008576 above 5.789?

Ans. 4.219576.

18. From $11.\dot{4}$ take $1.\dot{4}\dot{8}$, and there remains to six places 9.959596.

19. What is the excess of 7.8 above $1.37546\dot{5}\dot{8}$?

Ans. $6.42453\dot{4}\dot{1}$.

20. What is the difference between $9.46\dot{5}7\dot{4}$, and $4.18\dot{3}4\dot{5}$?

Ans. $5.28\dot{2}2\dot{9}$.

21. Express, decimally, the difference between $\frac{2}{3}+\frac{3}{4}+\frac{4}{5}+\frac{5}{6}+\frac{6}{7}$, and $\frac{1}{3}+\frac{4}{7}+\frac{21}{32}$. Ans. 2.34613+.

22. What is the difference, according to the decimal notation, between $\frac{7}{9}$ and $\frac{13}{99}$ true to six places of decimals? Ans. .636363.

23. What is the difference between $\frac{1}{2}$ and $\frac{4}{7}$ expressed decimally true to six decimal places? Ans. .071428.

24. What is the difference between the vulgar fractions corresponding to $.4\dot{9}$ and .5 ? Ans. 0.

25. Find the value of .786425+.975324+.176009+.32+.62519375—3.28295175+.4. Ans. 0.

26. What is the difference between 138.6012, and 128.8512 ? Ans. 9.75

27. What is the excess of 31.6322 above 5.674+1.83+.3125+18.62+4.3+.395—.5. Ans. 1.0007.

28. What is the excess, expressed decimally, of 5.83 above $4\frac{17}{99}$. Ans. $1.65\dot{8}\dot{2}$.

29. What is the difference between 8.375 and $7\frac{3}{7}$ true to six decimal places? Ans. .946428.

30. What is the value of 601.050725—441.001—.00625—3.818475—156.1+.125. Ans. .25.

V.—MULTIPLICATION OF DECIMALS.

If we multiply a decimal by a whole number, the process is precisely the same as if the multiplicand were a whole number, but care must be taken to keep the decimal point in the same relative position. Thus, in the annexed example, as there are three decimal places in the multiplicand, we make three also in the product. If we have to multiply a whole number by a decimal, we must mark off a decimal in the product for each decimal in the multiplier.—The reason of this will be manifest from the consideration that if we multiply 8 units by .6, or $\frac{6}{10}$, we get $\frac{48}{10}$, or 4.8, *i. e.*, 4 units and 8-tenths; and again, when we multiply 7 tens by .6 or $\frac{6}{10}$, we get $\frac{420}{10}$=42 units, which with the 4 units already obtained, make 46 units, and we now have arrived at whole numbers. The same illustration will apply to multiplying by .66, which requires two decimal places to be laid off from the right. Therefore, for every decimal place in the multiplier one must be cut off in the product, and we saw already that for every decimal place in the multiplicand, a deci-

```
 5.678
     6
------
34.068

  5678
    .6
------
3406.8
```

mal place must be cut off in the product, and therefore we conclude that for every decimal place in both factors, a decimal place must be marked in the product. It may be well to vary the illustration by observing that as the tenth of a tenth is a one-hundredth, tenths multiplied by tenths give hundredths; so also the product of tenths and hundredths is thousandths, and so on. Thus: .2 or $\frac{2}{10}$, multiplied by .3 or $\frac{3}{10}$, is $\frac{6}{100}$. Now, .6 would not represent this, for that would mean $\frac{6}{10}$; hence, it is necessary to prefix a cipher, and write .06, and this agrees with what has been already noted (Art. 3) regarding whole numbers, viz., that we are compelled by the nature of the notation to introduce a zero character, and in the present instance the cipher means that there are no *tenths*, just as it indicated in the case referred to that there were no tens. So, also, $\frac{6}{1000}$ would be written decimally .006, which would mean that there are no tenths, no hundredths, but 6 thousandths. From these explanations we deduce the

RULE:

Multiply, as in whole numbers, and cut off from the right a decimal place for every one in both multiplier and multiplicand.

EXAMPLES.

Multiply .78 by .42. Here we multiply as if the quantities were whole numbers, and in the product point off a decimal figure for each one in both multiplier and multiplicand. In Ex. 1, the number of figures in the product is the same as the number in both factors, and therefore we have no whole number in the result, but four decimal places. In Ex. 2 there are four decimal places in the factors, and there are six figures in the product, and consequently two figures represent whole numbers. In Ex. 3, when we multiply 6 by 3, we obtain 18, but if we had carried the repitend out one place farther we should have had 5 to be multiplied by 3, and consequently 1 to carry, so we add 1 to the 18, and in like manner we must allow 2 when multiplying by 4, and 1 when multiplying by 2.

(1.)
```
  .78
  .42
 ----
  156
 312
 ----
.3276
```

(2.)
```
    .674
    34.6
 -------
    4044
   2696
  2022
 -------
 23.3204
```

(3.) $4.\dot{5}\dot{6}$
```
    4.56
    2.43
 -------
    1369
   1826
   913
 -------
 11.0929
```

EXERCISES.

1. Multiply 7.49 by 63.1. Ans. 472.619.
2. Multiply .156 by .143. Ans. .022308.
3. Multiply 1.05 by 1.05, and the product by 1.05. Ans. 1.157625.
4. Find the continual product of .2, .2, .2, .2, .2, .2. Ans. .000064.
5. Multiply .0021 by 21. Ans. .0441.
6. Multiply 3.18 by 41.7. Ans. 132.606.
7. Multiply .08 by .036. Ans. .00288.
8. Multiply .13 by .7. Ans. .091.
9. Multiply .31 by .32 Ans. .0992.
10. Find the continual product of 1.2, 3.25, 2.125. Ans. 8.2875.
11. Multiply 11.4 by 1.14. Ans. 12.996.
12. Find the continual product of .1, .1, .1, .1, .1, .1. Ans. .000001.
13. Multiply 1240 by .008. Ans. 9.92.
14. Find the continual product of .101, .011, .11, 1.1 and 11. Ans. .001478741.
15. Multiply 7.43 by .862 to six places of decimals. Ans. .640839.
16. Multiply 3.18 by 11.7, and the product by 1000. Ans. 132606.
17. Multiply .144 by .144. Ans. .020736.
18. What is the continual product of 13.825, 5.128 and .001? Ans. .0708946.
19. What is the continual product of 4.2, 7.8 and .01? Ans. .3276.
20. What is the continual product of .0001, 6.27 and 15.9? Ans. .0099693.

CONTRACTED METHOD.—In many instances where long lines of figures are to be multiplied together, the operation may be very much shortened, and yet sufficient accuracy attained. We may instance what the student will meet with hereafter, calculations in compound interest and annuities, involving sometimes most tedious operations. By the following method the results in such cases may be obtained with great ease, and correct to a very minute fraction. If we are computing dollars and cents, and extend our calculation to four places of decimals, we are treating of the one-hundredth part of a cent, or the ten-thousandth part of a dollar, a quantity so minute as to become relatively valueless. Hence we conclude that three or four decimal places are sufficient for all ordinary purposes. There are cases, indeed, in which it is necessary to carry out the decimals farther, as, for instance, in the case of Logarithms to be considered hereafter. The principle of the contracted method will be best explained by comparing the two subjoined operations on the same quantities.

Let it be required to find the product of 6.35642 and 47.6453, true to four places of decimals:

EXTENDED OPERATION.		CONTRACTED OPERATION.
6.35	642	6.35642.
47.6	453	3546.74
19	06926	2542568
317	8210	444949
2542	568	38138
38138	52	2542
444949	4	317
2542568		19
		2 carried.
302.8535	37826	302.8535

RULE FOR THE CONTRACTED METHOD.

Place the units' figure of the whole number under the last required decimal place of the multiplicand, and the other integral figures to the right of that in an inverted order, and the decimal figures, also in an inverted order, to the left of the integral unit; multiply by each figure of the inverted multiplier, beginning with the figure of the multiplicand immediately above it, omitting all figures to the right, but allowing for what would have been carried if the decimal had been carried out one place farther—place the first figure of each partial product in the same vertical column, and the others in vertical columns to the left; the sum of these columns will be the required product.

Thus, in the above example, we are required to find the product correct to four decimal places, therefore we set the units' figure, 7, under the fourth decimal figure, and the tens' figure, 4, to the right, and the decimal figures, 6453, to the left in reversed order; then we multiply the whole line by 4, and then we multiply by .7, omitting the 2 which stands to the right, but allowing 1 for what would have been carried, that is, we say 7 times 4 is 28, and 1 is 29, and we write the nine under the 8, the first figure of the first partial product. By comparing the contracted method with the figures of the extended form, which are to the left of the vertical line drawn after the fourth decimal figures, it will be seen that the figures of each column are the same but placed in reversed order, which makes no difference in the sum, as 5+3=3+5=8. This is the same principle as the contracted method of multiplying by 17, 71, &c., suggested in the article on simple multiplication *

The object of writing the multiplier in a reversed order is simply to make the work come in the usual form, as otherwise we should be crossing and recrossing, so to speak, as will be seen by the operation in the margin.—Beginning with the left hand figure of the multiplier, and the right hand figure of the multiplicand, we find the first partial product; then taking the second figure of the multiplier from the left, (7) and the second figure of the multiplicand from the right, we get the second partial product, and so on, moving one place each time towards the right in the multiplier, and one place towards the left in the multiplicand. This is so different from the ordinary mode of operation, as to be excessively awkward and puzzling, and this gave rise to the idea of reversing the order of the digits. We append this remark as most persons cannot at first sight comprehend the reason of the inversion.

```
6.35642
47.6453
-----------
2542568
 444949
  38138
   2542
    317
     19
      2 allowed.
-----------
302.8535
```

* Let the learner observe that all the figures of the first column are of the same rank, viz., ten-thousandths, and therefore may be added together, and as the value of each figure is increased or decreased 10 times according to its position to left or right, it follows that all figures at equal distances from the decimal point, whether to right or left, are of the same rank, *i. e.*, units will be under units, tens under tens, tenths under tenths, hundredths under hundredths, &c., &c. The contracted method is not of much use in terminating decimals which extend to only a few places, but it saves a vast deal of labour in questions which involve either repetends or terminating decimals expressed by a long line of decimal figures

ADDITIONAL EXERCISES.

21. Multiply .26736 by .28758 to four decimal places Ans. .0769.

22. Multiply $7.\dot{2}8571\dot{4}$ by 36.74405 to five decimal places. Ans. 267.70665.

23. Multiply 2.656419 by $1.\dot{7}2\dot{3}$ to six decimal places. Ans. 4.578932.

24. What decimal fraction, true to six places, will express the product of $\frac{9}{14}$ multiplied by $\frac{3}{17}$? Ans. .113445.

25. What decimal fraction is equivalent to $\frac{23}{27}\times\frac{45}{82}$? Ans. .46748.

26. What is the second power of .841 ? Ans. .707281.

27. What is the product of $1.\dot{6}\dot{5}$ by $1.\dot{4}\dot{8}$, true to five places ? Ans. 2.45975.

28. Express decimally $2\frac{9}{13}\times\frac{8}{9}$. Ans. 2.393162.

29. What is the product of $73.6\dot{3}7\dot{1}$ by 8.143 ? Ans. $599.6272\dot{0}7\dot{7}$.

30. .681472×.01286, true to five places, will give .00876.

```
 .681472
 68210.0
 -------
   681
   136
    55
     1
 -------
 .00876
```

In the last exercise it must be observed that since there is no whole number, and five decimal places are required, we must place a cipher under the fifth decimal figure, and write .01286 in reversed order. That the result is a sufficiently close approximation will be evident from the consideration that the last figure 6 is only six one-hundred-thousandths of the unit, and consequently the next figure would be only one-millionth part of the unit.

VI.—DIVISION OF DECIMALS.

We have already seen (1) that we cannot perform any operation except the numbers concerned are of the same denomination, or one of them be abstract; (2) that when a denominate number is used either as a multiplier or a divisor, it ceases to be denominate, and becomes abstract, and (3) that the rules for addition, subtraction, multiplication and division of integers apply equally to decimals, the only additional requirement being the placing and moving of the decimal point.

Suppose then we are required to divide 1.2321 by 11.1, we must by (1) bring both quantities to the same denomination. Now the dividend is carried down to ten-thousands for $1.2321=1+\frac{2321}{10000}$, and therefore we express 11.1 in the corresponding form, ten-thousandths or $11+\frac{1000}{10000}$, or 11.1000, so that we change the form, but not the value of 11.1, the divisor. Again, by (2) the .1, which originally expressed *a tenth* of some unit, and therefore was in reality denominate, now becomes abstract as one of the figures of the given factor of 1.2321, by means of which we are to find the other factor. Hence by (3) we can now divide 1.2321 by 11.1000, as if both were whole numbers, and this is the reason for omitting the decimal point when we have made the number of decimal places equal. Beginners generally feel a difficulty in conceiving how a fraction divided by a fraction can give a whole number. The difficulty may be easily removed by noticing that $\frac{1}{4}$ is contained *twice* in $\frac{1}{2}$ for $\frac{2}{4}=\frac{1}{2}$, *e. g.*, a half dollar contains, or is equivalent to, two quarter dollars. Thus the fraction $\frac{1}{2}$ divided by the fraction $\frac{1}{4}$, gives the whole number 2. So, also, $\frac{1}{8}$ is contained 4 times in $\frac{1}{2}$, and therefore $\frac{1}{2}\div\frac{1}{8}=4$, a whole number. Hence, when we have reduced the divisor and dividend to the same denomination, we may omit the decimal point, as we have only to find *how often the one is contained in the other.* Hence the

RULE.

If the number of decimal places in the divisor and dividend be not equal, make them equal by supplying ciphers or repetends, and then divide as in whole numbers, and the quotient so far will be a whole number, but if there is a remainder, annex ciphers or repetends, and the part of the quotient thus obtained will be a decimal.

The decimal places may be supplied as the work proceeds, as it is easy to see how many ciphers or repetends must be supplied; for we have seen in multiplication that the number of decimal places in any product must be equal to all the decimal places in the factors, and, since a dividend must always be viewed as a product, it follows that the difference between the number of decimal places in dividend and divisor will indicate how many ciphers or repetends must be supplied.

EXERCISES.

1. Divide 47.58 by 26.175 to six decimal places.

Ans. 1.817765.

2. Divide 70.8946 by 13.825 to three places.

Ans. 5.128.

3. Divide $468.\dot{7}$ by 3.365 to six places of decimals.
Ans. 139.309889.

4. Express decimally $1 \div \frac{3}{700}$. Ans. $233.\dot{3}$.

5. Express in the decimal form $\frac{7}{8}$ of $\frac{6}{7} \div \frac{4}{5}$ of $\frac{8}{9}$ true to six places of decimals. Ans. 1.054687.

6. Divide the whole number 9 by the fraction .008. Ans. 1125.

7. What is the quotient of $5.\dot{0}\dot{9}$ by $6.\dot{2}$? Ans. $.\dot{8}\dot{1}$ nearly.

8. Divide .54439 by 7777. Ans. .00007.

9. What decimal is obtained by dividing 1 by 10.473654 ?
Ans. .09547766.

10. What is the difference between $\frac{2}{3} \div \frac{5}{7}$ and $\frac{5}{6} \div \frac{10}{11}$ in the decimal form? Ans. $.2458\dot{3}$.

CONTRACTED METHOD.

The work may often be much abbreviated in the manner exhibited by the following example:

```
.14736).23748|(1.611          14736)23748(1.611
        14736|                  .... 14736
        -----|-                      -----
         9012|0                       9012
         8841|6                       8842
         ----|-                       ----
          170|40                       170
          147|36                       147
          ---|---                      ---
           23|040                       23
           14|736                       15
           --|---                       --
            8|304                        8
```

Here it is required to divide .23748 by .14736. Since both divisor and dividend contain the same number of decimal places, no alteration is needed, and so we can at once reject the decimal point, and divide as in whole numbers. The principle of the contraction is simply what has been already explained, viz., that all we look for in such calculations is a sufficiently close approximation, by which we mean an approximation sufficient for all practical purposes. For this reason, when we have obtained the integral part of the quotient, we may omit one figure of the divisor in succession after each operation, as the value of each figure decreases in a tenfold degree as we descend towards the right, and after three decimal figures the error, or deficit rather, becomes only thousandths, which are very rarely worth taking into account. For example, if the calculation regards dollars and cents, the error at the fourth decimal place would be only the *one-thousandth* part of a cent.

RULE.

Arrange the fractions as in the ordinary mode; find the first figure of the quotient and the first remainder; then, instead of annexing a periodic figure or a cipher, cut off the right hand figure of the divisor, and use the remaining figures to find the next figure of the quotient, and so on.

It is usual to mark the figures as they are successively cut off by placing a point below each. In multiplying by each figure of the quotient, allowance must be made for what would have been carried from the figure of the divisor last cut off, had it been used in the division.

The vertical line drawn through the ordinary form shows how closely the two modes correspond. As has already been remarked, it is desirable, in order to secure accuracy, to carry the figures of repetends to one or two places more than are required.

EXERCISES.

```
        (1.)                              (2.)
43232323)73640000(170.3355.
  ······ 43232323
         --------
         30407677               54637 43682(.7995
         30262626                ···· 38246
         --------                     -----
           145051                      5436
           129697                      4917
           ------                      ----
            15354                       519
            12970                       491
            -----                       ---
             2384                        28
             2162                        27
             ----                        --
              222                         1
              216
              ---
                6
```

Divide 73.64 by .432, and .43682 by .54637 to 4 decimal places each. To show that there will be three integral places in the quotient of Ex. 1, we must consider that there are two places of whole numbers in the dividend and none in the divisor, and, therefore, if we divide 73 and 6, the first decimal place of the dividend by .4, the first figure cf the divisor, we get three integral places. Hence, since we are to have four decimai places, we shall have seven figures in all. This contraction is extremely useful when there are many decimal places.

3. Find the quotient of 8.6134÷7.3524 to four decimal places. Ans. 1.1715.

4. Divide .$\dot{6}\dot{1}$ by 13.543516 to five decimal places. Ans. .04549.

5. Divide .58 by 77.482 to five decimal places. Ans. .00756.

6. Divide .812.54567 by 7.$\dot{3}\dot{4}$ to three decimal places. Ans. 110.649.

7. Divide 1 by 10.473654 to six decimal places. Ans. .09547.

8. Divide 7.126491 by .531 to six decimal places. Ans. 13.420887.

9. Divide 1.77975 by the whole number 25425. Ans. .00007.

10. Divide to eight places .879454 by .897. Ans. .98043924.

VII.—DENOMINATE DECIMALS.

To express one denominate number as a fraction of another of the same kind, reduce both to the lowest denomination contained in either, make the former the numerator and the latter the denominator of a common fraction, and reduce the fraction so found to a decimal in the manner already pointed out.

EXAMPLES.

To express 16 cents as a fraction of a dollar: Here the lowest denomination mentioned is cents, and we reduce a dollar to cents and write $\frac{16}{100}=\frac{4}{25}$, and, dividing 4 by 25, we get .16. To express 11s. $4\frac{1}{2}$d. as a decimal of £1, we reduce both to half-pence, and obtain $\frac{273}{480}=\frac{91}{160}$, which, reduced to a decimal, is .56875.

EXERCISES.

1. Reduce 5s. $10\frac{1}{2}$d. to the decimal of £1. Ans. £ .29375.
2. Reduce $10\frac{1}{2}$d. to the decimal of £1. Ans. £ .04375.
3. Reduce 15s. $9\frac{3}{4}$d. to the decimal of £1. Ans. £ .790625.
4. Express 3 roods and 11 rods as a decimal of an acre. Ans. .81875.

5. Express 3 cwt., 1 qr., 7 lbs., as a decimal of a ton. Ans. .166.

6. Reduce 37 rods to the decimal of a mile. Ans. .115625.

7. Reduce 7 ozs. 4 dwts., to the decimal of a pound. Ans. .6.

8. Reduce a pound troy to the decimal of a pound avoirdupois; correct to six decimal places.* Ans. .822857+.

9. Reduce 5 hours, 48 minutes, 49.7 seconds, to the decimal of a day, taken as 24 hours. Ans. .2422419.

10. Express an ounce avoirdupois as a decimal of a pound troy.
Ans. .9114583.

VIII.—REDUCTION TO DENOMINATIONS.

To find the value of a fraction in the lower denominations, expressed as a decimal of any given denomination, multiply in succession by the numbers which express the given and lower denominations, and after each multiplication cut off from the right as many decimal figures as are contained in the given decimal, and the figures to the left of the decimal point will give the required value.

EXAMPLES.

1. To find the value of .64379 of a pound (apothecary). We multiply by 12, by 8, by 3 and by 20, which gives 7 ozs., 5 drs., 2 scrs., and a little over 8 grs. Repetends must be reduced to common fractions, or found approximately.

```
 .64379
     12
-------
7.72548
      8
-------
5.80384
      3
-------
2.41152
     20
-------
8.23040
```

2. To find the value of $.\dot{7}$: of a day, which is 18 hours, 39 min. and nearly $59\frac{3}{4}$ secs.

```
 .77777 } carry 1.
     24 }
--------
 311109
 155555
--------
18.66659
      60
--------
39.99540
      60
--------
59.72400
```

*The standard pounds are meant here, viz.: troy, 5760 grains, and avoirdupois 7000 grains. Taking the ounces would give $\frac{12}{16}=\frac{3}{4}=.75$

EXERCISES.

1. What is the vaiue of £.475 ? Ans. 9s. 6d.

2. What is the value of $.\dot{7}$ of a cwt. ?

Ans. 3 qrs., 3 lbs., 1 oz., $12\frac{4}{7}$ drs.

3. What is the value of $.541\dot{6}$ of a shilling sterling ? Ans. $6\frac{1}{2}$d.

4. What is the value of .6845 of s cwt. ?

Ans. 2 qrs., 20 lbs., 10 oz., $9\frac{123}{125}$.

5. What is the value of $.\dot{4}$ of 9s. $4\frac{1}{2}$d ? We have $.4=\frac{4}{9}$ and 9s. $4\frac{1}{2}$d., multiplied by 4, and the product, divided by 9, gives 4s. 2d., tho exact value.

6. What is the value of $.02\dot{6}$ of 1° 15′ ? Reducing $.02\dot{6}$ to a vulgar fraction, wc gct $\frac{24}{900}=\frac{2}{75}$, and multiplying 1° 15′ by 2, and dividing by 75, we find 2′.

RATIO AND PROPORTION.

17.—Ratio is the relation which one quantity bears to another of the same kind with respect to magnitude, or the number of times that the less is contained in the greater. Thus, the ratio 7 to 21 is 3, because 7 is contained 3 times in 21, or 21 is 3 times 7. The same result is obtained if we divide 7 by 21, for we then find $\frac{7}{21}=\frac{1}{3}$, which means that 7 is $\frac{1}{3}$ of 21, and this expresses the very same relation as before; for, to say that 7 is $\frac{1}{3}$ of 21 is precisely the same as to say that 21 is 3 times 7. (See note under Inverse Proportion.) And, therefore, 3 is called the measure of the ratio. The numbers thus compared are called the terms of the ratio—the first the antecedent and the second the consequent, and the relation is written 7 : 21. The sign (:) originally indicated division.

That the magnitudes must be of the same kind will be obvious from the consideration that 7 bags of flour could have no ratio to 21 dollars, for multiplying 7 bags of flour by 3 would not make them 21 dollars, but 21 bags of flour, and multiplying 7 dollars by 3 would not make them 21 bags of flour, but 21 dollars. Hence, the less could not be increased to make the greater, except they are homogeneous, or of the same kind.

Proportion is the equality of ratios.

The ratio of 9 to 27 is 3, but we have seen that the ratio of 7 to 21 is also 3, therefore the ratios of 7 to 21 and of 9 to 27 are the same, or $7 \div 21 = 9 \div 27$, and these quantities are, therefore, called proportionals. The sign (: :) was formerly used for equality, and is still retained for equality of ratios, and the sign (=) is used for the actual equality of quantities, though occasionally used for equality of ratios. Hence, the usual mode of writing the equality of two ratios is 7 : 21 : : 9 : 27. Such a statement is called a proportion, or an analogy, and is read—7 is to 21 as 9 to 27, *i. e.*, 27 exceeds 9 as many times as 21 exceeds 7, and this is expressed by saying 27 is the same multiple of 9 that 21 is of 7, or that 9 is the same sub-multiple, measure, or aliquot part of 27 that 7 is of 21. The four quantities are called the *terms* of the proportion; the first and last are called the *extremes*, and second and third the *means;* also, the first and third are called *homologous*, or of the same name, *i. e.*, both are antecedents, and so the second and fourth are homologous, for they are both consequents. The last term is called a fourth proportional to the other three, and we shall denote it by F. P. There are two simple ways of testing the correctness of an analogy. The first is to divide the second term by the first, and the fourth by the third, and if the quotients are equal, the analogy is correct. This is manifest from what has been already said. The second principle is, that, if the analogy be correct, the product of the extremes is equal to the product of the means. To prove this, let us resume the analogy, 7 : 21 : : 9 : 27. We have seen that $21 \div 7 = 27 \div 9$, or $3 = 3$. Now, if each be multiplied by 63, we have (by Ax. II., Cor.,) $189 = 189$. But 189 is the product of 27 by 7, the extremes, and also of 21 by 9, the means—these products then are always equal. From this simple principle we readily deduce a rule for finding a fourth proportional to three given quantities. Let the quantities be 48, 96, and 132, written thus: 48 : 96 : : 132 : , the required quantity. Now, $132 \times 96 = 12672$, the product of the means are therefore equal to the product of the extremes. We have, therefore, a product, 12672, and one of its factors, 48, hence, dividing this product by the given factor, we find the other factor to be 264, which is therefore the fourth proportional, or fourth term of the proportion, and we can now write the whole analogy, thus:—48 : 96 : : 132 : 264. To prove the correctness of the operation, multiply 264 by 48, and 12672 is obtained, the same as before. Hence,

THE RULE.

Divide the product of the second and third terms by the first, and the quotient will be the required fourth term.

To show the order in which the three given quantities are to be arranged, let it be required to find how much 730 yards of linen will cost at the rate of \$30 for 50 yards. It is plain that the answer, or fourth term, must be dollars, for it is a price that is required, and in order that the third term may have a ratio to the fourth, the \$30 must be the third term. Again, since 730 yds. will cost more than 50 yds., the fourth term will be greater than the third, and therefore the second must be greater than the first, and therefore the statement is $\overset{\text{yds.}}{50} : \overset{\text{yds.}}{730} :: \overset{\$}{30}$: 4th proportional, and by the rule $\frac{730 \times 30}{50} = \frac{21900}{50} = 438$, the fourth term, and we can now write the whole analogy, 50 yds : 730 yds : : \$30 : \$438.

This may be called the ascending scale, for the second is greater than the first, and the fourth greater than the third. If the question had been to find what 50 yards of linen will cost at the rate of \$438 for 730 yards, we still find that the answer will be dollars, and that therefore, as before, dollars must be in the third place, but we see that the answer will now be less than 438, as 50 yards, of which the price is required, will cost much less than 730 yards, of which the price is given, and that therefore the second term must be less than the first. Hence the statement is 730 yds : 50 yds : : \$438 : F. P., and by the rule $\frac{438 \times 50}{730} = 30$, the fourth proportional. We now have the full analogy 730 yds : 50 yds : : \$438 : \$30. As the second is less than the first, and the fourth less than the third, this may be called the descending scale. If the first should turn out to be equal to the second, and therefore the third equal to the fourth, we should say that the quantities were to each other in the ratio of *equality.*

RULE FOR THE ORDER OF THE TERMS.

If the question implies that the consequent of the second ratio must be greater than the antecedent, make the greater term of the first ratio the consequent, and the less the antecedent, and vice versa.

The questions hitherto considered belong to what is called *Direct Proportion*, to distinguish it from another kind called *Inverse Proportion;* because, in the former, the greater the number given, the less will be the corresponding number required, and *vice versa;*

whereas, in the latter, the greater the number given, the less will be the number required, and *vice versa.* To illustrate this, let it be required to find how long a stack of hay will feed 12 horses, if it will feed 9 horses for 20 weeks. Here the answer required is time, and therefore 20 weeks will be the antecedent of the second ratio; but the greater the number of horses, the shorter time will the hay last, and therefore the fourth term will be less than the third, and therefore the statement will not be 9 : 12, but the reverse, 12 : 9; and hence the name INVERSE, because the term 9, for which the time (20 weeks,) is given, and which therefore we should expect to be in the first place, has to be put in the second; and the term 12, for which the time is required, and which therefore we should expect to be in the second place, has to be put in the first, and thus the whole analogy is 12 : 9 : : 20 : 15.*

The principal changes that may be made in the order of the terms, will be more readily and clearly understood by the subjoined scheme, than by any explanation in words:

Original Analogy: 8 : 6 : : 12 : 9 for 8×9=72=6×12.
Alternately: 8 : 12 : : 6 : 9 for 8×9=72=6×12.
By Inversion: 6 : 8 : : 9 : 12 for 6×12=72=8×9.
By Composition: 8+6 : 6 : : 12+9 : 9 or 14 : 6 : : 21 : 9 for 14×9=126=6×21.
By Division: 8—6 : 6 : : 12—9 : 9 or 2 : 6 : : 3 : 9 for 2×9=18=6×3.
By Conversion: 8 : 8—6 : : 12 : 12—9 or 8 : 2 : : 12 : 3 for 8×3=24=2×12.

Simple transposition is often of the greatest use. Let us take an easy practical example. In calculating what power will balance a given weight, when the arms of the lever are known, let P be the power, W the weight, A the arm of power, and B the arm of weight. The rule is, that the power and weight are inversely as the arms. This solves all the four possible cases by transposition.

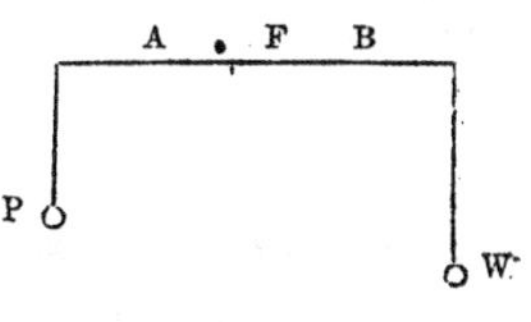

* Inverse ratio is sometimes spoken of, but in reality there is no such thing. It is true that Inverse Proportion requires the terms of one of the ratios to be inverted, but that is a matter of analogy, not of ratio, for we have seen already that 7÷21 expresses the very same relation as 21÷7.—(See in-

A : B : : W : P, gives the power when the others are known,
B : A : : P : W gives the weight when the others are known,
W : P : : A : B gives the arm of weight when the others are known,
P : W : : B : A gives the arm of power when the others are known.

The work may often be contracted in the following manner :— Resuming our example 48 : 96 : : 132 : fourth proportional, we see that 96 is double of 48, and therefore the ratio of 48 to 96 is the same as that of any two numbers, the second of which is double the first, and 48 : 96 is the same as 1 : 2, and we reduce the analogy to the simple form of 1 : 2 : : 132 : 4th prop., and we have $\frac{132\times2}{1}=264$, the term required, as before. In the example 50 : 730 : : 30 : 4th term, we have $\frac{730\times30}{50}=\frac{73\times30}{5}=\frac{73\times6\times5}{5}=73\times6=438$. This is equivalent to dividing the first and second by 10, and the first and third by 5. Hence we may divide the first and second, or first and third by any number that will measure both. The same principle will also be illustrated by the consideration that the second and third are multipliers, and the first a divisor; and if we first multiply, and then divide by the same quantity, the one operation will manifestly neutralize the other. Thus : 48 : 96 : : 132 : F. P. may be written 1×48 : 2×48 : : 132 : F. P.; where it is plain that since by first multiplying 132 by 48, and then dividing by the same, the one operation would neutralize the other, both may be omitted.

In proportion, when the means are equal, such as 4 : 12 : : 12 : 36, it is usual to write the analogy thus—4 : 12 : 36, and 12 is called a mean proportional between 4 and 36. To prove the correctness of this statement, we multiply 36 by 4 and 12 by itself, and as both give 144, the analogy is correct. Now, as 144 is the square or second power of 12, so 12 is called the second root, or square root of 144, or that which produced it, or the *root* from which it *grew* ; hence, to find a mean proportional between two given quantities, we have the following

RULE.

Multiply them together, and take the square root of the product.

Thus, in the above example, 4×36=144, the square root of which is 12. Again, to find a mean proportional between 9 and 49, we mul-

troductory remarks.) The term *Reciprocal Ratio* is liable to the same objection, for though 3 and $\frac{1}{3}$ are reciprocals, yet they express the same relation. When the expression *Inverse Ratio* is legitimately used, it does not refer to a *single* ratio, but means that *two* ratios are so related that *one* of them must be inverted.

tiply 49 by 9, which is 441, the square root of which is 21, which is a mean proportional between 9 and 49, *i. e.*, 9 : 21 : 49, or, written at full length, 9 : 21 : : 21 : 49. Proof: 49×9=441 and 21×21=441. As the learner is not supposed, at this stage, to know the method of finding the roots of quantities beyond the limits of the multiplication table, we append a table of squares and roots at the end of the book.

When each quantity in a series is a mean proportional between two adjacent quantities, the quantities are said to be continued, or continual proportionals. Thus: 2 : 4 : 8 : 16 : 32 : 64 : 128, and 3 : 9 : 27 : 81 : 243, are series in which each is a mean proportional between two adjacent ones. Let us take 16 and the two adjacent ones, 8 and 32—the analogy is 8 : 16 : : 16 : 32. Proof: 8×32=256, and 16×16=256. So also, 27 and the adjacent terms, 9 and 81. The analogy is 9 : 27 : : 27 : 81, and the proof, 9×81=729, and 27×27=729.

This subject will be treated of at length in a subsequent part of the work, but this explanation has been introduced here to fill up the outline and let the learner understand the *nature* of continued proportionals.

EXERCISES.

1. If 6 barrels of flour cost $32, what will 75 barrels cost? Ans. $400.

2. If 18 yards of cloth cost $21, what must be paid for 12 yards? Ans. $14.

3. How much must be paid for 15 tons of coal, if 2 tons can be purchased for $15? Ans. $112.50.

4. If you can walk 84 miles in 28 hours, how many minutes will you require to walk 1 mile? Ans. 20.

5. What will 14 horses cost, if 3 of the average value can be bought for $270? Ans. $1260.

6. What must be paid for a certain piece of cloth, if $\frac{2}{3}$ of it cost $9. Ans. $13.50.

7. If 5 men are required to build a wall in 5 days, how many men will do the same in $2\frac{1}{2}$ days? Ans. 10.

8. If 16 sheep are $\frac{2}{3}$ of a flock, how many are there in the same? Ans. 24.

9. What must be paid for $4\frac{1}{2}$ cords of wood, if the cost of 3 cords is $10? Ans. $15.

10. What is the height of a tree which casts a shadow of 125 feet, if a stake 6 feet high produces a shadow of 8 feet? Ans. $93\frac{3}{4}$.

11. How long will it take a train to run from Syracuse to Oswego (a distance of 40 miles), at the rate of 5 miles in $15\frac{5}{13}$ minutes?

12. If 15 men can build a bridge in 10 days, how many men will be required to erect three of the same dimensions in $\frac{1}{2}$ the time? Ans. 90.

13. If a man receive $4.50 for 3 days' work, how many days ought he to remain in his place for $25?

14. How much may a person spend in 94 days, if he wishes to save $73.50 out of a salary of $500 per annum?

15. If 3 cwt., 3 qrs., 14 lbs. of sugar cost $36.50, what will 2 qrs., 2 lbs. cost? Ans. $4.879+.

16. 5 men are employed to do a piece of work in 5 days, but after working 4 days they find it impossible to complete the job in less than 3 days more, how many additional men must be employed to do the work in the time agreed upon at first? Ans. 10.

17. A watch is 10 minutes too fast at 12 o'clock (noon) on Monday, and it gains 3 minutes 10 seconds a day, what will be the time by the watch at a quarter past 10 o'clock, A. M., on the following Saturday? Ans. 10 h. 40 m. $36\frac{7}{48}$ s.

18. A bankrupt owes $972, and his property, amounting to $607.50, is distributed among his creditors; what does one receive whose demand is $$11.33\frac{1}{3}$? Ans. $7.083+.

19. What is the value of .15 of a hhd. of lime, at $2.39 per hhd.? Ans. $.3585.

20. A garrison of 1200 men has provisions for $\frac{3}{4}$ of a year, at the rate of $\frac{7}{8}$ of a pound per day; how long will the provisions last at the same allowance if the garrison be reinforced by 400 men? Ans. $6\frac{3}{4}$ months.

21. If a piece of land 40 rods in length and 4 in breadth make an acre, how long must it be when it is 5 rods $5\frac{1}{2}$ feet wide? Ans. 30 rods.

22. A borrowed of B $745, for 90 days, and afterwards would return the favor by lending B $1341; for how long should he lend it?

23. If a man can walk 300 miles in 6 successive days, how many miles has he to walk at the end of 5 days? Ans. 50.

24. If 495 gallons of wine cost $394; how much will $72 pay for? Ans. 90 gal.

25. If 112 head of cattle consume a certain quantity of hay in 9 days; how long will the same quantity last 84 head? Ans. 12 days.

26. If 171 men can build a house in 168 days; in what time will 108 men build a similar house? Ans. 266 days.

27. It has been proved that the diameter of every circle is to the circumference as 113 : 355; what then is the circumference of the moon's orbit, the diameter being, in round numbers, 480,000 miles?

Ans. $1,507,964\frac{68}{113}$ m.

28. A round table is 12 ft. in circumference; what is its diameter?

Ans. 3 ft. $9\frac{297}{355}$ in.

29. A was sent with a warrant; after he had ridden 65 miles, B was sent after him to stop the execution, and for every 16 miles that A rode, B rode 21; How far had each ridden when B overtook A?

Ans. 273 miles.

30. Find a fourth proportional to 9, 19 and 99. Ans. 209.

31. A detective chased a culprit for 200 miles, travelling at the rate of 8 miles an hour, but the culprit had a start of 75 miles; at what rate did the latter travel? Ans. 5 miles an hour.

32. How much rum may be bought for $119.50, if 111 gallons cost $89.625? Ans. 148 gallons.

33. If 110 yards of cloth cost $18; what will $63 pay for?

Ans. 385 yards.

34. If a man walk from Rochester to Auburn, a distance of (say) 79 miles in 27 hours, 54 minutes; in what time will he walk at the same rate from Syracuse to Albany, supposing the distance to be 152 miles?

35. A butcher used a false weight $14\frac{3}{4}$ oz., instead of 16 oz. for a pound, of how many lbs. did he defraud a customer who bought 112 just lbs. from him? Ans. $9\frac{29}{59}$ lbs.

36. If 123 yards of muslin cost $205; how much will 51 yards cost? Ans. $85.

37. In a copy of Milton's Paradise Lost, containing 304 pages, the combat of Michael and Satan commences at the 139th page; at what page may it be expected to commence in a copy containing 328 pages?

Ans. The fourth proportional is $149\frac{37}{38}$; and hence the passage will commence at the foot of page 150

38. Suppose a man, by travelling 10 hours a day, performs a

journey in four weeks without desecrating the Sabbath; now many weeks would it take him to perform the same journey, provided he travels only 8 hours per day, and pays no regard to the Sabbath?

Ans. 4 weeks, 2 days.

39. A cubic foot of pure fresh water weighs 1000 oz., avoirdupois; find the weight of a vessel of water containing $217\frac{1}{2}$ cubic in.

Ans. 7 lbs., $13\frac{125}{144}$ oz.

40. Suppose a certain pasture, in which are 20 cows, is sufficient to keep them 6 weeks; how many must be turned out, that the same pasture may keep the rest 6 months? Ans. 15.

41. A wedge of gold weighing 14 lbs., 3 oz., 8 dwt., is valued at £514 4s.; what is the value of an ounce? Ans. £3.

42. A mason was engaged in building a wall, when another came up and asked him how many feet he had laid; he replied, that the part he had finished bore the same proportion to one league which $\frac{3}{17}$ does to 87; how many feet had he laid?

43. A farmer, by his will, divides his farm, consisting of 97 acres, 3 roods, 5 rods, between his two sons so that the share of the younger shall be $\frac{3}{4}$ the share of the elder; required the shares.

Here the ratio of the shares is 4 : 3, and we have shown that if four magnitudes are proportionals, the first term increased by the second is to the second as the third increased by the fourth is to the fourth. Now, 97 acres, 3 roods, 5 rods, being the sum of the shares, we must take the sum of 4 and 3 for first term, and either 4 or 3 for the second, and therefore 7 : 4 : : 97 acres, 3 roods, 5 rods : F.P., *i. e.*, the sum of the numbers denoting the ratio of the shares is to one of them as the sum of the shares is to one of them. This gives for the elder brother's share, 55 acres, 3 roods, 20 rods, and the younger's share is found either by repeating the operation, or by subtracting the share thus found from the whole, giving 41 acres, 3 roods, 25 rods.

44. A legacy of $398 is to be divided among three orphans, in parts which shall be as the numbers 5, 7, 11, the eldest receiving the largest share; required the parts?

23 : 5 : : 398 : $86\frac{12}{23}$, the share of the youngest.

23 : 7 : : 398 : $121\frac{3}{23}$, the share of the second.

23 : 11 : : 398 : $190\frac{8}{23}$, the share of the eldest.

45. Three sureties on $5000 are to be given by A, B and C, so that B's share may be one-half greater than A's, and C's one-half greater than B's; required the amount of the security of each?

Ans. A's share, 1052.63\frac{3}{19}$; B's, 1578.94\frac{14}{19}$; C's, 2368.42\frac{2}{19}$.

46. Suppose that A starts from Washington and walks 4 miles an hour, and B at the same time starts from Boston, to meet him, at the rate of 3 miles an hour, how far from Washington will they meet, the whole distance being 432 miles?

47. A certain number of dollars is to be divided between two persons, the less share being $\frac{2}{3}$ of the greater, and the difference of the shares $800, what are the shares, and what is the whole sum to be divided? Ans. Less share, $1600; greater, $2400; total, $4000.

48. A certain number of acres of land are to be divided into two parts, such that the one shall be $\frac{3}{7}$ of the other; required the parts and the whole, the difference of the parts being 716 acres?

Ans. the less part 537 acres; the greater, 1253 acres; the whole, 1790.

49. A mixture is made of copper and tin, the tin being $\frac{1}{3}$ of the copper, the difference of the parts being 75; required the parts and the whole mixture? Ans. tin, 37$\frac{1}{2}$; copper, 112$\frac{1}{2}$; the whole, 150.

50. Pure water consists of two gasses, oxygen and hydrogen; the hydrogen is about $\frac{2}{15}$ of the oxygen; how many ounces of water will there be when there are 764$\frac{12}{17}$ oz. of oxygen more than of hydrogen?

Ans. 1000 oz.

COMPOUND PROPORTION.

Proportion is called simple when the question involves only one condition, and compound when the question involves more conditions than one. As each condition implies a ratio, simple proportion is expressed, when the required term is found, by two ratios, and compound, by more than two. Thus, if the question be, How many men would be required to reap 65 acres in a given time, if 96 men, working equally, can reap 40 acres in the same time? Here there is but one condition, viz., that 96 men can reap 40 acres in the given time, which implies but one ratio, and when the question has been stated 40 : 65 : : 96 : F.P., and the required term is found to be 156, and the proportion 40 : 65 : : 96 : 156, we have the proportion, expressed by two ratios. But, suppose the question were, If a man walking 12 hours a day, can accomplish a journey of 250 miles in 9 days, how many days would he require walking at the same rate, 10 hours each day, to travel 400 miles? Here there are two conditions, viz.: *first*, that, in the one case, he travels 12 hours a day, and in the other 10 hours; and, *secondly*, that the distances are 250 and 400 miles. The statement, as we shall presently show, would be $\left.\begin{matrix}10 : 12 \\ 250 : 400\end{matrix}\right\} :: 9 : 17\tfrac{7}{25}$. Here each condition implies one ratio, 10 : 12 and 250 : 400, and when the required term, which is $17\tfrac{7}{25}$, is found, there are four ratios, viz., the two already noted, and 9 : $17\tfrac{7}{25}$, gives two more, one in relation to 10 : 12, and one in relation to 250 : 400. This will be evident, when we have shown the method of statement and operation.

EXPLANATORY STATEMENT AND OPERATION.

11 : 33 : : 12 : F. P.
1 : 3 : 12 : 36

18 : 5 : : 36 : F. P.
1 : 5 : : 2 : 10.

PRACTICAL STATEMENT AND OPERATION.

$\left.\begin{matrix}11 : 33 \\ 18 : 5\end{matrix}\right\} :: 12 : \text{F. P.}$

$\left.\begin{matrix}1 : 3 \\ 3 : 5\end{matrix}\right\} :: 2 : \text{F. P.}$

$\left.\begin{matrix}1 : 1 \\ 1 : 5\end{matrix}\right\} :: 2 : 10.$

Let the question be, How many men would be required to reap 33 acres in 18 days, if 12 men, working equally, can reap 11 acres in 5 days?

We first proceed, as on the left margin, as if there were only one condition in the question; or, in other words, as if the number of days were the same in both cases, and the question were—If 12 men can reap 11 acres in a given time, how many men will be required to reap 33 acres in the same time. This, then, is a question in simple proportion, and by that rule we have the statement—11 : 33 : : 12 : F. P., which, by contraction, becomes 1 : 3 : : 12 : F. P.; and thus, we find F. P. to be 36, the number of men required, if the time were the same in both cases. The question is now resolved into this: How many men will be required to reap, in 18 days, the *same quantity* of crop that 36 men can reap in 5 days? This is obviously a case of inverse proportion, for the longer the time allowed the less will be the number of men required, and hence the statement, 18 : 5 : 36 : F. P., which, by contraction, becomes 1 : 5 : : 2 : F. P., which gives 10 for the number of men. The work may be shortened by making the two statements at once, as on the right margin. We first notice that the last term is to represent a certain number of men, and, therefore, we place 12 in the third place; next, we see that, *other things being equal*, it will take more men to reap 33 than to reap 11 acres, and that, therefore, as far as that is concerned, the fourth term will be greater than the third, and so we put 11 in the first place, and 33 in the second. Again we see that, *other things being equal*, a less number of men will be required when 18 days are allowed for doing the work, than when it is required to be done in 5 days, and that therefore the fourth term, as far as that is concerned, will be less than the third, and therefore we write 18 : 5 below the other ratio as on the margin. Then by contraction we get $\left.\begin{matrix}1:3\\3:5\end{matrix}\right\}$: : 2 : F. P. Now, as 3 in the first term is to be a multiplier, and 3 in the second a divisor, we may omit these also, and we obtain $\left.\begin{matrix}1:1\\1:5\end{matrix}\right\}$: : 2 : 10, the answer as before.

$$\frac{11\times18}{198} : \frac{33\times5}{165} : : 12 : \text{F. P.}$$

$$\frac{165\times12}{198}=10$$

The full uncontracted operation would be to multiply 18 by 11, which gives 198, then to multiply 33 by 5, which gives 165, then multiply 165, the product of the two second terms, by 12, and divide the result, 1980, by 198, the product of the two first terms, which gives 10 as before.

Because in the analogy 198 : 165 : : 12 : 10, the first two terms are products, this kind of proportion has been called *compound*, and the ratio of 19 to 165 is called a *compound ratio*. We can show the strict and original meaning of the term *compound ratio* more easily by an example, than by any explanation in words. Let us take any series of numbers, whole, fractional or mixed, say 5, $\frac{7}{8}$, $\frac{3}{5}$, 19, 12, 1, 17, 11, $\frac{15}{16}$, 25, then the ratio of the first to the last is said to be compounded of the ratio of the first to the second, the second to the third, the third to the fourth, &c., &c., &c., to the end. Now the ratio of 5 to 25 is $\frac{25}{5}=5$, and the several ratios are in this order, $\frac{\frac{7}{8}}{5}\times\frac{\frac{3}{5}}{\frac{7}{8}}\times\frac{19}{\frac{3}{5}}\times\frac{12}{19}\times\frac{1}{12}\times\frac{17}{1}\times\frac{11}{17}\times\frac{\frac{15}{16}}{11}\times\frac{25}{\frac{15}{16}}$ which leaving finally $\frac{25}{5}=5$ as before. If we took them in reverse order, viz., $\frac{5}{25}=\frac{1}{5}$, it is obvious that all therein could be cancelled, as each would in succession be a multiplier and a divisor.

We would also remark that compound proportion is nothing else than a number of questions in simple proportion solved by one operation. This will be evident from our second example by comparing the two operations on the opposite margins. Again, we remarked that every condition implies a ratio, and that therefore the third and fourth terms of our first example really involve two ratios, one in relation to each of the preceding. Hence universally the number of ratios, expressed and implied, must always be double the number of conditions, and therefore always even. As the third ratio is only written once, the number of ratios appears to be odd, but is in reality even.

RULE:

Place, as in simple proportion, in the third place the term that is the same as the required term. Then consider each condition separately to see which must be placed first, and which second, other things being equal.

EXAMPLE.

1. If $35.10 pay 27 men for 24 days; how much will pay 16 men 18 days? Here we first observe that the answer will be money, and therefore $35.10 must be in the third place. Again, it will take less money to pay 16 men than 27 men, and therefore, other things being equal, the answer, as far as this is concerned, will be less than $35.10, and therefore we put the less quantity, 16, in the second place. So also because it will take less to pay any given number of men for 18 days than for 24 days, therefore we put the less quantity in the second place, which the statement shows in the margin.

27 : 16 : : $35.10
24 : 18
―――――
3 : 2
3 : 2
―――――
9 : 4 : : $35.10
4
―――――
9)140.40
―――――
Ans. $15.60

EXERCISES.

1. If 15 men, working 12 hours a day, can reap 60 acres in 16 days; in what time would 20 boys, working 10 hours a day, reap 98 acres, if 7 men can do as much as 8 boys in the same time?

Ans. $26\frac{22}{25}$ days.

2. If 15 men, by working $6\frac{2}{3}$ hours a day, can dig a trench 48 feet long, 8 feet broad, and 5 feet deep, in 12 days; how many hours a day must 25 men work in order to dig a trench 36 feet long, 12 feet broad, and 3 feet deep, in 9 days? Ans. $3\frac{3}{5}$.

3. If 48 men can build a wall 864 feet long, 6 feet high, and 3 feet wide, in 36 days; how many men will be required to build a wall 36 feet long, 8 feet high, and 4 feet wide, in 4 days? Ans. 32.

4. In what time would 23 men weed a quantity of potato ground which 40 women would weed in 6 days, if 7 men can do as much as 9 women? Ans. $8\frac{8}{69}$ days.

5. Suppose that 50 men can dig in 27 days, working 5 hours a day, 18 cellars which are each 48 feet long, 28 feet wide, and 15 feet deep; how many days will 50 men require, working 3 hours each day, to dig 24 cellars which are each 36 feet long, 21 feet wide, and 20 feet deep? Ans. 45 days.

6. If 15 bars of iron, each 6 ft. 6 in. long, 4 in. broad, and 3 in. thick weigh 20 cwt., 3 qrs., (28 lbs.) 16 lbs.; how much will 6 bars 4 ft. long, 3 in. broad, and 2 in. thick, weigh?

Ans. 2 cwt., 2 qrs., 8 lbs.

7. If 112 men can seed 460 acres, 3 roods, 8 rods, in 6 days; how many men will be required to seed 72 acres in 5 days?

Ans. 21.

8. If the freight by railway of 3 cwt. for 65 miles be $11.25; how far should $35\frac{5}{24}$ cwt. be carried for $18.75?

9. If a family of 9 persons can live comfortably in Philadelphia for $2500 a year; what will it cost a family of 8 to live in Chicago, all in the same style, for seven months, prices supposed to be $\frac{4}{5}$ of what they would be in Philadelphia?

10. If 126 lbs. of tea cost $173.25; what will 68 lbs. of a different quality cost, 9 lbs. of the former being equal in value to 10 lbs. of the latter?

11. If 120 yards of carpeting, 5 quarters wide, cost $60; what will be the price of 36 yards of the same quality, but 7 quarters wide? Ans. $25.20.

12. If 48 men, in 5 days of $12\frac{1}{2}$ hours each, can dig a canal $139\frac{3}{4}$ yards long, $4\frac{1}{2}$ yards wide, and $2\frac{1}{2}$ yards deep; how many hours per day must 90 men work for 42 days to dig $491\frac{1}{16}$ yards long, $4\frac{7}{8}$ yards wide, and $3\frac{1}{5}$ yards deep? Ans. 4.

13. A, standing on the bank of a river, discharges a cannon, and B, on the opposite bank, counts six pulsations at his wrist between the flash and the report; now, if sound travels 1142 feet per second,

and the pulse of a person in health beats 75 strokes in a minute, what is the breadth of the river? Ans. 1 mile, 201$\frac{3}{5}$ feet.

14. If 264 men, working 12 hours a day, can make 240 yards of a canal, 3 yards wide, and 12 yards deep, in 5 days; how long will it take 24 men, working 9 hours a day, to make another portion 420 yards long, 5 yards wide, and 3 yards deep?

15. If the charge per freight train for 10800 lbs. of flour be $16 for 20 miles; how much will it be for 12500 lbs. for 100 miles? Ans. 92\frac{16}{27}$.

16. If $42 keep a family of 8 persons for 16 days; how long, at that rate, will $100 keep a family of 6 persons? Ans. 50$\frac{50}{63}$ days.

17. If a mixture of wine and water, measuring 63 gallons, consist of four parts wine, and one of water, and be worth $138.60; what would 85 gallons of the same wine in its purity be worth? Ans. $233.75.

18. If I pay 16 men $62.40 for 18 days work; how much must I pay 27 men at the same rate? Ans. $140.40.

19. If 60 men can build a wall 300 feet long, 8 feet high, and 6 feet thick, in 120 days, when the days are 8 hours long; in what time would 12 men build a wall 30 feet long, 6 feet high, and 3 feet thick, when the days are 12 hours long? Ans. 15 days.

20. If 24 men, in 132 days, of 9 hours each, dig a trench of four degrees of hardness, 337$\frac{1}{2}$ feet long, 5$\frac{3}{5}$ feet wide, and 3$\frac{1}{2}$ feet deep; in how many days, of 11 hours each, will 496 men dig a trench of 7 degrees of hardness, 465 feet long, 3$\frac{2}{3}$ feet wide, and 2$\frac{1}{3}$ feet deep? Ans. 5$\frac{1}{2}$.

21. If 50 men, by working 3 hours each day, can dig, in 45 days, 24 cellars, which are each 36 feet long, 21 feet wide, and 20 feet deep; how many men would be required to dig, in 27 days, working 5 hours each day, 18 cellars, which are each 48 feet long, 28 feet wide, and 15 feet deep? Ans. 50.

22. If 15 men, 12 women, and 9 boys, can complete a certain piece of work in 50 days; what time would 9 men, 15 women, and 18 boys, require to do twice as much, the parts performed by each, in the same time, being as the numbers 3, 2 and 1? Ans. 104 days.

23. If 12 oxen and 35 sheep eat 12 tons, 12 cwt. of hay, in 8 days; how much will it cost per month (of 28 days,) to feed 9 oxen and 12 sheep, the price of hay being $40 per ton, and 3 oxen being supposed to eat as much as 7 sheep? Ans. $924.

24. A vessel, whose speed was $9\frac{1}{4}$ miles per hour, left Belleville at 8 o'clock, a. m., for Gananoque, a distance of 74 miles. A second vessel, whose speed was to that of the first as 8 is to 5, starting from the same place, arrived 5 minutes before the first; what time did the second vessel leave Belleville? Ans. 55 min. past 10 o'clock, a. m.

25. If 9 compositors, in 12 days, working 10 hours each day, can compose 36 sheets of 16 pages to a sheet, 50 lines to a page, and 45 letters in a line; in how many days, each 11 hours long, can 5 compositors compose a volume, consisting of 25 sheets, of 24 pages in a sheet, 44 lines in a page, and 40 letters in a line? Ans. 16 days.

MISCELLANEOUS EXERCISES ON THE PRECEDING RULES.

1. What is the value of .7525 of a mile?
Ans. 6 fur., 0 rd, 4 yds, 1 ft., $2\frac{2}{5}$ in.
2. What is the value of .25 of a score? Ans. 5.
3. Reduce 1 ft. 6 in. to the decimal of a yard. Ans. .5.
4. What is the value of 14 yards of cloth, at \$3.375 per yard?
Ans. \$47.15.
5. What part of 2 weeks is $\frac{5}{14}$ of a day? Ans. $\frac{5}{196}$.
6. What part of £1 is 13s. 4d? Ans. $\frac{2}{3}$.
7. Reduce $\frac{9}{75}$ of a day to hours, minutes and seconds.
Ans. 2 hours, 52 min., 48 sec.
8. Add $\frac{2}{3}$ of a furlong to $\frac{8}{9}$ of a mile.
Ans. 7 fur., 31 rds, 0 yd., 1 ft., 10 in.
9. What is the value of $.857\frac{1}{7}$ of a bushel of rye?
Ans. 48 pounds.
10. Reduce 47 pounds of wheat to the decimal of a bushel.
Ans. $.783\frac{1}{3}$.
11. Reduce 9 dozen to the decimal of a gross. Ans. .75.
12. Add $\frac{7}{10}$ of a cwt. to $\frac{3}{5}$ of a quarter. Ans. 3 qrs., 10 lbs.
13. Subtract $\frac{7}{8}$ of a day from $\frac{5}{7}$ of a week. Ans. 4 days, 3 hrs.
14. From $\frac{11}{18}$ of 5 tons take $\frac{3}{7}$ of 9 cwt.
Ans. 2 tons, 17 cwt., 1 qr., $\frac{25}{63}$ lbs.
15. How many yards of cloth, at $\$3\frac{1}{2}$ a yard, can be bought for $\$48\frac{1}{7}$? Ans. $13\frac{37}{49}$ yards.
16. A man bought $\frac{7}{8}$ of a yard of cloth for \$2.80; what was the rate per yard? Ans. \$3.20.
17. How many tons of hay, at $\$16\frac{1}{2}$ per ton, can be bought for $\$196\frac{1}{8}$? Ans. $11\frac{39}{44}$ tons.

18. At $\$17\frac{3}{5}$ per week, how many weeks can a family board for $\$765\frac{3}{5}$? Ans. $43\frac{1}{2}$ weeks.

19. What number must be added to $26\frac{3}{5}$, and the sum multiplied by $7\frac{3}{4}$, that the product may be 496? Ans. $37\frac{2}{5}$.

20. A man owns $\frac{3}{4}$ of an oil well. He sells $\frac{2}{3}$ of his share for $3500; what part of his share in the well has he still, and what is it worth at the same rate?

21. How long will $119\frac{3}{7}$ hhds. of water last a company of 30 men, allowing each man $\frac{2}{5}$ of a gallon a day? Ans. 627 days.

22. Reduce $\frac{2}{7}$ of $2\frac{4}{5}$, $\frac{8}{12}$ of $1\frac{5}{6}$, and $3\frac{1}{2}$ of $2\frac{2}{7}$, to equivalent fractions having the *least* common denominator. Ans. $\frac{36}{45}$, $\frac{55}{45}$, $\frac{360}{45}$.

23. From $\frac{2}{7}$ of $2\frac{4}{5}$ of 4, take $\frac{9}{17}$ of $6\frac{4}{5}$ of $\frac{1}{9}$. Ans. $2\frac{4}{5}$.

24. What is the sum of $\frac{1}{2}$, $\frac{1}{3}$, $\frac{1}{4}$, $\frac{1}{5}$, $\frac{1}{6}$, $\frac{1}{7}$, $\frac{1}{8}$, and $\frac{1}{9}$? Ans. $1\frac{2089}{2520}$.

25. What is the sum of $\frac{21}{35}$ of $3\frac{5}{8}+\frac{11}{45}$ of 85? Ans. $22\frac{2401}{2520}$.

26. How long will it take a person to travel 442 miles, if he travels $3\frac{1}{4}$ miles per hour, and $8\frac{1}{2}$ hours a day? Ans. 16 days.

27. Find the sum of $2\frac{1}{2}$ of $\frac{7}{10}$, $3\frac{1}{3}$ of $\frac{7}{9}$ of $\frac{6}{17}$ of $4\frac{1}{4}$ and $\frac{1}{2}$.
Ans. $6\frac{5}{36}$.

28. A has $2\frac{1}{7}$ times $8\frac{5}{6}$ dollars, and B $6\frac{1}{2}$ times $9\frac{3}{4}$ dollars; how much more has B than A? Ans. $\$44\frac{25}{56}$.

29. If I sell hay at $1.75 per cwt.; what should I give for $9\frac{3}{5}$ tons, that I may make $7 on my bargain. Ans. $329.

30. If 7 horses eat $93\frac{1}{3}$ bushels of oats in 60 days; how many bushels will one horse eat in $87\frac{3}{7}$ days? Ans. $19\frac{3}{7}$.

31. Bought $14\frac{7}{10}$ yards of broadcloth for $102.90; what was the value of $87\frac{3}{7}$ yards of the same cloth? Ans. $612.

32. How many bushels of wheat, at $\$2\frac{2}{3}$ per bushel, will it require to purchase $168\frac{8}{99}$ bushels of corn worth 75 cents per bushel?
Ans. $47\frac{3}{11}$.

33. If in $82\frac{1}{2}$ feet there are 5 rods; how many rods in one mile?
Ans. 320.

34. Suppose I pay $55 for $\frac{5}{8}$ of an acre of land; what is that per acre? Ans. $88.

35. If $\frac{5}{6}$ of a pound of tea cost $\$1.66\frac{1}{3}$; what will $\frac{7}{9}$ of a pound cost? Ans. $\$1.55\frac{11}{45}$.

36. Subtract the sum of $2\frac{1}{2}$ and $1\frac{1}{12}$, from the sum of $\frac{3}{4}$, $7\frac{4}{9}$ and 3, and multiply the remainder by $3\frac{3}{11}$. Ans. $24\frac{10}{11}$.

37. If $\frac{7}{8}$ lb. cost $23\frac{3}{14}$ cents; what will $2\frac{11}{12}$ cost?
Ans. $77\frac{8}{21}$ cents.

38. What is the difference between $2\frac{1}{10}\times3\frac{1}{9}$ and $2\frac{1}{9}\times3\frac{1}{10}$?
Ans. $\frac{1}{90}$.

39. If $\frac{7}{8}$ lb. cost $\$\frac{3}{8}$; what will $\frac{11}{12}$ lb. cost? Ans. $39\frac{2}{7}$ cents.

40. What is the difference between $\frac{3}{4}$ of $\frac{1}{3}+\frac{1}{5}+\frac{1}{7}\times\frac{1}{9}$, and $\frac{1}{4}+\frac{1}{6}+\frac{1}{8}$?

41. If $4\frac{7}{11}$ yards cost $\$1\frac{1}{33}$, what will $2\frac{1}{8}$ yards cost?
Ans. $47\frac{2}{9}$ cents.

42. Bought $\frac{3}{7}$ of 2000 yards of ribbon, and sold $\frac{2}{3}$ of it; how much remains? Ans. $285\frac{5}{7}$ yards.

43. Divide the sum of $\frac{1}{2}$, $\frac{3}{4}$, $\frac{7}{8}$, $\frac{15}{16}$, $\frac{31}{32}$, $\frac{63}{64}$, $\frac{127}{128}$ by the sum of $\frac{1}{2}$, $\frac{1}{4}$, $\frac{1}{8}$, $\frac{1}{16}$, $\frac{1}{32}$, $\frac{1}{64}$, $\frac{1}{128}$, and divide the quotient by $6\frac{7}{127}$, and multiply the result by $\frac{3}{4}$ of $\frac{5}{6}$. Ans. $\frac{5}{8}$.

44. I bonght $\frac{7}{8}$ of a lot of wood land, consisting of 47 acres, 3 roods, 20 rods, and have cleared $\frac{1}{2}$ of it; how much remains to be cleared? Ans. 20 acres, 3 roods, $31\frac{1}{4}$ rods.

45. What is the difference between $1\frac{25}{168}$ and $1\frac{23}{36}$? Ans. $\frac{247}{504}$.

46. If $\$\frac{11}{12}$ pay for a $1\frac{1}{2}$ st. of flour; for how much will $\$\frac{5}{8}$ pay?
Ans. $1\frac{1}{44}$ st.

47. Mount Blanc, the highest mountain in Europe, is 15,872 feet above the level of the sea; how far above the sea level is a climber who is $\frac{3}{16}$ of the whole height from the top, *i. e.*, $\frac{3}{16}$ of perpendicular hight? Ans. 12896 feet.

48. What will 45.94375 tons cost if 12.796875 tons cost $54.64?
Ans- $196.17.

49. If I gain $37.515625 by selling goods worth $324.53125; what shall I gain by selling a similar lot for $520.6635416̇. ?
Ans. $60.1884.

50. If 52.815 cwt. cost $22.345; what will 192.664 cwt. cost at the same rate? Ans. $81.512+

51. Required, the sum of the surfaces of 5 boxes, each of which is $5\frac{1}{2}$ feet long, $2\frac{1}{4}$ feet high, and $3\frac{1}{6}$ feet wide, and also the number of cubic feet contained in each box. The box supposed to be made from inch lumber?

52. If I pay $\$\frac{9}{10}$ for sawing into three pieces wood that is 4 ft. long; how much more should I pay, per cord, for sawing into pieces of the same length, wood that is 8 feet long? Ans. $22\frac{1}{2}$ cents.

53. A sets out from Oswego, on a journey, and travels at the rate of 20 miles a day; 4 days after, B sets out from the same place, and travels the same road, at the rate of 25 miles per day; how many days before B will overtake A? Ans. 16.

54. A farmer having $56\frac{1}{2}$ tons of hay, sold $\frac{3}{5}$ of it at $\$10\frac{5}{8}$ per ton, and the remainder at $9.75 per ton; how much did he receive for his hay? Ans. $\$580\frac{43}{80}$.

55. If the sum of $87\frac{11}{12}$ and $117\frac{16}{27}$ is divided by their difference; what will be the quotient? Ans. $6\frac{593}{641}$.

56. If $8\frac{3}{4}$ yards of silk make a dress, and 9 dresses be made from a piece containing 80 yards; what will be the remnant left?

Ans. $1\frac{1}{4}$ yards.

57. A merchant expended $840 for dry goods, and then had remaining only $\frac{37}{49}$ as much money as he had at first; how much money had he at first? Ans. $3430.

58. If a person travel a certain distance in 8 days and 9 hours, by travelling 12 hours a day; how long will it take him to perform the same journey, by traveling $8\frac{3}{4}$ hours a day? Ans. 12 days.

59. If 15 horses, in 4 days, consume 87 bushels, 6 qrts. of oats; how many horses will 610 bushels, 1 peck, 2 qrts, keep for the same time? Ans. 105.

60. Reduce 1 pound troy, to the fraction of one pound avoirdupois. Ans. $\frac{144}{175}$.

61. Reduce $\frac{\frac{2}{5}\times\frac{10}{12}}{4\frac{1}{2}\text{ of }\frac{2}{9}}$ to a simple fraction. Ans. $\frac{1}{3}$.

62. What will be the cost of 8 cwt., 3 qrs., $12\frac{1}{2}$ lbs. of beef, if 4 cwt. cost $34? Ans. $\$75\frac{7}{16}$.

63. If 4 men, working 8 hours a day, can do a certain piece of work in 15 days; how long would it take one man, working 10 hours a day, to do the same piece of work? Ans. 48 days.

64. Divide $1728 among 17 boys and 15 girls, and give each boy $\frac{7}{11}$ as much as a girl; what sum will each receive?

Ans. Each girl, $\$66\frac{66}{71}$; each boy, $\$42\frac{42}{71}$.

65. If A can cut 2 cords of wood in $12\frac{1}{3}$ hours, and B can cut 3 cords in $17\frac{1}{2}$ hours; how many cords can they both cut in $24\frac{1}{2}$ hours?

Ans. $8\frac{32}{185}$.

66. If it requires 30 yards of carpeting, which is $\frac{3}{4}$ of a yard wide, to cover a floor; how many yards, which is $1\frac{1}{4}$ yards wide, will be necessary to cover the same floor? Ans. 18.

67. A person bought 1000 gallons of spirits for $1500; but 140 gallons leaked out; at what rate per gallon must he sell the remainder so as to make $200 by his bargain?

68. What must be the breadth of a piece of land whose length is $40\frac{1}{2}$ yards, in order that it may be twice as great as another piece of

land whose length is $14\frac{5}{8}$ yards, and whose breadth is $13\frac{2}{13}$ yards?

Ans. $9\frac{1}{2}$ yards.

69. If 7 men can reap a rectangular field whose length is 1,800 feet, and breadth 960 feet, in 9 days of 12 hours each; how long will it take 5 men, working 14 hours a day, to reap a field whose length is 800 feet, and breadth 700 feet? Ans. $3\frac{1}{2}$ days.

70. 124 men dug a trench 110 yards long, 3 feet wide, and 4 feet deep, in 5 days of 11 hours each; another trench was dug by one-half the number of men in 7 days of 9 hours each; how many feet of water was it capable of holding? Ans. 2268 cubic feet.

71. If 100 men, by working 6 hours each day, can, in 27 days, dig 18 cellars, each 40 feet long, 36 feet wide, and 12 feet deep; how many cellars, that are each 24 feet long, 27 feet wide, and 18 feet deep, can 240 men dig in 81 days, by working 8 hours a day?

Ans. 256.

72. A gentleman left his son a fortune, $\frac{1}{5}$ of which he spent in 2 months, $\frac{1}{4}$ of the remainder lasted him 3 months longer, and $\frac{3}{8}$ of what then remained lasted him 5 months longer, when he had only $895.50 left; how much did his father leave him? Ans. $4477.50.

73. A farmer having sheep in two different fields, sold $\frac{1}{4}$ of the number from each field, and had only 102 sheep remaining. Now 12 sheep jumped from the first field into the second; then the number remaining in the first field, was to the number in the second field as 8 to 9; how many sheep were there in each field at first?

Ans. 80 in first field; 56 in second.

74. A and B paid $120 for 12 acres of pasture for 8 weeks, with an understanding that A should have the grass that was then on the field, and B what grew during the time they were grazing; how many oxen, in equity, can each turn into the pasture, and how much should each pay, providing 4 acres of pasture, together with what grew during the time they were grazing, will keep 12 oxen 6 weeks; and in similar manner, 5 acres will keep 35 oxen 2 weeks?

Ans. { A should turn into the field 18 oxen, and pay $72.
B should turn into the field 12 oxen, and pay $48. }

ANALYSIS AND SYNTHESIS.

Analysis is the act of separating and comparing all the different parts of any compound, and showing their connection with each other, and thereby exhibiting all its elementary principles.

The converse of Analysis is Synthesis. The meaning and use of these terms will probably be most readily comprehended by reference to their derivation.

They are both pure Greek words. Analysis means *loosing up*. The general reader would here probably expect *loosing down*, as employed in most popular definitions; but we may illustrate the Greek term, *loosing up*, by our own everyday phrase, *tearing up*, which means *rending into shreds*, the English *up* conveying the same idea here as the Greek *ana* in analysis. The Greek synthesis means literally placing together; that is, the component parts being known, the word synthesis indicates the act of combining them into one. We might give many illustrations, but one will suffice, and we choose the one which will be most generally understood. When we analyse a sentence, we loose it *up*, or tear it *up*, into its component parts, and by synthesis we write or compose, *i. e.*, put together the parts, which, by analysis, we have found it to consist of.

When we commence to analyse a *problem* we reason from a given quantity to its unit, and then from this unit to the required quantity; hence, all our deductions are self-evident, and we therefore require *no rule* to solve a problem by analysis.

Although this part of arithmetic is usually called analysis, yet, as it is really both analysis and synthesis, we have given it a title in accordance with the principles now laid down.

EXAMPLE.

1. If 12 pounds of sugar cost $1.80, what will 7 pounds cost?

SOLUTION.

12)1.80 —— .15 7 —— $1.05	If 12 lbs. cost $1.80, one pound will cost the $\frac{1}{12}$ of $1.80=15 cents. Now, if 1 lb. cost 15 cents, 7 lbs. will cost 7 times 15 cents=to $1.05. Therefore, 7 lbs. of sugar will cost $1.05, if 12 lbs. cost $1.80.

NOTE.—The work may be somewhat shortened, especially in long questions, by arranging it in the following manner, so as to admit of cancelling, if possible:—

$$\frac{1}{\not{12}}\times\frac{\overset{15}{\not{180}}}{1}\times\frac{7}{1}=\frac{105}{1}=\$1.05. \quad \text{Ans.}$$

2. If 5 bushels of pease cost $5.50, for what can you purchase 19 bushels? Ans. $20.90.

3. If 9 men can perform a certain piece of labor in 17 days, how long will it take 3 men to do it? Ans. 51 days.

4. How many pigs, at $2 each, must be given for 7 sheep, worth $4 a head? Ans. 14.

5. If $100 gain $6 in 12 months, how much would it gain in 40 months? Ans. $20.

6. If $4\frac{2}{3}$ bushels of apples cost $\$3\frac{1}{9}$, what will be the cost of $7\frac{1}{2}$ bushels?

SOLUTION.

In the first place, $4\frac{2}{3}$ bushels$=\frac{14}{3}$ bushels, and $\$3\frac{1}{9}=\$\frac{28}{9}$. Now, since $\frac{14}{3}$ bushels cost $\$\frac{28}{9}$, one bushel will cost $\$\frac{28}{9}\div\frac{14}{3}=\frac{28}{9}\times\frac{3}{14}=\$\frac{2}{3}$, and $7\frac{1}{2}$ or $\frac{15}{2}$ bushels will cost $\frac{15}{2}$ times $\$\frac{2}{3}=\frac{2}{3}\times\frac{15}{2}=$ $5, the value of $7\frac{1}{2}$ bushels of apples, if $4\frac{2}{3}$ bushels are worth $\$3\frac{1}{9}$.

OPERATION

$$\frac{\overset{2}{\not{28}}}{\underset{3}{\not{9}}}\times\frac{\not{3}}{\not{14}}\times\frac{\overset{5}{\not{15}}}{\not{2}}=\frac{5}{1}=\$5$$

7. If $\frac{2}{3}$ of $3\frac{3}{4}$ lbs. of tea cost $\$1\frac{7}{8}$; what will be the cost of $5\frac{1}{2}$ pounds? Ans. $\$4.12\frac{1}{2}$.

8. 100 is $\frac{2}{3}$ of what number? Ans. 150.

9. If $\frac{4}{9}$ of a mine cost $2800; what is the value of $\frac{2}{3}$ of it? Ans. $4200.

10. $\frac{2}{3}$ of 24 is $1\frac{3}{5}$ times what number? Ans. 10.

11. $\frac{3}{4}$ of 40 is $\frac{5}{12}$ of how many times $\frac{1}{2}$ of $\frac{4}{5}$ of 20? Ans. 9.

12. A is 16 years old, and his age is $\frac{2}{3}$ times $\frac{2}{3}$ of his father's age; how old is his father? Ans. 36.

13. A and B were playing cards; A lost $10, which was $\frac{1}{3}$ times $\frac{3}{8}$ as much as B then had; and when they commenced $\frac{2}{3}$ of A's money was equal to $\frac{3}{4}$ of B's; how much had each when they began to play? Ans. A $50; B $40.

14. A man willed to his daughter $560, which was $\frac{1}{3}$ of $\frac{3}{4}$ of what he bequeathed to his son; and 4 times the son's portion was $\frac{2}{3}$ the value of the father's estate; what was the value of the estate? Ans. $13,440.

15. A gentleman spent $\frac{1}{4}$ of his life in St. Louis, $\frac{1}{3}$ of it in Boston, and the remainder of it, which was 25 years, in Washington; what age was he when he died? Ans. 60 years.

16. A owns $\frac{1}{8}$, and B $\frac{1}{12}$ of a ship; A's part is worth $650 more than B's; what is the value of the ship? Ans. $15,600.

17. A post stands $\frac{1}{4}$ in the mud, $\frac{1}{3}$ in the water, and 15 feet above the water; what is the length of the post? Ans. 36 feet.

18. A grocer bought a firkin of butter containing 56 pounds, for $11.20, and sold $\frac{3}{4}$ of it for 8\frac{2}{5}$; how much did he get a pound?

Ans. 20 cents.

19. The head of a fish is 4 feet long, the tail as long as the head and $\frac{1}{2}$ the length of the body, and the body is as long as the head and tail; what is the length of the fish? Ans. 32 feet.

20. A and B have the same income; A saves $\frac{1}{7}$ of his; B, by spending $65 a year more than A, finds himself $25 in debt at the end of 5 years; what did B spend each year? Ans. $425.

21. A can do a certain piece of work in 8 days, and B can do the same in 6 days; A commenced and worked alone for 3 days, when B assisted him to complete the job; how long did it take them to finish the work?

SOLUTION.

If A can do the work in 8 days, in one day he can do the $\frac{1}{8}$ of it, and if B can do the work in 6 days, in one day he can do the $\frac{1}{6}$ of it, and if they work together, they would do $\frac{1}{8}+\frac{1}{6}=\frac{7}{24}$ of the work in one day. But A works alone for 3 days, and in one day he can do $\frac{1}{8}$ of the work, in 3 days he would do 3 times $\frac{1}{8}=\frac{3}{8}$ of the work, and as the whole work is equal to $\frac{8}{8}$ of itself, there would be $\frac{8}{8}-\frac{3}{8}=\frac{5}{8}$ of the work yet to be completed by A and B, who, according to the conditions of the question, labour together to finish the work. Now A and B working together for one day can do $\frac{7}{24}$ of the entire job, and it will take them as many days to do the balance $\frac{5}{8}$ as $\frac{7}{24}$ is contained in $\frac{5}{8}$, which is equal $\frac{5}{8}\times\frac{24}{7}=2\frac{1}{7}$ days.

22. A and B can build a boat in 18 days, but if C assists them, they can do it in 8 days; how long would it take C to do it alone?

Ans. $14\frac{2}{5}$ days.

23. A certain pole was $25\frac{1}{2}$ feet high, and during a storm it was broken, when $\frac{3}{4}$ of what was broken off, equalled $\frac{2}{3}$ of what remained; how much was broken off, and how much remained?

Ans. 12 feet broken off, and $13\frac{1}{2}$ remained.

24. There are 3 pipes leading into a certain cistern; the first will fill it in 15 minutes, the second in 30 minutes, and the third in one hour; in what time will they all fill it together?

Ans. 8 min., $34\frac{2}{7}$ sec.

25. A. and B. start together by railway train from Buffalo to Erie a distance of (say) 100 miles. A goes by freight train, at the rate of 12 miles per hour, and B by mixed train, at the rate of 18 miles per hour, C leaves Erie for Buffalo at the same time by express train, which runs at the rate of 22 miles per hour, how far from Buffalo will A and B each be when C meets them.

26. A cistern has two pipes, one will fill it in 48 minutes, and the other will empty it in 72 minutes; what time will it require to fill the cistern when both are running? Ans. 2 hours, 24 min.

27. If a man spends $\frac{5}{12}$ of his time in working, $\frac{1}{3}$ in sleeping, $\frac{1}{16}$ in eating, and $1\frac{1}{2}$ hours each day in reading; how much time will be left? Ans. 3 hours.

28. A wall, which was to be built 32 feet high, was raised 8 feet by 6 men in 12 days; how many men must be employed to finish the wall in 6 days? Ans. 30 men.

29. A and B can perform a piece of work in $5\frac{5}{11}$ days; B and C in $6\frac{2}{3}$ days; and A and C in 6 days; in what time would each of them perform the work alone, and how long would it take them to do the work together?

Ans. A, 10 days; B, 12 days; C, 15 days; and A. B, and C, together, in 4 days.

30. My tailor informs me that it will take $10\frac{1}{4}$ square yards of cloth to make me a full suit of clothes. The cloth I am about to purchase is $1\frac{7}{8}$ yards wide, and on sponging it will shrink $\frac{1}{20}$ in width and length; how many yards of this cloth must I purchase for my "new suit?" Ans. $6\frac{662}{1083}$ yards.

31. If A can do $\frac{2}{3}$ of a certain piece of work in 4 hours, and B can do $\frac{3}{4}$ of the remainder in 1 hour, and C can finish it in 20 min.; in what time will they do it all working together?

Ans. 1 hour, 30 min.

32. A certain tailor in the City of Brooklyn bought 40 yards of broadcloth, $2\frac{1}{4}$ yds wide; but on sponging, it shrunk in length upon every 2 yards, $\frac{1}{16}$ of a yard, and in width, $1\frac{1}{2}$ sixteenths upon every $1\frac{1}{2}$ yards. To line this cloth, he bought flannel $1\frac{1}{4}$ yards wide, which, when wet, shrunk $\frac{1}{2}$ the width on every 10 yards in length, and in width it shrunk $\frac{1}{2}$ of a sixteenth of a yard; how many yards of flannel had the tailor to buy to line his broadcloth?

Ans. $71\frac{7}{13}$ yards.

33. If 6 bushels of wheat are equal in value to 9 bushels of barley, and 5 bushels of barley to 7 bushels of oats, and 12 bushels of

oats to 10 bushels of pease, and 13 bushels of pease to $\frac{1}{2}$ ton of hay, and 1 ton of hay to 2 tons of coal, how many tons of coal are equal in value to 80 bushsls of wheat?

SOLUTION.

If 6 bushels of wheat are equal in value to 9 bushels of barley, or 9 bushels of barley to 6 bushels of wheat, one bushel of barley would be equal to $\frac{1}{9}$ of 6 bushels of wheat, equal to $\frac{6}{9}$, or $\frac{2}{3}$ of a bushel of wheat, and 5 bushels of barley would be equal to 5 times $\frac{2}{3}$ of a bushel of wheat, equal to $\frac{2}{3}\times5=\frac{10}{3}=3\frac{1}{3}$ bushels of wheat. But 5 bushels of barley are equal to seven bushels of oats; hence, 7 bushels of oats are equal to $3\frac{1}{3}$ bushels of wheat, and one bushel of oats would be equal to $3\frac{1}{3}\div7=\frac{10}{21}$ bushels of wheat, and 12 bushels of oats would be equal to 12 times $\frac{10}{21}=\frac{120}{21}=5\frac{5}{7}$ bushels of wheat. But 12 bushels of oats are equal in value to 10 bushels of pease, hence, 10 bushels of pease are equal to $5\frac{5}{7}$ bushels of wheat, and one bushel of pease would equal $5\frac{5}{7}\div10=\frac{4}{7}$ of a bushel of wheat, and 13 bushels of pease would equal $\frac{4}{7}\times13=\frac{52}{7}=7\frac{3}{7}$ bushels of wheat. But 13 bushels of pease equal in value $\frac{1}{2}$ ton of hay, hence, $\frac{1}{2}$ ton of hay equals $7\frac{3}{7}$ bushels of wheat, and one ton would equal $7\frac{3}{7}\times2=14\frac{6}{7}$ bushels of wheat. But one ton of hay equals 2 tons of coal, hence, 2 tons of coal are equal in value to $14\frac{6}{7}$ bushels of wheat, and one ton would equal $14\frac{6}{7}\div2=7\frac{3}{7}$ bushels of wheat. Lastly, if $7\frac{3}{7}$ bushels of wheat be equal in value to one ton of coal, it would take as many tons of coal to equal 80 bushels of wheat, as $7\frac{3}{7}$ is contained in 80, which gives $10\frac{10}{13}$ tons of coal.

NOTE.—This question belongs to that part of arithmetic usually called Conjoined Proportion, or, by some, the "Chain Rule," which has each antecedent of a compound ratio equal in value to its consequent. We have thought it best not to introduce such questions under a head by themselves, on account of their *theory* being more easily understood when exhibited by Analysis than by Proportion. Questions that do occur like this will most probably relate to Arbitration of Exchange. Although they may all be worked by Compound Proportion as well as by Analysis, yet the most expeditious plan, and the one generaly adopted, is by the following

RULE.

Place the antecedents in one column and the consequents in another, on the right, with the sign of equality between them. Divide the continued product of the terms in the column containing the odd term by the continued product of the other column, and the quotient will be the answer.

Let us now take our last example (No. 33), and solve it by this rule:

6 bushels of wheat=9 bushels of barley.
5 bushels of barley=7 bushels of oats.
12 bushels of oats=10 bushels of pease.
13 bushels of pease=$\frac{1}{2}$ ton of hay.
1 ton of hay=2 tons of coal.
— tons of coal=80 bushels of wheat.

$$\begin{array}{l} \qquad\qquad\qquad\quad 20 \\ \cancel{3},\quad \cancel{2},\qquad\quad \cancel{40} \\ \dfrac{\cancel{9},\ 7,\ \cancel{10},\ \cancel{1}\text{-}\cancel{2},\ \cancel{2},\ \cancel{80}}{\cancel{6},\ \cancel{5},\ \cancel{12},\ 13,\ \cancel{1},} = \frac{140}{13} = 10\frac{10}{13}.\quad \text{Ans.} \\ \cancel{2},\quad \cancel{6},\quad \cancel{2}, \\ \qquad \cancel{3}, \end{array}$$

34. If 12 bushels of wheat in Boston are equal in value to $12\frac{1}{2}$ bushels in Albany, and 14 bushels in Albany are worth $14\frac{1}{2}$ bushels in Syracuse; and 12 bushels in Syracuse are worth $12\frac{1}{2}$ bushels in Oswego; and 25 bushels in Oswego are worth 28 bushels in Cleveland; how many bushels in Cleveland are worth 60 bushels in Boston? Ans. $75\frac{2}{4}\frac{5}{8}$.

35. If 12 shillings in Massachusetts are worth 16 shillings in New York, and 24 shillings in New York are worth $22\frac{1}{2}$ shillings in Pennsylvania, and $7\frac{1}{2}$ shillings in Pennsylvania are worth 5 shillings in Canada; how many shillings in Canada are worth 50 shillings in Massachusetts? Ans. $41\frac{2}{3}$.

36. If 6 men can build 125 rods of fencing in 4 days, how many days would seven men require to build 210 rods?

SOLUTION.

If 6 men can build 120 rods of fencing in 4 days, one man could do $\frac{1}{6}$ of 120 rods in the same time; and $\frac{1}{6}$ of 120 rods is 20 rods. Now, if one man can build 20 rods in 4 days, in one day he would build $\frac{1}{4}$ of 20 rods, and $\frac{1}{4}$ of 20 rods is 5 rods. Now, if one man can build 5 rods in one day, 7 men would build 7 times 5 rods in one day, and 7 times 5 rods=35 rods. Lastly, if 7 men can build 35 rods in one day, it would take them as many days to build 210 rods as 35 is contained in 210, which is 6; therefore, if 6 men can build 120 rods of fencing in 4 days, 7 men would require 6 days to build 210 rods.

37. If 12 men, in 36 days, of 10 hours each, build a wall 24 feet long, 16 feet high, and 3 feet thick; in how many days, of 8

hours each, would the same lot of men build a wall 20 feet long, 12 feet high, and $2\frac{1}{2}$ feet thick? Ans. $23\frac{7}{16}$.

38. If 5 men can perform a piece of work in 12 days of 10 hours each; how many men will perform a piece of work four times as large, in a fifth part of the time, if they work the same number of hours in a day, supposing that 2 of the second set can do as much work in an hour as 3 of the first set? Ans. $66\frac{2}{3}$ men.

NOTE.—Such questions as this, where the answer involves a fraction, may frequently occur, and it may be asked how $\frac{2}{3}$ of a man can do any work. The answer is simply this, that it requires 66 men to do the work, and one man to continue on working $\frac{2}{3}$ of a day more.

39. Suppose that a wolf was observed to devour a sheep in $\frac{7}{8}$ of an hour, and a bear in $\frac{3}{4}$ of an hour; how long would it take them together to eat what remained of a sheep after the wolf had been eating $\frac{1}{2}$ an hour? Ans. $10\frac{5}{13}$ min.

40. Find the fortunes of A, B, C, D, E, and F, by knowing that A is worth $20, which is $\frac{1}{4}$ as much as B and C are worth, and that C is worth $\frac{1}{3}$ as much as A and B, and also that if 19 times the sum of A, B and C's fortune was divided in the proportion of $\frac{3}{4}$, $\frac{1}{2}$ and $\frac{1}{3}$, it would respectively give $\frac{3}{4}$ of D's, $\frac{1}{2}$ of E's, and $\frac{1}{3}$ of F's fortune.

Ans. A, 20; B, 55; C, 25; and D, E and F, 1200 each.

41. A and B set out from the same place, and in the same direction. A travels uniformly 18 miles per day, and after 9 days turns and goes back as far as B has travelled during those 9 days; he then turns again, and pursuing his journey, overtakes B $22\frac{1}{2}$ days after the time they first set out. It is required to find the rate at which B uniformly travelled. Ans. 10 miles per day.

42. A hare starts 40 yards before a greyhound, and is not perceived by him until she has been running 40 seconds, she scuds away at the rate of 10 miles an hour, and the dog pursues her at the rate of 18 miles an hour; how long will the chase last, and what distance will the hare have run? Ans. $60\frac{5}{22}$ sec.; 490 yards.

43. A can do a certain piece of work in 9 days, and B can do the same in 12 days; they work together for 3 days, when A is taken sick and leaves, B continues on working alone, and after 2 days he is joined by C, and they finish it together in $1\frac{1}{2}$ days; how long would C be doing it alone? Ans. 12 days.

44. A, in a scuffle, seized on $\frac{2}{3}$ of a parcel of sugar plums; B caught $\frac{3}{8}$ of it out of his hands, and C laid hold on $\frac{3}{10}$ more; D ran off with all A had left, except $\frac{1}{7}$ which E afterwards secured slyly for himself; then A and C jointly set upon B, who, in the conflict, let

fall $\frac{1}{2}$ he had, which were equally picked up by D and E, who lay perdu. B then kicked down C's hat, and to work they all went anew for what it contained; of which A got $\frac{1}{4}$, B $\frac{1}{3}$, D $\frac{2}{7}$, and C and E equal shares of what was left of that stock. D then struck $\frac{3}{4}$ of what A and B last acquired, out of their hands; they, with some difficulty, recovered $\frac{5}{8}$ of it in equal shares again, but the other three carried off $\frac{1}{8}$ a piece of the same. Upon this, they called a truce, and agreed that the $\frac{1}{3}$ of the whole left by A at first, should be equally divided among them; how many plums, after this distribution, had each of the competitors?

Ans. A had 2863; B, 6335; C, 2438; D, 10294 and E, 4950.

PRACTICE

The rule which is called Practice is nothing else tnan a particular case of simple proportion, viz., when the first term is unity. Thus: if it is required to find the price of 28 tons of coal, at $7 a ton—as a question in proportion, it would be, if 1 ton of coal costs $7, what will 28 tons cost? and the statement would be 1 : 28 : : 7 : F. P. Here the first term being 1, the question becomes one of simple multiplication, but the answer, $196, is really the fourth term of an analogy.

```
 $7.62½
    46
 -------
    23
  4572
 3048
 -------
$350.75
```

Again, to find the price of 46 barrels of flour, at $7.62½ per barrel, we have only to multiply $7.62½ by 46. In many cases, however, it is more convenient to multiply the 46 by 7, which will give the price of 46 barrels at $7 each. Now, 50 cents being half a dollar, the price of 46, at 50 cents, will be $23, and 12½ cents being $\frac{1}{4}$ of 50 cents, the price at 12½ cents will be the fourth of that at 50 cents, or $5.75, and the whole comes to $350.75.

```
50  | ½ |   46
    |   |    7
    |   | -------
12½ | ¼ |  322
    |   |   23
    |   |    5.75
    |   | -------
    |   | $350.75
```

To find the price of 36 cwt., 2 qrs., 15 lbs., at $4.87½. Here the question stated at length would be, if 1 cwt. cost $4.87½, what will 36 cwt., 2 qrs., 15 lbs. cost? The statement would be 1 : 36., 2., 15 : : $4.87½ : F. P. This becomes a question of multiplication because the first term is unity, and divided by 1 would not alter the product of the other two terms. Thus:

2 qrs.	½ of 1 cwt.	4.87½	
		36	
		18	
		2922	
		.1461	
		175.50	= price of 3 cwt., @ $4.87½ per cwt.
10 lbs.	⅕ of 2 qrs.	2.437	= " 2 qrs. " " "
5 "	½ of 10 lbs.	.487	= " 10 lbs. " " "
		.243	= " 5 " " " "
		$178.667	= " 36 cwt., 2 qrs., 15 lbs.

We would call the learner's special attention to the following direction, as the neglect of it is a fertile source of error. Whenever you take any quantity as an aliquot part of a higher to find the price of the former, *be sure you divide the line which is the price at the rate of that higher denomination.*

To find the rent of 189 acres, 2 roods, 32 rods, at $4.20 per acre.

2 roods=½ of 1 acre,	4.20
	189
20 rods=¼ of 2 roods,	210
	525
10 rods=½ of 20 rods,	2625
	525
2 rods=⅓ of 10 rods,	3780
	3360
	420
	$696.74

Since the rent of 1 acre is $4.20, the half of it, $2.10, will be the rent of 2 roods, the rent of 20 rods will be .525, the ¼ of the rent of 2 roods, the half of that, .2625, will be the rent of 10 rods, and, lastly, .0525 will be the rent of 2 rods, which is the ⅕ of 10 rods. We then multiply by 189, and set the figures of the product in the usual order, so that the first figure of the product by 9 shall be under the units of cents, &c., and then adding all the partial results, we find the final answer, $796.74, the rent of 189 acres, 2 roods and 32 perches.

EXERCISES.

1. What is the price of 187 cwt. at $5.37½ per cwt.?

Ans. $1005.12½.

2. What is the value of 1857 lbs., at \$3.87½ per lb.?
Ans. \$7195.87½.

3. What will 4796 tons amount to at \$14.50 per ton?
Ans. \$21582.

4. What is the price of 29 score of sheep, at \$7.62½ each?
Ans. \$4422.50.

5. Sold to a cattle dealer 196 head of cattle at \$18.75 each, find the amount. Ans. \$3675.

6. Sold to a dealer 97 head of cattle, at \$16.12½ each, on the average; find the price of all. Ans. \$1564.12½.

7. What is the price of 16 tons, 17 cwt., 2 qrs. of coal, at \$8.62½ per ton?

8. What is the yearly rent of 97 acres, 3 roods, 20 rods, at \$4.37½ per acre?

9. If a man has \$12.50 per week; how much has he per year?
Ans. \$650.

10. If a clerk has \$2.12½ salary for every working day in the year; what is his yearly income? Ans. \$665.12½.

11. If a tradesman earn \$1.64 per day; how much does he earn in the year, the Sabbaths not being reckoned? Ans. \$513.32.

12. If an officer's pay is a guinea and a half per day; how much has he a year? Ans. £574 17s. 6d.

13. What is the price of 479 cwt. of sugar, at \$17.90 per cwt.
Ans. \$8574.10.

14. Find the price of 879 articles, at \$1.19 each.

15. Find the cost of 1793 tons of coal, at \$7.87½ per ton.

16. What is the value of 2781 tons of hay, at \$8.62½ per ton?

17. What is the rent of 189 acres, 2 roods, 32 rods, at \$4.20 per acre? Ans. \$795.74.

18. What is the price of 879 hogs, at \$4.25 each?

19. What will 366 tons of coal come to at \$8.12½ per ton?

20. What is the price of 118 acres, 3 roods and 20 rods of cleared land, at \$36.75 per acre? Ans. \$4368.66.

21. What is the price of 286 acres, 1 rood, 24 rods of uncleared land, at \$7.25 per acre? Ans. \$2076.40.

22. A has 84 acres, 2 roods, 36 rods of cleared land, worth \$24.60 an acre; B has 298 acres, 3 roods, 24 rods of uncleared land, worth \$4.40 an acre—they exchange, the difference of value to be paid in cash; which has to pay, and how much? Ans. B \$989.08.

ACCOUNTS AND INVOICES.

ACCOUNTS are statements from merchants to customers that have purchased goods on credit, and are generally made out periodically, unless specially called for.

An invoice is simply a statement rendered by the seller to the buyer, at time of purchase, showing the articles bought, and the prices of each.

1. NEW YORK, July 1st, 1866.

MR. JAMES ANDERSON,
To FRENCH, WHITE & Co., *Dr.*

1866.

2.25 1.35 2.00
Jany. 4, To 2 lbs. tea, 1.12½ ; 3 lbs. coffee, 45c. ; 20 lbs. rice, 10c....
4.87½ 2.25
" 29, " 2½ yds. Amer. tweed, 1.95 ; 1 vest....................
1.75 2.00
Feb. 10, " 14 lbs. Mus. sugar, 12½c. ; 10 lbs. crus. white sugar, 20c.
60c. 28c. 1.80
" 22, " 1 lb. bk. soda, ; 1 lb. car. soda, ; 4 lbs. coffee, 45c...
3.00 87½c.
Mar. 11, " 10 yds. print, 30c. ; trimming, &c., per bill ....
1.80 85c. 2.00
" 19, " 2 lbs. tobacco, 90c. ; 1 gal coal oil, ; 2 gals. syrup, 1.00.
1.75 1.65½
Aprl 12, " ½ yd. blk. silk, 3.50 ; ¼ yd. blk. velvet, 6.62½..........
3.25 40c. 60c.
May 6, " 2 lbs. tea, 1.62½ ; 1 bottle pickles, ; 1 lb. pepper, ..
35c. 1.00 1.50
" 20, " 1 bag salt, ; 10 lbs. sugar, 10c. ; 3 lbs. raisins, 50c....
75c. 2.50
" 31, " 3 lbs. currants, 25c. ; 10 lbs. white sugar, 25c.........
1.50 12½c. 2.00
June 10, " 2 lbs. tobacco, 75c. ; ½ lb. B. soda, 25c. ; 20 lbs. rice, 10c..
40c. 10c. 30c. 1.75
" 17, " 1 lb. cloves, ; ¼ lb. nutmegs, ; ½ cinnamon, ; 1 lb. tea,

$47.61

---

2. BALTIMORE, Oct. 1st, 1866.

MR. WILLIAM PATTERSON,
To MOFFAT & MURRAY, *Dr.*

1866.

July 3, To 14 yds. fancy print, 20c. ; 12 yds. col'd silk, 2.75.......
" 14, " 2 ladies' felt hats, 2.00; 2 prs. kid gloves, 1.80........
" 22, " 4 prs. cotton hose, 40c. ; 3 yds. red flannel, 80c........
Aug. 19, " 2½ yds. blk. cassimere, 2.95 ; 2¼ yds. cotton, 20c.......
" 27, " 1¼ yds. white flannel, 75c. ; buttons, 10c. ; twist, 15c....
Sept. 1, " 2 suits boys' clothes, 9.00 ; 2 felt hats, 1.80...........
" 8, " 2 prs gloves 80c. ; 2 neckties, 62½c..................
" 22, " ½ doz. prs. cotton hose, 7.50 ; ½ doz. shirts, 26.00......

Contra. *Cr.*

20.00 15.00
Aug. 18, By Cash, ; 27, Cash, ...$35.00
" 25. " firkin butter, 95 lbs., at 22c....... .... 20.90 55.90

Balance due.......................... $41.71½

Received payment in full,

MOFFAT & MURRAY.

ROCHESTER, Jan. 2nd, 1866.

MR. JOHN DEANS.

To WOOD & FUDGER, *Dr.*

1866.

July 4, To 12 lbs. sugar, 10c.; 3 lbs. tea, $1.^{25}$; 2 lbs. tobacco, 87½c.
" 11, " 1 bbl. salt, 2^{25}; 2 lbs. indigo, 25c.; 1½ lbs. pepper, 30c.
" 18, " 2 prs. socks, 45c.; 1 neck-tie, 75c.; 2 scarfs, 25c.......
" 25, " 10 lbs. sugar, 11c.; 20 lbs. dr'd apples, 10c.; 2 lbs. coffee 28c
" " " 18 lbs. dried peaches, 12½c.; 1 bush. onions, $1^{12½}$.......
Aug. 4, " 12 lbs. rice, 7c.; 2 gals. syrup, 75c.; 14 lbs. sugar, 12c...
" " " 13 lbs. mackerel, 12c.; 2 lbs. ginger, 20c.; 2 lbs. tea, $1.^{25}$
" 21. " 2 prs. kid gloves, 1^{25}; 2 boxes collars, 37½c...........
Sept. 12, " 10 lbs. sugar, 15c.; 2 lbs. coffee, 35c.; 1 lb. chocolate, 40c.
Oct. 4, " 2 felt hats, 1^{25}; shoe blacking, 25c....................
" 21. " 2 lbs. pepper, 15c.; soda, 40c.; salpetre, 30c.; salt, 75c.

Contra. *Cr.*

Sept. 14. By Cash, $10.^{00}$; Oct. 4, Cash $5.^{00}$ ....
Oct. 17. " 2 bbls. winter apples, 2^{25}......................

$ 18.42

BOSTON, Nov. 1st, 1866.

MR. WM. REID.

To CAMPBELL, LINN & CO., *Dr.*

Aug. 4, To 2 prs. kip boots, 3^{25}; 2 prs. cobourgs, 2^{25}.............
" 17. " 7 yds. fancy tweed, 2^{25}; trimmings, 1^{00}; buttons 25c..
Sept. 4, " 2 prs. gloves, 75c.; 3 prs. socks, 35c.; 2 straw hats, 40c,
" 26. " 10 yds. print, 35c.; trimmings, 1^{25}; ribbons, 75c.......
Oct. 11, " 3 neck-ties, 62½c.; 2 prs. boys' gaiters, 2^{75}; shoe ties, 12½c.
" 22, " 1 business coat, 14^{00}; 2 felt hats, 1^{75}; 1 umbrella, 2^{50}
" 27, " 2 flannel shirts, 4^{25}; 1 pr. pants, 8^{50}; over-coat, 16^{00}.
" 30. " 2 lace scarfs, 2^{25}; 3 prs. woollen mits 75c.; pins, 25c.

Contra. *Cr.*

Sept. 12. By Cash 10^{00}; Oct. 4, Cash, 8^{00} ....
Oct. 24. " 300 lbs. cheese, 10c.; 75 lbs. butter, 25c........

Balance due........ $37.60

Received payment.

CAMPBELL, LINN & CO.

AUBURN, Sept. 1st, 1866.

MR. S. SMITH

To WILSON, RAY & Co., *Dr.*

1866.

Jan. 15, To 6 yds B. cloth, $4.^{50}$; 2 doz. buttons, 30c.; 9 ozs. thread, 15c.
" 20, " 40 yds. fac. cot., 16c.; 7 spools cot., 4c.; 12 yds. rib., 35c.
" 30. " 15 yds. B. silk, $2.^{30}$; 16 yds. lining, 15c.; 3 silk spools, 11c.
Feb. 20. " 3 yds. drill, 31c.; 5 yds. cob'rg, 34c.; 2 papers need. 18c.
Mar. 18, " 9 yds. coating, $5.^{10}$; $1\frac{1}{2}$ yds. vesting, $1.^{90}$; 5 pr. hose, 40c.
" 31. " 21 yds. print, 20c.; $19\frac{1}{2}$ yds. muslin, 30c.; 2 prs. gloves, $1.^{40}$
Apr. 15, " 4 prs. gloves, $1.^{10}$; 16 yds. ribbon, 18c.; 6 hand'k. 36c.
" 25. " 3 prs. blankets $6.^{30}$; 4 counterpanes, $3.^{20}$; 15 yds. cot., 25c.
May 29, " 2 summer hats, $1.^{05}$; 6 yds. ribbon, 40c.; 2 feathers, 2^{30}
June 5, " 4 prs. slippers, $1.^{40}$; 4 prs. hose, 60c.; 3 prs. hose, 40c.
" 15. " 3 wool shawls, $5.^{30}$; 1 B. suit, $30.^{50}$; 9 ozs. thread, 18c.
July 6. " 40 yds. cotton, 30c.; 3 spools, 12c.; 2 spools, 10c........
Aug. 10. " 13 yds. flannel, 75c.; 4 hand'ks., 35c.; 12 yds. tape, 13c.

Contra. *Cr.*

Jan. 15. By Cash, $15.^{00}$; 22. Cash, $10.^{00}$ ....
Feb. 20. " 50 lbs. butter, 40c.; 6 cwt. pork, 10^{40}............
May 15. " 6 geese, 80c.; 14 fowls, 40c ....
June 5. " 60 lbs. wool, 50c.; 16 lbs. wool, 60c.............
July 6. " Cash, $30.^{00}$; Aug. 10, Cash, $10.^{00}$ ....

Balance due...................... $82.73

BROOKLIN, July 15th, 1866.

MR. R. R. HILLIS.

To J. WILLIAMS, *Dr.*

1866.

Jan. 10, To 10lbs. M. sugar, 15c.; 16lbs. W. sugar, 20c.; 12lbs. C. sugar, 18c.
" 30. " 15 lbs. raisins, 16c.; 13 lbs. raisins, 15c.; 10 lbs. raisins, 18c.
Feb. 12. " 9 lbs. cur'nts, 13c.; 12 lbs. cur'nts, 14c.; 6 lbs. cur'nts, 20c.
Mar. 30. " 60 lbs. salt, 2c.; 2 lbs. wash. soda, 23c.; 1 lb. bak. soda, 25c.
Apr. 5, " 6 lbs. D. apples, 12c.; 10 lbs. bisc'ts, 17c.; 5 lbs. bisc'ts, 21c.
" 25. " 3 cwt. flour, $4.^{20}$; 2 cwt. C. meal, $2.^{30}$; 3 lbs. butter, 25c.
May 1. " 16 lbs. pork, 20c.; 19 lbs. cheese, 10c.; 14 lbs. sugar, 15c.
June 15. " 5 lbs. tea, $1.^{38}$; 9 gals. molasses, 40c.; 6 doz. eggs, 12c.
July 12, " 5 lbs. sugar, 16c.; $9\frac{1}{2}$ lbs. raisins, 16c.; 10 lbs. cur'nts, $12\frac{1}{2}$c.
" 29, " 14 lbs. bacon, 12c.; 5 lbs. cheese, 16c.; 4 lbs. butter, 25c.
" 31, " 4 lbs. tea, $1.^{60}$; 2 lbs. tea, $1.^{30}$; 6 lbs. coffee, 35c......
" " " 40 lbs. salt, $1\frac{1}{4}$c.; 3 lbs. indigo, 90c.; $1\frac{1}{2}$ lbs. blue, 30c.
" " " 3 lbs. salt petre, 35c.; 4 doz. eggs, $12\frac{1}{2}$c.; 6 lbs. butter, 15c.

$83.16

Received payment.

J. WILLIAMS.

ALBANY, Dec. 1, 1866

MR. GEO. SIMPSON,

To TAYLOR & GRANT, *Dr.*

1866.

July 7, To 12 lbs. sugar, 15c. ; 2 lbs. tea, $1.^{25}$; 3 lbs. coffee, 35c ...

" 12, " 2 lbs.tobacco,87½c.; 3 lbs.raisins,30c.; 12 lbs.currants, 15c.

" 24, " 3 lbs. gunpowder, 62½c.; 6 lbs. shot, 18c. ; 2 lbs. glue, 25c.

Aug. 4, " 12 lbs. washing soda, 15c. ; 4 lbs. baking soda, 25c.......

" 12, " 1 box mustard, $1.^{50}$; 2 lbs. filberts, 30c.; 2 lbs. alm'ds, 35c.

Sept. 21, " 8 lbs. sugar, 14c. ; 1 lb. tea, $1.^{12½}$; 3 lbs. chocolate, 40c.

Oct. 12, " 4 lbs. figs, 15c. ; 2 lbs. orange peel, 30c. ; spices 40c.....

" 20, " 2 lbs. but. blue, 18c.; 2 lbs. sulphur, 20c.; 3 lbs. soda, 35c.

Nov. 4, " 2 lbs. smok. tobacco, 90c.; 2 lbs. snuff, 20c.; 1 business suit, $18.^{00}$

Contra. *Cr.*

Aug. 12, By Cash, $8.^{00}$; Sept 21, Cash, $5.^{00}$;..................

Oct. 20, " 100 lbs. dried apples, 15c. ; 50 lbs. peaches, 20c...

Balance due.... .... **$7.91**

DETROIT, Sept. 30th, 1866.

MR. S. SMITH,

To RAY, HILL & CO., *Dr.*,

1866.

Jan. 1, To 5 lbs. tea, $1.^{70}$; 15 lbs. sugar, 15c.; 1½ lbs. cinnamon, $2.^{50}$.

" 10, " 18 lbs. rice, 10c. ; 16 lbs. salt, 4c. ; 34 lbs. oat meal, 6c...

" 13, " 12 lbs. raisins, 18c. ; 3 lbs. tobacco, 58c. ; ½ lb. snuff, 34c..

Feb. 2, " 10 lbs. cur'nts, 17c.; 10 lbs. ginger, 41c.; 5 lbs. mustard, 42c.

" 8, " 6 lbs. sugar, 18c.; 13 lbs. rice, 8c.; 21 lbs. dr'd apples, 16c.

" 13, " 25 lbs. raisins, 18c. ; ½ lb. B. soda, 30c. ; ½ lb. nutmegs, 22c.

Mar. 4, " 12 lbs. coffee, 36c.; 6 lbs. M. sugar, 15c.; 4 lbs. W. sugar, 20c.

" 15, " 4 lbs. mustard, 30c.; 3 lbs. tobacco, 30c.; 12 lbs. ginger, 27c.

Aprl. 6, " 2 lbs. currants, 20c. ; 14 lbs. rice, 8c. ; 9 lbs. tur. seed, 45c.

" 14, " 1½ lbs. cin'mon, 70c.; 12 lbs. sago, 31c.; 14 lbs. sugar, 21c.

May 10, " 16 lbs. salt, 3c. ; 2 lbs. indigo, 90c. ; 61 lbs. corn starch, 14c.

June 12, " 40 lbs. flour, 4c. ; 30 lbs. corn meal, 3c. ; 25 lbs. coffee, 38c.

$88.46

31. CHICAGO, Jan. 4th, 1866.

MR. ELIAS G. CONKLIN,

Bought of J. BUNTIN & Co.,

12 reams of foolscap paper	@	$3.25
15 dozen school books	@	4.50
23 " slates	@	1.30
7 " photograph albums	@	15.00
3 " Bullion's grammar	@	7.00
8 " fifth reader	@	3.50
5 gallons of black ink	@	1.10
4 dozen American Commercial Arithmetic	@	18.00
		$367.90

Received payment,

J. BUNTIN & Co.

---

32 TORONTO, Jan. 12th, 1866.

MR. JAMES H. BURRITT,

Bought of MORRISON, TAYLOR & Co.,

15 cwt. of cheese	@	$9.00
4 cwt. of flour	@	4.25
120 pounds of bacon	@	0.14
7 bushels of corn meal	@	0.75
12 firkins of butter	@	13.50
20 bushels of dried apples	@	2.25
13 " " peaches	@	4.00
11 cwt. of buck-wheat flour	@	5.50
15 cwt. maple sugar	@	8.00
25 bags of common salt	@	1.15
57 barrels of mess pork	@	13.00
68 " beef	@	9.75
13 bushels of clover seed	@	7.50
		$2143.80

Received payment by note at 30 days.

FOR MORRISON, TAYLOR & Co.,

A. C. HENRY.

33 HAMILTON, January 2nd, 1866.

MR. M. MCCULLOCH,

To JOSEPH LIGHT, Stationer, *Dr.*

For	500 French envelopes	@	$3.00 per thousand.
"	12 doz. British American copy books	@	1.15
"	6 " B. B. lead pencils	@	.50
"	5 gross mourning envelopes	@	1.05
"	2 reams mourning note paper	@	3.15
"	4 " tinted note paper	@	3.15
"	2½ " Foreign note paper	@	1.40
"	3 " " letter paper	@	3.00
"	1 doz. First Books	@	.15
"	5 boxes Gillott's No. 303 pens	@	.90
"	5 doz. Third Books	@	1.62½
"	10 quires blank books, half bound	@	.35
"	2 packs visiting cards	@	.37½
			$71.98.

NOTE.—Bills should not be signed until settled.

---

34. BROCKVILLE, Jan. 5th, 1866.

N. D. GALBREAITH,

To R. FITZSIMMONS & CO., *Dr.*

For	24 lbs. Mackerel	@	05½c.	
"	3 gallons Molasses	@	45	
"	13 lbs. Young Hyson Tea	@	87½	
"	13 lbs. brown Sugar	@	11	
"	15 bushels of Potatoes	@	45	
				$22.23

CR.

For	10 lbs. Butter	@	17c.	
"	5 doz. Eggs	@	12½	
"	3 gallons Maple Molasses	@	95	
"	Note at 20 days, to balance			17.05
				$22.23

R. FITZSIMMONS & Co.

NOTE.—Such a Bill as this would be termed a Barter Bill.

35 KINGSTON, Jan. 2nd, 1866.

JAMES THOMPSON, ESQ.,

To A. JARDINE & CO., *Dr.*

For 3 doz. Buttons	@	$0.12	
" 5½ yards of black Broadcloth	@	5.50	
" 20 yards Sheeting	@	.15	
" 1 chest Y. H. Tea, 83 lbs.	@	.95	
" 18 yards French Print	@	.20	
" 2 skeins of Silk Thread	@	.09	
" 5 yards black Silk Velvet	@	3.50	
" 20 lbs. Loaf Sugar	@	.18	
" 2 gallons Molasses	@	.40	
" 1 bag of common Salt	@	1.15	
" 25 lbs. Rice	@	.09	
" 3 sacks Coffee, 70 lbs. each	@	.12	
CR.			$166.74
By Cash			50.00
Balance due			$116.74

---

36 ALGONQUIN, Jan. 15th, 1865.

W. FLEMING & CO.,

Bought of J. & A. WRIGHT,

1500 lbs. Canadian Cheese	@	$ .09	
300 bushels Fall Wheat	@	1.25	
9 brls Pot Ash, net 7056 lbs.	@	5.75 per cwt.	
150 bushels Spring Wheat	@	1.15	
200 " Potatoes	@	.45	
600 " Oats	@	.37½	
150 " Pease	@	.65	
50 " Indian Corn	@	.50	
60 " Apples	@	.60	
3 kegs Butter, 110 lbs. each	@	.18	
50 bushels Rye	@	.70	
40 " Barley	@	.80	
			$1688.12

Received payment,

J. & A. WRIGHT.

PERCENTAGE.

18.—PERCENTAGE is an allowance, or reduction, or estimate of a certain portion of each 100 of the units that enter into any given calculation. The term is a contraction of the Latin expression for one hundred, and means literally *by the hundred.* In calculating dollars and cents, 6 per cent. means 6 dollars for every 100 dollars, or 6 cents for every $1, or 100 cents. If we are estimating the rate of yearly increase of the population of a rising village, and find that at the end of a certain year it was 100, and at the end of the next it was 106, we say it has increased 6 per cent. *i. e.*, 6 persons have been added to the 100. So, also, if a large city has a population of 100,000 at the end of a certain year, and it is found that it has 106,000 at the end of the following year, we say it has increased 6 per cent., which means that if we count the population by hundreds we shall find that for every 100 at the end of the one year, there are 106 at the end of the next; because one hundred thousands is the same as one thousand hundreds, and we have supposed the increase in every 100 to be 6, the total increase will be one thousand *sixes* or 6,000, giving a total population of 106,000 as above, or an increase at the rate of 6 per cent. A decrease would be estimated in the same manner. Thus, a falling off in the population of 6 persons in the hundred would be denoted by 100—6=94, as an increase of 6 in the hundred would be denoted by 100+6=106. So, also, in our first example, a deduction of $6 in $100 would be $100—6=$94, and a gain would be $100+$6=$106.

The portion of 100 so allowed or estimated, is called the *rate per cent.*, as in the examples given, 6 denotes the *rate per cent.*, or the allowance or estimate on every 100. Should the sum on which the estimate is made not reach 100, we can, nevertheless, estimate what is to be allowed on it at the same rate. Thus, if 6 is to be allowed for 100, then 3 must be allowed for 50, and $1\frac{1}{2}$ for 25, &c.

The number on which the percentage is estimated is called the *basis.* Thus, in the example given regarding the population of a city, 100,000 is the basis.

When the basis and percentage are combined into *one*, the result is called the *amount.* If the rate per cent. be an *increase* or *gain*, it is to be added to the basis to get the amount, and if it is a *decrease*, or *loss*, it is to be subtracted from the basis to get the amount. This latter result is sometimes called the *remainder.*

From what has been said, it is plain that percentage is nothing else than taking 100 as a standard unit of measure—(See Art. 1)—and making the rate a fraction of that unit, so that 6 per cent. is $\frac{6}{100}$=(Art. 15, V.) .06. We may obtain the same result by the rule of proportion. Thus, in our illustrative example of an increase of 6 persons for every 100 on a population of 100,000, the analogy will be 100 persons : 100,000 persons : : 6 (the increase on 100) : 6,000, the increase on 100,000. It is manifest that the same result will be obtained whether we multiply the third by the second, and divide by the first, or whether we divide the third by the first, and multiply the result by the second; or, which is the same thing, multiply the second by the result. Now, we already found that $6\div100=\frac{6}{100}$=.06, the same as before. So also, 7 per cent. of any loss is seven one-hundredths of it, *i. e.*, $\frac{7}{100}$=.07. It should be carefully observed that such decimals represent, *not the rate per cent.*, *but the rate per unit.*

Though this is easily comprehended, yet we know by experience that learners are constantly liable to commit errors by neglecting to place the decimal point correctly. We would therefore direct particular attention to the above caution, which, with the rule already laid down, under the head of decimal fractions, should be sufficient to guide any one who takes even moderate pains.

EXERCISES ON FINDING THE RATE PER UNIT.

At $\frac{1}{4}$ per cent., what is the rate per unit?	Ans. .00$\frac{1}{4}$.
At $\frac{1}{2}$ per cent., what is the rate per unit?	Ans. .00$\frac{1}{2}$.
At 1 per cent., what is the rate per unit?	Ans. .01.
At 2 per cent., what is the rate per unit?	Ans. .02.
At 4 per cent., what is the rate per unit?	Ans. .04.
At 7$\frac{1}{4}$ per cent., what is the rate per unit?	Ans. .07$\frac{1}{4}$.
At 10 per cent., what is the rate per unit?	Ans. .10.
At 12$\frac{1}{2}$ per cent., what is the rate per unit?	Ans. .12$\frac{1}{2}$.
At 17 per cent., what is the rate per unit?	Ans. .17.
At 25 per cent., what is the rate per unit?	Ans. .25.
At 33$\frac{1}{3}$ per cent., what is the rate per unit?	Ans. .33$\frac{1}{3}$.
At 66$\frac{2}{3}$ per cent., what is the rate per unit?	Ans. .66$\frac{2}{3}$.
At 75 per cent., what is the rate per unit?	Ans. .75.
At 100 per cent., what is the rate per unit?	Ans. 1.00.
At 112$\frac{1}{2}$ per cent., what is the rate per unit?	Ans. 1.12$\frac{1}{2}$.
At 150 per cent., what is the rate per unit?	Ans. 1.50.
At 200 per cent., what is the rate per unit?	Ans. 2.00.

I. To find the percentage on any given quantity at a given rate:

On the principles of proportion, we have as 100 : given quantity : : rate : percentage, and as the third term, divided by the first, gives the rate per unit, we have the simple

RULE:

Multiply the given quantity by the rate per unit, and the product will be the percentage.

EXAMPLES.

To find how much 6 per cent. is on 720 bushels of wheat, we have $6 \div 100 = .06$, the rate per unit, and $720 \times .06 = 43\frac{1}{5}$ bushels, the percentage.

To find 8 per cent. of $7963-75, in like manner, we have .08, the rate per unit, and $7963.75×.08 gives $637.10, the percentage.

Instead of *per cent* the mark (%) is now commonly used.

EXERCISES ON THE RULE.

1. What does 6 per cent. of 450 tons of hay amount to? Ans. 27.
2. What is 10 per cent. of $879.62½? Ans. $87.96.
3. If 12 per cent. of an army of 47,800 men be lost in killed and wounded; how many remain? Ans. 42,064.
4. What is 5 per cent. of 187 bushels of potatoes? Ans. 9.35.
5. What is 2½ per cent. of a note for $870? Ans. 21.75.
6. Find 12½ per cent. of 97 hogsheads? Ans. 12.12½.

II. To find what rate per cent. one number is of another given number:—Let us take as an example, to find what per cent. 24 is of 96. Here the basis is 96, and we take 100 as a standard basis, and these are magnitudes of the same kind, and 24 is a certain rate on 96, and we wish to find what rate it is on 100, and by the rule of proportion, we have the statement 96 : 100 : : 24 : F. P. $= \frac{2400}{96} = 25$. Therefore 24 is 25 per cent. of 96.

From this we can deduce the simple

RULE.

Annex two ciphers to the given percentage, and divide that by the basis, the quotient will be the rate per cent.

7. What per cent. of 150 is 15? Ans. 10.
8. What per cent. of 240 is 36? Ans. 15.

9. What per cent. of 18 is 2? Ans. $11\frac{1}{9}$.
10. What per cent. of 72 is 48? Ans. $66\frac{2}{3}$.
11. What per cent. of 576 is 18? Ans. $3\frac{1}{8}$.
12. What per cent. is 12 of 480? Ans. $2\frac{1}{2}$.
13. Bought a block of buildings in King street for $1719, and sold it at a gain of 18 per cent.; what was the gain?
Ans. $309.42.

14. Vested $325 in an oil well speculation, and lost 8 per cent.; what was the loss? Ans. $26.00.

15. In 1841 the population of Cleveland was about 15,000, it is now about 50,000; what is the rate of increase? Ans. $233\frac{1}{3}$.

16. An estate worth $4,500 was sold; A bought 30 per cent. of it; B, 25 per cent.; C, 20 per cent.; and D purchased the remainder; what per cent. of the whole was D's share? Ans. 25.

17. If a man walk at the rate of 4 miles an hour; what per cent. is that of a journey of 32 miles? Ans. $12\frac{1}{2}$.

18. What is the percentage on $1370 at $2\frac{3}{4}$ per cent.?
Ans. $37.67\frac{1}{2}$.

III. Given, a number, and the rate per cent. which it is of another number, to find that other number, .400 is 40 per cent. of a certain number, to find that number. As 40 : 100 : : 400 : F. P.= $\frac{400\times100}{40}$=1,000. Hence we derive the

RULE.

Annex two ciphers to the given number, and divide by the rate per cent.

EXERCISES.

1. A bankrupt can pay $2600, which is 80 per cent of his debts; how much does he owe? Ans. $3250.

2. A clerk pays $8 a month for rent, which is 16 per cent. of his salary; what is his yearly salary? Ans. $600.

3. In a manufacturing district in England, 40,000 persons died of cholera in 1832, this was 25 per cent. of the population; what was the population? Ans. 160,000.

4. Bought a certain number of bags of flour, and sold 124 of them, which is $12\frac{1}{2}$ per cent. of the whole. Required, the number of bags purchased. Ans. 992.

5. In a shipwreck 480 tons are lost, and this amount is 15 per cent. of the whole cargo. Find the cargo. Ans. 3200 tons.

6. A firm lost $1770 by the failure of another firm; the loss was 30 per cent. of their capital; what was their capital? Ans. $5900.

IV. To find the basis when the amount and rate are given:—Suppose a man buys a piece of land for a certain sum, and by selling it for $300, gains 25 per cent.; what did he pay for it at first?—Here it is plain that for every dollar of the cost, 25 cents are gained by the sale, *i. e.*, 125 cents for every 100, which gives us the analogy, 125 : 100 : : 300 : F. P.; or, dividing the two terms by 100, 1.25 : 1.00 : : 300 : F. P., which by the rules for the multiplication and division of decimals, gives $\frac{30000}{125}$=$240, the original cost.

Again, suppose the farm had been sold at a loss of 25 per cent. This being a loss, we subtract 25 from 100, and say, as 75 : 100 : : 300 : F. P.=$\frac{30000}{75}$=$400, the prime cost in this case.

Hence we derive the

RULE.

Divide the given amount by one increased or diminished by the given rate per unit, according as the question implies increase or decrease, gain or loss.

EXERCISES.

1. Given the amount $198, and the rate of increase 20 per cent. to find the number yielding that percentage. Ans. $165.

2. A field yields 840 bushels of wheat, which is 250 per cent. on the seed; how many bushels of seed were sown? Ans. 240 bushels.

3. At 5 per cent. gain; what is the basis if the amount be $126? Ans. $120.

4. At 10 per cent. loss; what is the basis, the amount being $328.5? Ans. $365.

5. A ship is sold for $12045, which is a gain of $\frac{3}{8}$ per cent. on the sum originally paid for it; for how much was it bought at first? Ans. $12000.

6. A gambler lost 10 per cent. of his money by a venture, and had $279 left; how much had he at first, and how much did he lose? Ans. He lost $31, and had $310 at first.

7. A grocer bought a lot of flour, and having lost 20 per cent. of the whole, had 160 bags remaining; how many bags did he buy? Ans. 200.

8. A merchant lost 12 per cent. of his capital by a bankruptcy, and had still $2200 left; what was his whole capital? Ans. $2500.

9. Sold a sheep for $5, and gained 25 per cent.; what did I pay for it? Ans. $4.

10. Lost $12000 on an investment, which was 30 per cent. of the whole; what was the investment? Ans. $40000.

INTEREST.

From a transition common in language, the word interest has been inappropriately applied to the *sum paid* for the use of money, but its original and true meaning is simply the *use* of money. To illustrate this, we will suppose that A borrows of B $100 for one year, and at the end of the year, when A wishes to settle the account, he gives B $107. Were we to ask the question of almost any person except an accountant, whether A or B received the interest, we should undoubtedly receive for an answer that B received it. But such is not the case. A having had the *use* of that money for one year, paid B $7 for that *use* or *interest;* hence A received the *interterest* or *use* of that money, and B received $7 in cash for the same. It is only by considering this subject in its true light that accountants are able to determine upon the proper debits and credits that arise from a transaction where interest is involved. If an individual borrows money, he *receives* the use of that money, and when he pays for that use or interest, he places the sum so paid to that side of his "interest account" which represents interest received, and if he lends money, he *has parted with* the use of that money, and when he receives value for that use or interest, he places the sum so received to that side of his "interest account" which represents interest delivered.

We think that this explanation is sufficiently clear to illustrate the difference between *interest* and the *value received* or *paid* for it.

It will also be noticed that we have given many of the exercises in the usual form, *e. g.*, we say what is the interest on $100 for one year, instead of saying *what must be paid for the interest* of $100 for one year, but we have done this more in accordance with custom than from any intention to deviate from the true meaning of the word interest.

Interest is reckoned on a scale of so many units on every $100 for one year, and hence it is called so much *per cent. per annum*, from the Latin *per centum*, by the hundred, and *per annum*, by the year. Thus, $6 a year for every $100, is called *six per cent. per annum.* The term is also extended to designate the return accruing from any investment, such as shares in a joint stock company.

To show the object and use of such transactions, we may suppose a case or two.

A person feels himself cramped or embarrassed in his circumstances and operations, and he applies to some friendly party that lends him $100 for a year, on the condition that at the expiration of the year he is to receive $106, that is, the $100 lent, and $6 more as a return for the use of the $100; or, if the borrower gets $600, he pays at the and of the stipulated time not only the $600, but also $36 ($6 for each $100) in return for the use of the $600. By this means the borrower gets clear of his difficulty, and maintains his credit at a small sacrifice.

The sum on which interest is paid is called the *principal.*

The sum paid for the use of money is called the *interest.*

The sum paid on each $100 is called the *rate.*

The sum of the principal and interest is called the *amount.*

When interest is charged on the principal only, it is called *simple interest.*

When interest is charged on the amount, it is called *compound interest.*

When a certain rate per cent. is established by law, it is called *legal interest.*

When a higher rate per cent. is charged than is allowed by law, it is called *usury.*

The legal rate per cent. differs in different States and in different countries, so also does the mode of calculation differ. In some States it is considered *legal,* to reckon the month as consisting of 30 days, in the calculating of interest on any sum for a short period, in others it is considered *illegal.* We have given the different modes of calculation in order to make the work applicable to all the States. For the legal rate per cent. of each State, see "Laws of the States," at the end of this work.

SIMPLE INTEREST.

As simple interest, when calculated for one year, differs in no way from a percentage on a given sum, we have only four things to consider, viz., the principal, the rate (100 being the basis), the interest, and the time, any three of which being known, the fourth can be found. The finding of the interest includes by far the greatest number of cases.

We shall first show the general principle, and from it deduce an easy practical rule.

Let it be required to find the interest on $468 for one year, at 6 per cent.

As 100 is taken as the *basis principal* in relation to which all calculations are made, it is plain that 100 will have the same ratio to any given principal that the rate, which is the interest on 100, has to the interest on the given principal. Hence, in the question proposed, we have as \$100 : \$468 : : \$6 : interest=$\$468\times\frac{6}{100}=$ $\$468\times.06=\$28.08$. Now .06 is the rate *per unit*, and from this we can deduce rules for all cases.

CASE I.

To find the interest of any sum of money for one year, at any given rate per cent.

RULE.

Multiply the principal by the rate per unit.

EXERCISES.

1. What is the interest on $15, for 1 year, at 3 per cent.?
Ans. $0.45.
2. What is the interest on $35, for 1 year, at 5 per cent.?
Ans. $1.75.
3. What is the interest on $100, for 1 year, at 7 per cent.?
Ans. $7.00.
4. What is the interest on $2.25, fer 1 year, at 8 per cent.?
Ans. $0.18.
5. What is the interest on $6.40, for 1 year, at 8½ per cent.?
Ans. $0.54.
6. What is the interest on $250, for 1 year, at 9½ per cent.?
Ans. $23.75.
7. What is the interest on $760.40, for 1 year, at 7½ per cent.?
Ans. $57.03.
8. What is the interest on $964.50, for 1 year, at 6½ per cent.?
Ans. $62.69.
9. What is the interest on $568.75, for 1 year, at 7¼ per cent.?
Ans. $41.23.

CASE II.

To find the interest of any sum of money, for any number of years, at a given rate per cent.

RULE.

Find the interest for one year, and multiply by the number of years.

EXERCISES.

10. What is the interest of $4.60, for 3 years, at 6 per cent.? Ans. $0.83.

11. What is the interest of $570, for 5 years, at 7½ per cent.? Ans. $213.75.

12. What is the interest of $460.50, for 3 years, at 6¼ per cent.? Ans. $86.34.

13. What is the interest of $17.40, for 3 years, at 8⅓ per cent.? Ans. $4.35.

14. What is the interest of $321.05, for 8 years, at 5¾ per cent.? Ans. $147.68.

15. What is the interest of $1650.45, for 2 years, at 9 per cent.? Ans. $297.08.

16. What is the interest of $964.75, for 4 years, at 10 per cent.? Ans. $385.90.

17. What is the interest of $1674.50, for 3 years, at 10½ per cent.? Ans. $527.47.

18. What is the interest of $640.80, for 5 years, at 4¾ per cent.? Ans. $152.19.

19. What is the interest of $965.50, for 7 years, at 5½ per cent.? Ans. $371.72.

20. What is the interest of $2460.20, for 4 years, at 7 per cent.? Ans. $688.86.

CASE III.

To find the interest on any sum of money for any number of months, at a given rate per cent.

RULE.

Find the interest for one year, and take aliquot parts for the months; or,

Find the interest for one year, divide by 12, and multiply by the number of months.

EXERCISES.

21. What is the interest on $684.20, for 4 months, at 6 per cent.? Ans. $13.68.

22. What is the interest on $760.50, for 5 months, at 7 per cent.? Ans. $22.18.

23. What is the interest on $899.99, for 2 months, at 8 per cent.? Ans. $12.00.

24. What is the interest on $964.50, for 4 months, at 9 per cent.? Ans. $28.94.

25. What is the interest on $1500, for 7 months, at 10 per cent.? Ans. $87.50.

26. What is the interest on $1560, for 11 months, at 7½ per cent.? Ans. $107.25.

27. What is the interest on $1575.54, for 8 months, at 6¼ per cent.? Ans. $65.65.

28. What is the interest on $1728.28, for 9 months, at 8½ per cent.? Ans. $110.18.

29. What is the interest on $268.25, for 13 months, at 7 per cent.? Ans. $20.34.

30. What is the interest on $1569.45, for 1 year, 3 months, at 8 per cent.? Ans. $156.95.

31. What is the interest on $642.99, for 1 year, 5 months, at 10 per cent.? Ans. $91.09.

32. What is the interest on $560.45, for 1 year, 6 months, at 9½ per cent.? Ans. $79.86.

33. What is the interest on $48.50, for 3 years, 9 months, at 10½ per cent.? Ans. $19.10.

34. What is the interest on $560.80, for 2 years, 8 months, at 11¾ per cent.? Ans. $175.72.

35. What is the interest on $2360.40, for 19 months, at 12 per cent.? Ans. $448.48.

CASE IV.

To find the interest on any sum of money, for any number of months and days, at a given rate per cent.

RULE.

Find the interest for the months, and take aliquot parts for the days, reckoning the month as consisting of 30 *days.*

EXAMPLE.

36. What is the interest on $875.50, for 8 months, 18 days, at 11 per cent.?

SOLUTION.

Principal	$875.50
Rate per unit	.11
Interest for 1 year	96.3050
Interest for 6 months; or, ½ of interest for 1 year	48.1525
Interest for 2 months; or, ⅓ of interest for 6 months	16.0508
Interest for 15 days; or, ¼ of interest for 2 months	4.0127
Interest for 3 days; or, ⅕ of interest for 15 days	.8025
Interest for 8 months, 18 days	$69.0185

We find the interest for 1 year to be $96.305, and as 6 months are the ½ of 1 year, the interest for 6 months will be the ½ of the interest for 1 year; likewise the interest for 2 months will be the ⅓ of the interest for 6 months, and as 15 days are the ¼ of 2 months or 60 days, the interest for 15 days will be the ¼ of the interest for 2 months, and likewise the interest for 3 days, will be the ⅕ of the interest for 15 days. Adding the interest for the *months* and *days* together, we obtain $69.02, the sum to be paid for the use of $875.50, for 8 months, 18 days, at 11 per cent.

EXERCISES.

37. What is the interest on $468.75, for 4 months, 15 days, at 7 per cent.? Ans. $12.30.

38. What is the interest on $1654.40, for 3 months, 8 days, at 5 per cent.? Ans. $22.52.

39. What is the interest on $345.65, for 11 months, 25 days, at 6 per cent.? Ans. $20.45.

40. What is the interest on $74.85, for 5 months, 22 days, at 9 per cent.? Ans. $3.22.

41. What is the interest on $673.75, for 8 months, 19 days, at 7½ per cent.? Ans. $36.35.

42. What is the interest on $57.45, for 1 year, 2 months, 12 days, at 6 per cent.? Ans. $4.14.

43. What is the interest on $2647, for 1 year, 5 months, 18 days, at 6¼ per cent.? Ans. $242.64.

44. What is the interest on $268.40, for 2 years, 1 month, 1 day, at 8 per cent.? Ans. $44.79.

45. What is the interest on $2345.50, for 3 years, 7 months, 20 days, at 10 per cent.? Ans. $853.50.

46. What is the interest on $4268.45, for 4 years, 11 months, 11 days, at 11¾ per cent.? Ans. $2481.24.

47. What is the interest of $642.20, for 2 years, 7 months, 24 days, at 12 per cent.?

48. What is the interest of $64.50, for 2 years, 11 months, 2 days, at 7 per cent.? Ans. $13.19.

49. What is the amount of $746.25, for 1 year, 10 months, 12 days, at 5 per cent.?

50. What is the interest of $680, for 4 years, 1 month, 15 days, at 6 per cent.? Ans. $168.30.

CASE V.

To find the interest on any sum of money, for any number of days, at a given rate per cent.*

RULE.

Find the interest for one year, and say, as one year (365 days,) is to the given number of days, so is the interest for one year to the interest required; or,

Having found the interest for one year, multiply it by the given number of days, and divide by 365.

EXERCISES.

51. What is the interest on $464, for 15 days, at 6 per cent.? Ans. $1.14.

52. What is the interest on $364, for 12 days, at 7 per cent.? Ans. 84 cents.

53. What is the interest on $56.82, for 14 days, at 8 per cent.? Ans. 17 cents.

---

* To find how many years elapse between any two dates, we have only to subtract the earlier from the later date. Thus, the number of years from 1814 to 1865 is 51 years. To find months, we must reckon from the given date in the first named month, to the same date in each successive month. Thus, five months from the 10th of March brings us on to the 10th of August. To find days, we require to count how many days each month contains, for to consider every month as consisting of 30 days, in the calculation of interest, is not strictly correct, although for portions of a single month it causes no serious error. Thus, the correct time from March 2nd to June 14th, would be 104 days, viz., 29 for March, 30 for April, 31 for May, and 14 for June. A very convenient plan for reckoning time between two given dates is to count the number of months and odd days that intervene. Thus, from June 14th to November 20th, would be 5 months and 6 days.

54. What is the interest on $75.50, for 18 days, at 8½ per cent.? Ans. 32 cents.

55. What is the interest on $125.25, for 20 days, at 5 per cent.? Ans. 34 cents.

56. What is the interest on $150.40, for 33 days, at 6 per cent.? Ans. 82 cents.

57. What is the interest on $56.48, for 45 days, at 6½ per cent.? Ans. 45 cents.

58. What is the interest on $75.75, for 65 days, at 7 per cent.? Ans. 94 cents.

59. What is the interest on $268.40, for 70 days, at 7½ per cent.? Ans. $3.86.

60. What is the interest on $464.45, for 80 days, at 8 per cent.? Ans. $8.14.

61. What is the interest on $15.84, for 120 days, at 9 per cent.? Ans. 47 cents.

62. What is the interest on $240, for 135 days, at 9½ per cent.? Ans. $8.43.

63. What is the interest on $2460, for 145 days, at 10 per cent.? Ans. $97.73.

64. What is the interest on $1568, for 170 days, at 11 per cent.? Ans. $80.33.

65. What is the interest on $2688, for 235 days, at 11¾ per cent.? Ans. $203.35.

66. What is the amount of $364.80, for 320 days, at 11½ per cent.? Ans. $401.58.

CASE VI.

To find the interest on any sum of money, for any time, at 6 per cent.

Since .06 would be the rate per unit, or the interest of $1 for 1 year, it follows that the interest for *one month* would be the $\frac{1}{12}$ of .06, or $\frac{6}{12}$ of a cent, equal to ½ cent or .005, and for 2 months it would equal ½ cent, or .005×2=.01. Therefore, when interest is at the rate of 6 per cent., the interest of $1, for every 2 months, is *one cent*. Again, if the interest of $1, for *one month*, or 30 days, is ½ cent or .005, it follows that the interest for 6 days will be the $\frac{1}{5}$ of .005 or .001. Therefore, when interest is at the rate of 6 per cent., the interest of $1 for every 6 days is *one mill*. Hence the

RULE.

Find the interest of \$1 *for the given time by reckoning* 6 *cents for every year,* 1 *cent for every* 2 *months, and* 1 *mill for every* 6 *days; then multiply the given principal by the number denoting that interest, and the product will be the interest required.*

NOTE.—This method can be adopted for any rate per cent. by first finding the interest at 6 per cent., then adding to, or subtracting from the interest so found, such a part or parts of it, as the given rate exceeds, or is less than 6 per cent.

This method, although adopted by some, is not exactly correct as the year is considered as consisting of 360 days, instead of 365; so that the interest, obtained in this manner, is too large by $\frac{5}{365}$ or $\frac{1}{73}$, which for every \$73 interest, is \$1 too much, and must therefore be subtracted if the exact amount be required.

EXAMPLE.

67. What is the interest of \$24, for 4 months, 8 days, at 6 per cent.?

SOLUTION.

The interest of \$1, for 4 months, is..............................	.02
The interest of \$1, for 8 days, is	$.001\frac{1}{3}$
Hence the interest of \$1, for 4 months, 8 days, is..........	$.021\frac{1}{3}$

Now, if the interest of \$1, for the given time, is $.021\frac{1}{3}$, the interest of \$24 will be 24 times $.021\frac{1}{3}$, which is \$.512.

EXERCISES.

68. What is the interest on \$171, for 24 days, at 6 per cent.? Ans. 68 cents.

69. What is the interest on \$112, for 118 days, at 6 per cent.? Ans. \$2.20.

70. What is the interest on \$11, for 112 days, at 6 per cent.? Ans. 21 cents.

71. What is the interest on 50 cents, for 360 days, at 6 per cent.? Ans. 3 cents.

72. What is the interest on \$75.00, for 236 days, at 6 per cent.? Ans. \$2.95.

73. What is the interest on \$111.50, for 54 days, at 6 per cent.? Ans. \$1.00.

74. What is the interest on \$15.50, for 314 days, at 6 per cent.? Ans. 81 cents.

75. What is the interest on $174.25, for 42 days, at 6 per cent.? Ans. $1.22.

76. What is the interest on $10, for 1 month, 18 days, at 6 per cent. Ans. 8 cents.

77. What is the interest on $154, for 3 months, at 6 per cent.? Ans. $2.31.

78. What is the interest on $172, for 2 months, 15 days, at 6 per cent.? Ans. $2.15.

79. What is the interest on $25, for 4 months, at 6 per cent.? Ans. 50 cents.

80. What is the interest on $36, for 1 year, 3 months, 11 days, at 7 per cent.? Ans. $3.23.

81. What is the interest on $500, for 160 days, at 6 per cent.? Ans. $13.33.

82. What is the interest on $92.30, for 78 days, at 5 per cent.? Ans. $1.00.

83. What is the interest on $125, for 3 years, 5 months, 15 days, at 10 per cent. Ans. $43.23.

84. What is the amount of $200, for 9 months, 27 days, at 6 per cent.? Ans. $209.90.

85. What is the interest on $125.75, for 5 months, 17 days, at 7 per cent.? Ans. $4.08.

86. What is the interest on $84.50, for 1 month, 20 days, at 5 per cent.? Ans. 59 cents.

87. What is the amount of $45, for 1 year, 1 month, 1 day, at 8 per cent.? Ans. $48.91.

88. What is the interest on $175, for 7 months, 6 days, at 5½ per cent.? Ans. $5.78.

89. What is the interest on $225, for 3 months, 3 days, at 9 per cent.? Ans. $5.23.

90. What is the interest on $212.60, for 9 months, 8 days, at 8½ per cent.? Ans. $13.95.

CASE VII.

To find the interest on any sum of money, in pounds, shillings, and pence, for any time, at a given rate per cent.

RULE.

Multiply the principal by the rate per cent., and divide by 100.

EXAMPLE.

91. What is the interest of £47 15s. 9d., for 1 year, 9 months, 15 days, at 6 per cent.?

SOLUTION.

	£	S.	D.
Interest for 1 year..........................	2	17	4
Interest for 6 mos., or ½ of int. for 1 year,	1	8	8
Interest for 3 mos., or ½ of int. for 6 mos.,	0	14	4
Interest for 15 days, or ⅙ of int. for 3 mos.,	0	2	4½
Interest for 1 year, 9 months, 15 days....	£5	2	8½

£	S.	D.
47	15	9
		6
2)86	14	6
	20	
17)34		
12		
4)14		

92. What is the interest of £25, for 1 year, 9 months, at 5 per cent.? Ans. £2 3s. 9d.

93. What is the interest of £75 12s. 6d., for 7 months, 12 days, at 8 per cent.? Ans. £3 14s. 7½d.

94. What is the amount of £64 10s. 3d., for 3 months, 3 days, at 7 per cent.? Ans. £65 13s. 7d.

95. What is the interest of £35 4s. 8d., for 6 months, at 10 per cent.? Ans. £1 15s. 2¾d.

96. What is the amount of £18 12s., for 10 months and 3 days, at 6 per cent.? Ans. £19 10s. 9¾d.

CASE VIII.

To find the **PRINCIPAL**, the interest, the time, and the rate per cent. being given.

EXAMPLE.

97. What principal will produce $4.50 interest in 1 year, 3 months, at 6 per cent.?

SOLUTION.

If a principal of $1 is put on interest for 1 year, 3 months, at 6 per cent., it will produce .075 interest. Now, if in this example, .075 be the interest on $1, the number of dollars required to produce $4.50, will be represented by the number of times that .075 is contained in $4.50, which is 60 times. Therefore, $60 will produce $4.50 interest in 1 year, 3 months, at 6 per cent. Hence the

RULE.

Divide the given interest by the interest of $1 *for the given time, at the given rate per cent.*

EXERCISES.

98. What principal will produce 77 cents interest in 3 months, 9 days, at 7 per cent.? Ans. $40.

99. What principal will produce $10.71 interest in 8 months, 12 days, at 7½ per cent.? Ans. $204.

100. What principal will produce $31.50 interest in 4 years, at 3½ per cent.? Ans. $225.

101. What sum of money will produce $79.30 interest in 2 years, 6 months, 15 days, at 6½ per cent.? Ans. $480.

102. What sum of money is sufficient to produce $290 interest in 2 years and 6 months, at 7¼ per cent.? Ans. $1600.

CASE IX.

To find the RATE PER CENT., the principal, the interest, and the time being given.

EXAMPLE.

103. If $3 be the interest of $60 for 1 year, what is the rate per cent.?

SOLUTION.

If the interest of $60 for 1 year, at 1 per cent, is .60, the required *rate per cent.* will be represented by the number of times that .60 is contained in 3.00, which is 5 times. Therefore, if $3 is the interest of $60 for 1 year, the rate per cent. is 5. Hence the

RULE.

Divide the given interest by the interest of the given principal at 1 *per cent. for the given time.*

EXERCISES.

104. If the interest of $40, for 2 years, 9 months, 12 days, is $13.36; what is the rate per cent.? Ans. 12.

105. If I borrow $75 for 2 months, and pay $1 interest; what is the rate per cent.? Ans. 8.

106. If I give $2.25 for the use of $30 for 9 months; what rate per cent. am I paying? Ans. 10.

107. At what rate per cent. will $150 amount to $165.75, in 1 year, 4 months, 24 days? Ans. $7\frac{1}{2}$.

108. At what rate per cent. must $1, or any sum of money, be on interest to double itself in 12 years? Ans. Ans. $8\frac{1}{3}$.

109. At what rate per cent. must $425 be lent to gain $11.73 in 3 months, 18 days? Ans. $9\frac{1}{5}$.

110. At what rate per cent. will any sum of money amount to three times itself in 25 years? Ans. 8.

111. If I give $14 for the interest of $125 for 1 year, 7 months, 6 days; what rate per cent am I paying? Ans. 7.

CASE X.

To find the TIME, the principal, the interest, and the rate per cent. being given.

EXAMPLE.

112. How long must $75 be at interest, at 8 per cent., to gain $12?

SOLUTION.

The interest for $75, for 1 year, at 8 per cent., is $6. Now, if $75 require to be on interest for 1 year to produce $6, it is evident that the number of years required to produce $12 interest, will be represented by the number of times that 6 is contained in 12, which is 2. Therefore, $75 will have to be at interest for 2 *years* to gain $12. Hence the

RULE.

Divide the given interest by the interest of the principal for one year, at the given rate per cent.

EXERCISES.

113. In what time will $12 produce $2.88 interest, at 8 per cent? Ans. 3 years.

114. In what time will $25 produce 50 cents interest, at 6 per cent.? Ans. 4 months.

115. In what time will $40 produce 75 cents interest, at $6\frac{1}{4}$ per cent.? Ans. 3 months, 18 days.

116. In what time will any sum of money double itself, at 6 per cent.? Ans. 16 years, 8 months.

117. In what time will any sum of money quadruple itself, at 9 per cent.? Ans. 33 years, 4 months.

118. In what time will $125 amount to $138.75, at 8 per cent.? Ans. 1 year, 4 months, 15 days.

119. Borrowed, January 1, 1865, $60, at 6 per cent, to be paid as soon as the interest amounted to one-half the principal. When is it due? Ans. May 1, 1873.

120. A merchant borrowed a certain sum of money on January 2, 1856, at 9 per cent., agreeing to settle the account when the interest equalled the principal. When should he pay the same? Ans. Feb. 11, 1867.

MERCHANTS' TABLE

For showing in what time any sum of money will double itself, at any rate per cent., from one to twenty, simple interest.

Per cent.	Years.	Per cent.	Years.	Per cent.	Years.	Per cent.	Years.
1	100	6	$16\frac{2}{3}$	11	$9\frac{1}{11}$	16	$6\frac{1}{4}$
2	50	7	$14\frac{2}{7}$	12	$7\frac{1}{2}$	17	$5\frac{15}{17}$
3	$33\frac{1}{3}$	8	$12\frac{1}{2}$	13	$7\frac{9}{13}$	18	$5\frac{5}{9}$
4	25	9	$11\frac{1}{9}$	14	$7\frac{1}{7}$	19	$5\frac{5}{19}$
5	20	10	10	15	$6\frac{2}{3}$	20	5

MIXED EXERCISES.

121. What is the interest on $64.25 for 3 years, at 7 per cent.? Ans. $13.49.

122. What is the interest on $125.40 for 6 months, at 6 per cent.? Ans. 3.76.

123. What is the amount of $369.29 for 2 years, 3 months, 1 day, at 9 per cent.? Ans. $444.16.

124. What must be paid for the use of 75 cents for 6 years, 9 months, 3 days, at 10 per cent.? Ans. 51 cents.

125. What will $54 amount to in 254 days, at 10 per cent.?* Ans. $57.81.

* This and the following exercises (marked with a *) are to be worked by Case VI.

126. What must be paid for the interest of $45 for 72 days, at 9 per cent. ?* Ans. 81 cents.

127. What is the interest of $240 from January 1, 1866, to June 4, 1866, at 7 per cent. ? Ans. $7.14.

128. What will $140.40 amount to from August 29, 1865, to November 29, 1866, at $6\frac{1}{2}$ per cent. ? Ans. $151.83.

129. What principal will give $4.40 interest in 1 year, 4 months, 15 days, at 8 per cent. ? Ans. $40.

130. In what time will $40 amount to $44.40, at 8 per cent. ? Ans. 1 yr., 4 mos., 15 days.

131. At what rate per cent. will $40 produce in 1 yr., 4 mos., 15 days, $4.40 interest ? Ans. 8.

132. What must be paid for the interest of $145.50 for 240 days, at $9\frac{1}{2}$ per cent. ?* Ans. $9.22.

133. What will $160 amount to in 175 days, at 6 per cent. ?* Ans. $164.67.

134. At what rate per cent. must any sum of money be on interest to quadruple itself in 33 years and 4 months ? Ans. 9.

135. In what time will any sum of money double itself, at 10 per cent. ? Ans. 10 years.

CASE XI.

To find the interest on bonds, notes, or other documents drawing $7\frac{3}{10}$ per cent. interest.

Since $.07\frac{3}{10}$ or, .073 would be the rate per unit, or the interest of $1 for 1 year or 365 days, it follows that the interest for 1 day would be the $\frac{1}{365}$ part of .073 which is .0002, equal to two tenths of a mill, hence the

RULE.

Multiply the principal by the number of days, and the product by two tenths of a mill the result will be the answer in mills.

EXAMPLE.

What must be paid for the use of $75 for 36 days at $7\frac{3}{10}$ per cent. ?

SOLUTION.

The interest on $75 for 36 days would be the same as the interest on $75×36=$2700 for 1 day, and at $\frac{2}{10}$ of a mill per day would be $2700×.0002=54 cents.

2. What would be the interest on $118.30 for 42 days at $7\frac{3}{10}$ per cent. Ans. 99cts.

COMMERCIAL PAPER

COMMERCIAL paper is divided into two classes—NEGOTIABLE and NON-NEGOTIABLE.

NEGOTIABLE COMMERCIAL PAPER.

Negotiable commercial paper is that which may be freely transferred from one owner to another, so as to pass the right of action to the holder, without being subject to any set-offs, or legal or equitable defences existing between the original parties, if transferred for a valuable consideration before maturity, and received without any defect therein.

Negotiable paper is made payable to the payee therein named, or to his order, or to the payee or bearer, or to bearer; or some similar term is used; showing that the maker intends to give the payee authority to transfer it to a third party, free from all set-offs, or equitable or legal defences existing between himself and the payee.

NON-NEGOTIABLE COMMERCIAL PAPER.

Non-negotiable commercial paper is that which is made payable to the payee therein named, without authority to transfer it to a third party. It may be passed from one owner to another by assignment, or by indorsement, but it passes subject to all set-offs, and legal or equitable defences existing between the original parties.

HOW THE TITLE PASSES.

The title to negotiable paper passes from one owner to another by delivery, if made payable to payee or bearer, or to bearer. It passes by indorsement and delivery, if made payable to payee or order. The title to non-negotiable paper passes by a mere verbal assignment and delivery, or by indorsement and delivery.

PRIMARY DEBTOR.

In a promissory note there are two original parties—the maker and the payee. The obligation of the maker is absolute, and continues until the note is presumed to have been paid under the Statute of Limitations. The maker is the primary debtor. In a bill of exchange there are three parties. When the drawer accepts the bill, he becomes the primary debtor upon the bill of exchange.

PROMISSORY NOTE NOT PAYABLE IN MONEY.

When a promissory note is payable in anything but money, it does not come within the Statute. There is no presumption that it is founded upon a valuable consideration. A consideration must be alleged in the complaint, and proved on the trial. The acknowledgment of a consideration in such promissory note, by inserting the words "*value received*," is sufficient to cast upon the defendant the burden of proof that there was no consideration. The acknowledgment of "value received," raises the presumption that the note was given for value; but this presumption may be rebutted by the defendant.

A negotiable instrument is a written promise or request for the payment of a certain sum of money to order or bearer.

A negotiable instrument must be made payable in money only, and without any condition not certain of fulfillment.

The person, to whose order a negotiable instrument is made payable, must be ascertainable at the time the instrument is made.

A negotiable instrument may give to the payee an option between the payment of the sum specified therein, and the performance of another act.

A negotiable instrument may be with or without date; with or without seal; and with or without designation of the time or place of payment.

A negotiable instrument may contain a pledge of collateral security, with authority to dispose thereof.

A negotiable instrument must not contain any other contract than such as is specified. Two different contracts cannot be admitted.

Any date may be inserted by the maker of a negotiable instrument, whether past, present, or future, and the instrument is not invalidated by his death or incapacity at the time of the nominal date.

There are several classes of negotiable instruments, namely:—

1. Bills of Exchange; 2. Promissory Notes; 3. Bank Notes; 4. Cheques on Banks and Bankers; 5. Coupon Bonds; 6. Certificates of Deposit; 7. Letters of Credit.

A negotiable instrument that does not specify the time of payment, is payable immediately.

A negotiable instrument which does not specify a place of payment, is payable wherever it is held at its maturity.

An instrument, otherwise negotiable in form, payable to a person named, but adding the words, "or to his order," or "to bearer," or equivalent thereto, is in the former case payable to the written order of such person, and in the latter case, payable to the bearer.

A negotiable instrument, made payable to the order of the maker, or of a fictitious person, if issued by the maker for a valid consideration, without indorsement, has the same effect against him and all other persons having notice of the facts, as if payable to the bearer.

A negotiable instrument, made payable to the order of a person obviously fictitious, is payable to the bearer.

The signature of every drawer, acceptor and indorser of a negotiable instrument, is presumed to have been made for a valuable consideration, before the maturity of the instrument, and in the ordinary course of business, and the words "value received," acknowledge a consideration.

One who writes his name upon a negotiable instrument, otherwise than as a maker or acceptor, and delivers it, with his name thereon, to another person, is called an indorser, and his act is called an indorsement.

One who agrees to indorse a negotiable instrument is bound to write his signature upon the back of the instrument, if there is sufficient space thereon for that purpose.

When there is not room for a signature upon the back of a negotiable instrument, a signature equivalent to an indorsement thereof may be made upon a paper annexed thereto.

An indorsement may be general or special.

A general indorsement is one by which no indorser is named. A special indorsement specifies the indorsee.

A negotiable instrument bearing a general indorsement cannot be afterwards specially indorsed; but any lawful holder may turn a general indorsement into a special one, by writing above it a direction for payment to a particular person.

A special indorsement may, by express words for that purpose, but not otherwise, be so made as to render the instrument not negotiable.

Every indorser of a negotiable instrument warrants to every subsequent holder thereof, who is not liable thereon to him:

1. That it is in all respects what it purports to be;
2. That he has a good title to it;
3. That the signatures of all prior parties are binding upon them;
4. That if the instrument is dishonored, the indorser will, upon notice thereof duly given unto him, or without notice, where it is excused by law, pay so much of the same as the holder paid therefor, with interest.

One who indorses a negotiable instrument before it is delivered to the payee, is liable to the payee thereon, as an indorser.

An indorser may qualify his indorsement with the words, "without recourse," or equivalent words; and upon such indorsement, he is responsible only to the same extent as in the case of a transfer without indorsement.

Except as otherwise prescribed by the last section, an indorsement "without recourse" has the same effect as any other indorsement.

An indorsee of a negotiable instrument has the same right against every prior party thereto, that he would have had if the contract had been made directly between them in the first instance.

An indorser has all the rights of a guarantor, and is exonerated from liability in like manner.

One who indorses a negotiable instrument, at the request, and for the "accommodation" of another party to the instrument, has all the rights of a surety, and is exonerated in like manner, in respect to every one having notice of the facts, except that he is not entitled to contribution from subsequent indorsers.

The want of consideration for the undertaking of a maker, acceptor, or indorser of a negotiable instrument, does not exonerate him from liability thereon, to an indorsee in good faith for a consideration.

An indorsee in due course is one who in good faith, in the ordinary course of business, and for value, before its apparent maturity or presumptive dishonor, acquires a negotiable instrument duly indorsed to him, or indorsed generally, or payable to the bearer.

An indorser of a negotiable instrument, in due course, acquires an absolute title thereto, so that it is valid in his hands, notwithstanding any provision of law making it generally void or voidable, and notwithstanding any defect in the title of the person from whom he acquired it.

One who makes himself a party to an instrument intended to be negotiable, but which is left wholly or partly in blank, for the purpose of filling afterwards, is liable upon the instrument to an indorsee thereof in due course, in whatever manner, and at whatever time it may be filled, so long as it remains negotiable in form.

It is not necessary to make a demand of payment upon the principal debtor in a negotiable instrument in order to charge him; but if the instrument is by its terms payable at a specified place, and he is able and willing to pay it there at maturity, such ability and willingness are equivalent to an offer of payment upon his part.

Presentment of a negotiable instrument for payment, when necessary, must be made as follows, as nearly as by reasonable diligence it is practicable:

1. The instrument must be presented by the holder, or his authorized agent.

2. The instrument must be presented to the principal debtor, if he can be found at the place where presentment should be made, and if not, then it must be presented to some other person of discretion, if one can be found there, and if not, then it must be presented to some other person of discretion, if one can be found there, and if not, then it must be presented to a notary public within the State;

3. An instrument which specifies a place for its payment, must be presented there, and if the place specified includes more than one house, then at the place of residence or business of the principal debtor, if it can be found therein;

4. An instrument which does not specify a place for its payment, must be presented at the place of residence or business of the principal debtor, or wherever he may be found, at the option of the presentor; and,

5. The instrument must be presented upon the day of its apparent maturity, or, if it is payable on demand, at any time before its apparent maturity, within reasonable hours, and, if it is payable at a banking house, within the usual banking hours of the vicinity; but, by the consent of the person to whom it should be presented, it may be presented at any hour of the day.

The apparent maturity of a negotiable instrument, payable at a particular time, is the day on which by its terms it becomes due; or, when that is a holiday, it should be paid the previous day.

A bill of exchange, payable at a specified time after sight, which is not accepted within ten days after its date, in addition to the time which would suffice, with ordinary diligence, to forward it for acceptance, is presumed to have been dishonored.

The apparent maturity of a bill of exchange, payable at sight or on demand, is:

1. If it bears interest, one year after its date; or,

2. If it does not bear interest, ten days after its date, in addition to the time which would suffice, with ordinary diligence, to forward it for acceptance.

The apparent maturity of a promissory note, payable at sight or on demand, is:

1. If it bears interest one year after its date; or,

2. If it does not bear interest, six months after its date.

When a promissory note is payable at a certain time after sight or demand, such time is to be added to the periods mentioned in the last paragraph.

A party to a negotiable instrument may require, as a condition concurred to its payment by him:

1. That the instrument be surrendered to him, unless it is lost or destroyed, or the holder has other claims upon it; or,

2. If the holder has a right to retain the instrument, and does not retain it, then that a receipt for the amount paid, or an exoneration of the party paying, be written thereon; or,

3. If the instrument is lost, then that the holder give to him a bond, executed by himself and two sufficient sureties, to indemnify him against any lawful claim thereon; or

4. If the instrument is destroyed, then that proof of its destruction be given to him.

A negotiable instrument is dishonored when it is either not paid, or not accepted, according to its tenor, or presentment for the purpose, or without presentment, where that is excused.

Notice of the dishonor or protest of a negotiable instrument may be given:

1. By a holder thereof; or,

2. By a party to the instrument who might be compelled to pay it to the holder, and who would, upon taking it up, have a right to reimbursement from the party to whom the notice is given.

A notice of dishonor may be given in any form which describes the instrument with reasonable certainty, and substantially informs the party receiving it that the instrument has been dishonored.

A notice of dishonor may be given :

1. By delivering it to the party to be charged, personally, at any place; or,

2. By delivering it to some person of discretion at the place of residence or business of such party, apparently acting for him ; or,

3. By properly folding the notice, directing it to the party to be charged, at his place of residence, according to the best information that the person giving the notice can obtain, depositing it in the post-office most conveniently accessible from the place where the presentment was made, and paying the postage thereon.

In case of the death of a party to whom notice of dishonor should otherwise be given, the notice must be given to one of his personal representatives; or, if there are none, then to any member of his family who resided with him at his death, or, if there is none, then it must be mailed to his last place of residence, as prescribed by subdivision 3 of the last paragraph.

A notice of dishonor sent to a party after his death, but in ignorance thereof, and in good faith, is valid.

Notice of dishonor, when given by the holder of an instrument, or his agent, otherwise than by mail, must be given on the day of dishonor, or on the next business day thereafter.

When notice of dishonor is given by mail, it must be deposited in the post-office in time for the first mail which closes after noon of the first business day succeeding this dishonor, and which leaves the place where the instrument was dishonored, for the place to which the notice should be sent.

When the holder of a negotiable instrument, at the time of its dishonor, is a mere agent for the owner, it is sufficient for him to give notice to his principal in the same manner as to an indorser, and his principal may give notice to any other party to be charged, as if he were himself an indorser. And if an agent of the owner employes a sub-agent, it is sufficient for each successive agent or sub-agent to give notice in like manner to his own principals.

Every party to a negotiable instrument, receiving notice of its dishonor, has the like time thereafter to give similar notice to prior parties, as the original holder had after its dishonor. But this additional time is available only to the particular party entitled thereto.

A notice of the dishonor of a negotiable instrument, if valid in favor of the party giving it, inures to the benefit of all other parties thereto, whose right to give the like notice has not then been lost.

FORMS OF FOREIGN BILLS OF EXCHANGE.

French.

Lille, le 28 *Septembre,* 1848. *Bou pour* £158 9 *Sterlings.*

Au vingt-cinq Décembre prochain, Il vous plaira payer par ce mandat à l'ordre de nousmêmes la somme de cent cinquante-huit livres sterlings 9 *shellings valeur en nousmêmes et que passerez suivant l'avis de*

____

4 *Messieurs*____________________
à Londres.

German.

Nürnberg, den 28 *October,* 1838. *Pro* £100 *Sterling.*

*Zwei monate nach dato zahlen Sie gegen diesen Prima Wechsel an die Ordre des Herrn*____________________*Ein Hundert Vfund Sterling den Werth erhalten. Sie bringen solche auf Rechnung laut Bericht von*

____

*Herrn*____________________
London.

Italian.

Livorno, le 25 *Settembre,* 1848. *Per* £500 *Sterline.*

A Tre mesi data pagate per questa prima de Cambio (una sol volta) all' ordine ____________________*, la somma di Lire cinque cento sterline valuta cambiata, e ponete in conto M. S. secondo l'avviso Addio.*

____

*Al*____________________
Londra.

Spanish.

Malaga, á 20 *de Setb*[re] *de* 1848, *Son* £300.

A noventa dias fecha se servíran V[s] *mandar pagar por esta primera de cambio á la orden de los S*[res]____________________*Tres cientas libras Esterlinas en oro o plata valor recibido de dhos S*[res] *que anotaran valor en cuenta segun aviso de* ____________________

A los S[res]____________________
Londres.

Portuguese.

£600 *Esterlinas.* *Lisbon, aos* 8 *de Dezembro de* 1848.

*A Sessenta dias de vista precizos pagará V*____________________*por esta nossa unica via de Letra Segura, à nossa Ordem a quantia acima de Seis Centas Livras Esterlinas valor de nos recibido em Fazendas, que passera em Conta segundo o aviso de* ____________________

*Ao Sen*____________________
Londres.

Bill of Exchange on London.

£347 19*s.* 10*d.* *Philadelphia, Oct.* 25*th,* 1866.

Sixty days after sight of this, my first Bill of Exchange (second and third of the same date, and tenor unpaid), pay to the order of Williams & Mann, Three Hundred and Forty-seven Pounds, Nineteen Shillings and Ten peuce, Sterling, value received, with or without further advice.

KERR, BROWN & Co.

To R. H. Gladstone, Banker,
London.

Inland Draft.

\$971$\frac{25}{100}$ *Chicago, Sept.* 10*th,* 1866.

Ninety days after sight, pay to the order of Manning and Munson, Nine Hundred and Seventy-one and $\frac{25}{100}$ *Dollars, value received, and charge the same to our account.*

SMITH & EVANS.

To Samuel Small & Co.,
Baltimore, Md.

Bills of Exchange are the highest class of commercial paper known to the law, and it has never been the cherished object of the law merchant,—which has been permitted by the English courts to insinuate itself into the common law, till it now forms a part of that code,—to uphold them inviolate, as far as possible. While the *lex-mercatoria* (or mercantile law) is deeply impregnated with the principles of equity, those principles have been chiefly marked to enable courts of law to enforce equitable rights, and upon this principle was the negotiability of bills of exchange insisted upon and finally maintained at the common law; but when equitable principles have been invoked for the purpose of destroying the validity and security of bills of exchange, they have been listened to with great disfavor and only admitted as exceptional cases

CHECKS.

1. A check is substantially the same as an inland bill of exchange; it passes by delivery, when payable to bearer, and the rules as to presentment, diligence of the holder, &c., which are applicable to the one, are generally applicable to the other.

2. A check is an appropriation of the drawer's funds, in the hands of the banker, to the amount thereof, and, consequently, the drawee has no right to withdraw them before the check is paid.

3. The characteristics which distinguish checks from bills of exchange are, that checks are always drawn on a bank or banker; that they are payable immediately upon presentment, and without days of grace; and that they are not presentable for acceptance, but only for payment. The want of due presentment of a check, and notice of the non-payment thereof only exonerates the drawer in so far as actual damages have thereby resulted to him.

LETTERS OF CREDIT.

In addition to the commercial paper before mentioned, there is an extensive business done by the issue of "Letters of Credit." These are issued by prominent bankers in London, Paris, New York and other cities, to travellers who are about to visit foreign countries, and who are thus saved the risk and expense of carrying any large amount of cash about them.

These Letters of Credit are addressed by the banker to his correspondents abroad, authorizing any one or more of them to pay to the person named, any portion of the sum mentioned in the letter.

Thus a person leaving New York for the Pacific Ports, South America or Arctic Ports, or any city or place in Europe or other portions of the world, need carry very little cash. At the first port of arrival he is able to realize such funds as may be necessary to pay his expenses to a further port by using his Letters of Credit. A traveller may go round the world, with the aid of such a CREDIT, and never have more than one hundred dollars in his pocket. No loss from exchange need occur, in such cases: bills on London being in demand throughout the civilized world.

The usual charge by the bankers for such "Letters of Credit," is *one per cent.* where the trader does not pay the amount of the Letter in advance. Where he pays in advance, no charge is made; the use of the money in the banker's hands being an equivalent for the cost of the credit.

Letters of Credit are also extensively used by importers when travelling abroad for the purchase of goods; also by supercargoes and captains of vessels for the purchase of cargoes in foreign ports; also as remittances to distant ports in Asia, Australia, &c., for the purchase of cargoes of foreign goods. Before Letters of Credit were adopted or in circulation, it was the practice among American and other merchants to remit specie to remote parts for investment in foreign merchandize

DAYS OF GRACE.

1. In most countries, when a bill or note is payable at a certain time after date, or after sight, or after demand, it is not payable the precise time mentioned in the bill or note, but days of grace are allowed.

2. The days of grace are so called, because they were formerly gratuitous, and not to be claimed as a right by the person on whom it was incumbent to pay the bill, and were dependant on the inclination of the holder; they still retain the name of days of grace, though the custom of merchants, recognized by law, has long reduced them to a certainty, and established them as a right.

3. In England, Scotland, Wales, and Ireland, three days grace are allowed; in other countries they vary from three to twelve days.

4. The days of grace as allowed in England, are generally allowed in the United States, at least no traces can be found of a contrary decision, except in the State of Massachusetts, where it has been held that no days of grace are allowable, unless stipulated in the contract itself.

It is probable that a bill of exchange was, in its original, nothing more than a letter of credit from a merchant in one country, to his debtor, a merchant in another, requesting him to pay the debt to a third person, who carried the letter, and happened to be travelling to the place where the debtor resided. It was discovered, by experience, that this mode of making payments was extremely convenient to all parties:—to the creditor, for he could thus receive his debt without trouble, risk or expense—to the debtor, for the facility of payment was an equal accommodation to him, and perhaps drew after it faciiity of credit to the bearer of the letter, who found himself in funds in a foreign country, without the danger and incumbrance of carrying specie. At first, perhaps, the letter contained many other things besides the order to give credit. But it was found that the original bearer might often, with advantage, transfer it to another. The letter was then disencumbered of all other matter; it was opened and not sealed, and the page on which it was written, gradually shrunk to the slip now in use. The assignee was, perhaps, desirous to know beforehand whether the party to whom it was addressed would pay, and sometimes showed it to him for that purpose; his promise to pay was the origin of acceptances. These letters or bills, the representatives of debts due in a foreign country, were sometimes more, sometimes less, in demand; they became, by degrees, articles of traffic; and the present complicated and abstruse practice and theory of exchange was gradually formed.

PARTIAL PAYMENTS

Partial payments, as the term indicates, are the part payments of promissory notes, bonds, or other obligations.

When these payments are made the creditor specifies in writing, on the *back* of the note, or other instrument, the sum paid, and the time when it is paid, and acknowledges it by signing his name.

The method approved of by the Supreme Court of the United States, for casting interest upon bonds, notes, or other obligations, upon which partial payments have been made, is to apply the payment, in the first place, to the discharge of the interest then due. If the payment exceeds the interest, the surplus goes towards discharging the principal, and the subsequent interest is to be computed on the balance of the principal remaining due. If the payment be less than the interest, the surplus of interest must not be taken to augment the principal, but interest continues on the former principal until the time when the payments, taken together, exceed the interest due, and then the surplus is to be applied towards discharging the principal.

RULE.

Find the amount of the principal to the time of the first payment; subtract the payment from the amount, and then find the amount of the remainder to the time of the second payment; deduct the payment as before; and so on to the time of settlement.

But if any payment is less than the interest then due, find the amount of the sum due to the time when the payments, added together, shall be equal, at least, to the interest already due; then find the balance, and proceed as before.

EXAMPLE.

1. On the 4th of January, 1865, a note was given for $800, payable on demand, with interest at 6 per cent. The following payments were receipted on the back of the note:

February 7th, 1865,	received	....	$150
April 16th,	"	"	100
Sept., 30th,	"	"	180
January 4th, 1866.		"	170
March 24th,	"	"	100
June 12th,	"	"	50

Settled July 1st, 1867. How much was due?

SOLUTION:

Face of the note, or principal..................................	$800.00
Interest on the same to February 7th, 1865 (1 month, 3 days)..	4.40
Amount due at time of 1st payment.........................	804.40
First payment to be taken from this amount.........	150.00
Balance remaining due February 7th, 1865..........	654.40
Interest on the same from February 7th, 1865, to April 16th, 1865..	7.525
Amount due at time of 2nd payment........................	661.925
Second payment to be taken from this amount............	100.000
Balance remaining due April 16th, 1865.............	561.925
Interest on the same from April 16th, 1865, to September 30th, 1865..	15.359
Amount due at time of 3rd payment........................	577.284
Third payment to be taken from this amount..............	180.000
Balance remaining due Sept. 30th, 1865.............	397.284
Interest on the same from Sept. 30th, 1865, to January 4th, 1866	6.290
Amount due at time of 4th payment..........................	403.574
Fourth payment to be taken from this amount............	170.000
Balance remaining due January 4th, 1866...........	233.574

Interest on the same from Jan. 4th, 1866, to March 24th, 1866	3.114
Amount due at time of 5th payment	236.688
Fifth payment to be taken from this amount	100.000
Balance remaining due, March 24th, 1866	136.688
Interest on the same from March 24th, 1866, to June 12th, 1866	1.799
Amount due at time of 6th payment	138.487
Sixth payment to be taken from this amount	50.000
Balance remaining due June 12th, 1866	88.487
Interest on the same from June 12th, 1866, to July 1st, 1867	5.589
Amount due on settlement	94.076

2. $1600. CHARLESTON, February 16th, 1865.

On demand, I promise to pay Jacob Anderson, or order, one thousand six hundred dollars, with interest, at 7 per cent.

JOHN FORTUNE JR.

There was paid on this note,

April 19th, 1865	$460
July 22nd "	150
August 25th, 1866	50
Sept. 12th, "	100
Dec. 24th. "	700

How much was due December 31st, 1866?

SOLUTION.

Face of the note or principal	$1600.00
Interest on the same from Feb. 16th, 1865, to April 19th, 1865	19.60
Amount due at time of 1st payment	1619.60
First payment to be taken from this amount	460.00
Balance remaining due, April 19th. 1865	1159.60

Interest on the same from April 19th, 1865, to July 22nd, 1865	20.969
Amount due at time of 2nd payment	1180.569
Second payment to be taken from this amount	150.000
Balance remaining due, July 22nd, 1865	1030.569
Interest on the same from July 22nd, 1865, to Aug. 25th, 1866, greater than 3rd payment,*	
Interest on the same from July 22nd, 1865, to Sept. 12th, 1866	82.359
Amount due at time of 4th payment	1112.928
Third and fourth payments to be taken from this amount,	150.000
Balance remaining due Sept. 12th, 1866	962.928
Interest on the same from Sept. 12th, 1866, to Dec. 24th, 1866	19.098
Amount due at time of last payment	982.026
Last payment to be taken from this amount	700.000
Balance remaining due Dec. 24th, 1866	282.026
Interest on the same from Dec. 24th, 1866, to Dec. 31st, 1866	.382
Amount due at time of settlement, Dec. 31st, 1866	$282.408

3. $350. BOSTON, May 1st, 1864.

On demand I promise to pay William Brown, or order, three hundred and fifty dollars, with interest, at 6 per cent.

JAMES WESTON.

There was paid on this note,

December 25th, 1864	$50
June 30th, 1865	5

* The interest on $1030.569, from July 22nd, 1865, to August 25th, 1866, is $78.752, and the payment made at this date, is only $50, not enough to pay the interest, so if we proceeded, as in the former case, to add the interest to the principal, and subtract the payment from the amount obtained, we would be taking interest, until the next payment, on the excess of the interest, $78.752, over the payment, $50, which would be in effect interest upon interest, or compound interest which the law does not allow.

August 22nd, 1866.................. 15
June 4th, 1867.................. 100

How much was due April 5th, 1868? Ans. $251.67.

4. $609.65. BRANTFORD, June 8th, 1861.

Six months after date, we jointly and severally promise to pay John Anderson, or order, six hundred and nine $\frac{65}{100}$ dollars, at the Royal Canadian Bank in Toronto, with interest at 6 per cent. after maturity.

SAMUEL GRAHAM.
T. B. BEARMAN.

There was paid on this note,

October 4th, 1862.................... $25.00
March 15th, 1863.................... 16.25
August 24th, 1864.................... 36.56

What was due December 19th, 1865? Ans. 679.27.

5. $874.95. KINGSTON, May 9th, 1863.

Three months after date, I promise to pay Harmon Cummings, or order, eight hundred and seventy-four $\frac{95}{100}$ dollars, with interest after maturity at 6 per cent.

THOMAS GOODPAY.

There was paid on this note,

April 12th, 1864...................... $56.30
July 14th, 1865...................... 24.80
Sept. 18th, 1866...................... 240.60

What was due February 9th, 1868? Ans. $773.07.

When the interest accruing on a note is to be paid annually adopt the following

RULE.*

Compute the interest on the principal to the time of settlement, and on each year's interest after it is due, then add the sum of the

* When notes, bonds, or other obligations, are given, "with interest payable annually," the interest is due at the end of each year, and may be collected, but if not collected at that time, the interest due draws only *simple interest*, and the original principal must not be increased by any addition of yearly interest. If nothing has been paid until maturity on a note drawing annual interest, the amount due consists of the principal, the total annual interest, or the simple interest, and the simple interest on each item of annual interest from the time it became due until paid.

interests on the annual interests to the amount of the principal, and from this amount take the payments, and the interest on each, from the time they were paid to the time of settlement, the remainder will be the amount due.

6. $500. PRESCOTT, May 1st, 1864.

One year after date, for value received, I promise to pay Musgrove & Wright, or order, Five Hundred Dollars, at their office, in the city of Toronto, with interest at 6 *per cent., payable annually.*

JAMES MANNING.

There was paid on this note:

May 4th, 1865	$150
Dec. 18th, "	300

How much was due June 1st, 1866?

SOLUTION.

Face of note, or principal			$500.00
Interest on the same from May 1st 1864, to June 1st, 1866			62.50
Amount of the principal at time of settlement			562.50
First year's interest on principal	$30		
Interest on the same from May 1st, 1865, to June 1st, 1866		$1.95	
Second year's interest on principal	$30		
Interest on the same from May 1st, 1866, to June 1st, 1866		.15	
Amount of interest upon *annual interest*			2.10
Total amount of principal			$564.60
First payment, May 4th, 1865		$150.00	
Interest on the same from May 4th, 1865, to June 1st, 1866		9.70	
Second payment, December 18th, 1865		300.00	
Interest on the same from December 18th, 1865, to June 1st, 1866		8.20	
Payments and interest on the same			467.90
Amount due June 1st, 1866			$96.70

7. $700. CINCINNATI, January 2nd, 1863.

Eighteen months after date, I promise to pay to the order of J. H. Wilson, Seven Hundred Dollars, for value received, with interest at 6 per cent., payable annually.

THOS. A. BRYCE.

There was paid on this note:

January 15th, 1864.................... $350
July 2nd, 1864.......................... 300

What amount was due January 2nd, 1865? Ans. $107.22.

8. $950. INDIANAPOLIS, Jan. 3rd, 1863.

Two years after date, I promise to pay A. R. Tennison, or order, Nine hundred and Fifty Dollars, with interest at 9 per cent., payable annually, value received.

JAMES S. PARMENTER.

The following payments were receipted on the back of this note:

February 1st, 1864, received................ $500
May 14th, " " 100
January 12, 1865, " 300

What was due May 6th, 1865? Ans. $188.94.

9. $250. MOBILE, January 2nd, 1863.

Three years from date, for value received, I promise to pay Michael Wright, or order, Two Hundred and Fifty Dollars, with interest, payable annually, at 6 per cent.

CALVIN W. PEARSONS.

At First National Bank here.

What was the amount of this note at maturity? Ans. $297.70.

CONNECTICUT RULE.

The Supreme Court of the State of Connecticut has adopted the following

RULE.

Compute the interest on the principal to the time of the first payment; if that be one year or more from the time the interest commenced, add it to the principal, and deduct the payment from the sum total. If there be after payments made, compute the interest on the balance due to the next payment, and then deduct the payment as above, and in like manner from one payment to another, till all the payments are absorbed, provided the time between one payment and another be one year or more.

If any payments be made before one year's interest has accrued, then compute the interest on the principal sum due on the obligation for one year, add it to the principal, and compute the interest on the sum paid, from the time it was paid, up to the end of the year; add it to the sum paid, and deduct that sum from the principal and interest, added as above.

If any payments be made, of a less sum than the interest arising at the time of such payment, no interest is to be computed, but only on the principal sum for any period.

NOTE.—If a year extends beyond the time of *settlement*, find the amount of the remaining principal to the time of *settlement;* find also the amount of the payment or payments, if any, from the time they were paid to the time of settlement, and subtract their sum from the amount of the principal.

EXAMPLES.

10. $900. KINGSTON, June 1st, 1862.

On demand we promise to pay J. R. Smith & Co., or order, nine hundred dollars, for value received, with interest from date, at 6 per cent.

JONES & WRIGHT.

On the back of this note were receipted the following payments:

June 16th, 1863, received	....	$200
August 1st, 1864, "	....	160
Nov. 16th, 1864, "	....	75
Feby. 1st, 1866, "	....	220

What amount was due August 1st, 1866?

SOLUTION.

Face of note or principal	$900.00
Interest on the same from June 1st, 1862, to June 16th, 1863	56.25
Amount of principal and interest, June 16th, 1863	956.25
First payment to be taken from this amount	200.00
Balance due	756.25
Interest on the same from June 16th, 1863, to August 1st, 1864	51.046
Amount due August 1st, 1864	807.296

Second payment to be taken from this amount............	160.000
Balance due...	647.296
Interest on the same for *one year*............................	38.837
Amount due August 1st, 1865	686.133
Amount of 3rd payment from Nov. 16th, 1864, to August 1st, 1865...	78.187
Balance due...	607.946
Interest on the same from August 1st, 1865, to August 1st, 1866.................	36.476
Amount due August 1st, 1866..............................	644.422
Amount of 4th payment from February 1st, 1866, to August 1st, 1866...	226.600
Balance due August 1st, 1866................................	$417.822

MERCHANTS' RULE.

It is customary among merchants and others, when partial payments of notes or other debts are made, when the note or debt is settled within a year after becoming due, to adopt the following

RULE.

Find the amount of the principal from the time it became due until the time of settlement. Then find the amount of each payment from the time it was paid until settlement, and subtract their sum from the amount of the principal.

EXAMPLE.

11. $400. MAITLAND, January 1st, 1865.

For value received, I promise to pay J. B. Smith & Co., or order, on demand, four hundred dollars, with interest at 6 *per cent.* A. R. CASSELS.

The following payments were receipted on the back of this note:

February 4th, 1865,	received	....	$100
May 16th,	" "	....	75
August 28th	" "	....	100
November 25th,	" "	....	80

What was due at time of settlement, which was December 28th, 1865?

SOLUTION.

Principal or face of note.		$400.00
Interest on the same from Jan. 1st, 1865, to Dec. 28th, 1865		23.80
Amount of principal at settlement		423.80
First payment	$100.00	
Interest on the same from Feb. 4th, 1865, to Dec. 28th, 1865	5.40	
Second payment	75.00	
Interest on the same from May 16th, 1865, to Dec. 28th, 1865	2.77½	
Third payment	100.00	
Interest on the same from August 28th, 1865, to Dec. 25th, 1865	2.00	
Fourth payment	80.00	
Interest on the same from Nov. 25th, 1865, to Dec. 28th, 1865	.44	
Amount of payments to be taken from *amount* of principal		365.61½
Balance due, December 28th, 1865		$58.18½

12. $500. CLEVELAND, January 1st, 1865.

Three months after date, I promise to pay James Manning, or order, five hundred dollars, for value received, at the First National Bank of Buffalo. CYRUS KING.

Mr. King paid on this note, July 1st 1865, $200.

What was due April 1st, 1866, the rate of interest being 7 per cent? Ans. $324.50.

13. $240. PHILADELPHIA, May 4th, 1865.

On demand, I promise to pay A. K. Frost & Co., or order, two hundred and forty dollars, for value received, with interest at 6 *per cent.* DAVID FLOOK.

The following payments were receipted on the back of this note:

September 10th, 1865, received	$60
January 16th, 1866, "	90

What was due at the time of settlement, which was May 4th, 1866? Ans. $100.44.

14. $340. LOWELL, June 16th, 1864.

Three months after date, I promise to pay Thomas Culverwell, or order, three hundred and forty dollars, with interest, at 6 per cent. WILLIAM MANNING.

On this note were receipted the following payments :

October 14th, 1864, received..............$86
February 12th, 1865, " 40

What was due at time of settlement, Aug. 10, 1865? Ans. $232.0.6

COMPOUND INTEREST.

When interest is unpaid at the end of the year, it may, by special agreement, be added to the principal, and in its turn bear interest, and so on from year to year. When added to the principal in this way, it is said to be *compound.*

A person may take compound interest and not be liable to the charge of usury, provided the person to whom he lends money chooses to pay compound interest, but he cannot legally collect it unless there has been a previous agreement to that effect.

EXAMPLE.

1. What is the compound interest of $60, for 4 years, at 7 per cent.?

SOLUTION.

Principal..	$60.00
Interest on the same for one year................................	4.20
New principal for 2nd year..	64.20
Interest on the same for one year...............................	4.494
New principal for 3rd year..	68.694
Interest on the same for one year..............................	4.808
New principal for 4th year...	73.502
Interest on the same for one year................................	5.145
Amount for 4 years...	78.647
Principal to be taken from same..................................	60.000
Compound interest for 4 years.......................................	$18647

The method of finding compound interest is usually much shortened by the following table, which shows the amount of $1 or £1 for any number of years not exceeding 50, at 3, 3½, 4, 5, 6 and 7 per cent. The amount of $1 or £1 thus obtained, being multiplied by the given principal, will give the required amount, from which, if the principal be taken, the remainder will be compound interest:

TABLE,

SHOWING THE AMOUNT OF ONE DOLLAR AT COMPOUND INTEREST FOR ANY NUMBER OF YEARS NOT EXCEEDING FIFTY.

No.	3 per cent.	3½ per cent.	4 per cent.	5 per cent.	6 per cent.	7 per cent.
1	1.030 000	1.035 000	1.040 000	1.050 000	1.060 000	1.070 000
2	1.060 900	1.071 225	1.081 600	1.102 500	1.123 600	1.144 900
3	1.092 727	1.108 718	1.124 864	1.157 625	1.191 016	1.225 043
4	1.125 509	1.147 523	1.169 859	1.215 506	1.262 477	1.310 796
5	1.159 274	1.187 686	1.216 653	1.276 282	1.338 226	1.402 552
6	1.194 052	1.229 255	1.265 319	1.340 096	1.418 519	1.500 730
7	1.229 874	1.272 279	1.315 932	1.407 100	1.503 630	1.605 781
8	1.266 770	1.316 809	1.368 569	1.477 455	1.593 848	1.718 186
9	1.304 773	1.362 897	1.423 312	1.551 328	1.689 479	1.838 459
10	1.343 916	1.410 599	1.480 244	1.628 895	1.790 848	1.967 151
11	1.384 234	1.459 970	1.539 454	1.710 339	1.898 299	2.104 852
12	1.425 761	1.511 069	1.601 032	1.795 856	2.012 196	2.252 192
13	1.468 534	1.563 956	1.665 074	1.885 649	2.132 928	2.409 845
14	1.512 590	1.618 694	1.731 676	1.979 932	2.260 904	2.578 534
15	1.557 967	1.675 349	1.800 944	2.078 928	2.396 558	2.759 032
16	1.604 706	1.733 986	1.872 981	2.182 875	2.540 352	2.952 164
17	1.652 848	1.794 675	1.947 901	2.292 018	2.692 773	3.158 815
18	1.702 433	1.857 489	2.025 817	2.406 619	2.854 339	3.379 932
19	1.753 506	1.922 501	2.106 849	2.526 950	3.025 600	3.616 526
20	1.806 111	1.989 789	2.191 123	2.653 298	3.207 135	3.869 684
21	1.860 295	2.059 431	2.278 768	2.785 963	3.399 564	4.140 562
22	1.916 103	2.131 512	2.369 919	2.925 261	3.603 537	4.430 402
23	1.973 587	2.206 114	2.464 716	3.071 524	3.819 750	4.740 530
24	2.032 794	2.283 328	2.563 304	3.225 100	4.048 935	5.072 367
25	2.093 778	2.363 245	2.665 836	3.386 355	4.291 871	5.427 433
26	2.156 591	2.445 959	2.772 470	3.555 673	4.549 383	5.807 353
27	2.221 289	2.531 567	2.883 369	3.733 456	4.822 346	6.213 868
28	2.287 928	2.620 177	2.998 703	3.920 129	5.111 687	6.648 838
29	2.356 566	2.711 878	3.118 651	4.116 136	5.418 388	7.114 257
30	2.427 262	2.806 794	3.243 398	4.321 942	5.743 491	7.612 255
31	2.500 080	2.905 031	3.373 133	4.538 039	6.088 101	8.145 113
32	2.575 083	3.006 708	3.508 059	4.764 941	6.453 387	8.715 271
33	2.652 335	3.111 942	3.648 381	5.003 189	6.840 590	9.325 340
34	2.731 905	3.220 860	3.794 316	5.253 348	7.251 025	9.978 114
35	2.813 862	3.333 590	3.946 089	5.516 015	7.686 087	10.676 581
36	2.890 278	3.450 266	4.103 933	5.791 816	8.147 252	11.423 942
37	2.985 227	3.571 025	4.268 090	6.081 407	8.636 087	12.223 618
38	3.074 783	3.696 011	4.438 813	6.385 477	9.154 252	13.079 271
39	3.167 027	3.825 372	4.616 366	6.704 751	9.703 507	13.994 820
40	3.262 038	3.959 260	4.801 021	7.039 989	10.285 718	14.974 458
41	3.359 899	4.097 834	4.993 061	7.391 988	10.902 861	16.022 670
42	3.460 696	4.241 258	5.192 784	7.761 588	11.557 033	17.144 257
43	3.564 517	4.389 702	5.400 495	8.149 667	12.250 455	18.344 355
44	3.671 452	4.543 342	5.616 515	8.557 150	12.985 482	19.628 460
45	3.781 596	4.702 358	5.841 176	8.985 003	13.764 611	21.002 452
46	3.895 044	4.866 941	6.074 823	9.434 258	14.590 487	22.472 623
47	4.011 895	5.037 284	6.317 816	9.905 971	15.465 917	24.045 707
48	4.132 252	5.213 589	6.570 528	10.401 270	16.393 872	25.728 907
49	4.256 219	5.396 065	6.833 349	10.921 333	17.377 504	27.529 930
50	4.383 906	5.584 927	7.106 683	11.467 400	18.420 154	29.457 025

NOTE.—If each of the numbers in the table be diminished by 1, the remainder will denote the interest of $1, instead of its amount.

EXERCISES.

2. What is the compound interest on $75, for 2 years, at 7 per cent.? Ans. $10.87.

3. What will $50 amount to in 3 years, at 6 per cent., compound interest? Ans. $59.55.

4. What is the compound interest on $600, for 2 years, at 6 per cent., payable half-yearly? Ans. $75.31.

5. What will $320 amount to in $2\frac{1}{2}$ years, at 7 per cent., compound interest? Ans. $379.19.

6. What is the compound interest of $150, for 3 years, at 9 per cent.? Ans. $44.25.

7. What is the compound interest on $1,000, for 2 years, at $3\frac{1}{2}$ per cent, payable quarterly? Ans. $72.18.

8. What will $460 amount to in 3 years, 4 months, 10 days, at 6 per cent., compound interest? Ans. $559.74.

9. What is the compound interest on $1860, for 8 years, at 7 per cent.? Ans. $1335.83.

10. What will be the compound interest on $75.20, for 20 years, at $3\frac{1}{2}$ per cent.? Ans. $74.43.

11. How much more will $500 amount to at compound than simple interest, for 20 years, 3 months, 15 days, at 7 per cent.? Ans. $764.14.

12. What sum will $50, deposited in a savings bank, amount to at compound interest, for 21 years, at 3 per cent, payable half-yearly? Ans. $173.03.

13. If a note of $60.60, dated October 25th, 1856, with the interest payable yearly, at 6 per cent., be paid October 25th, 1860; what will it amount to at compound interest? Ans. $76.51.

14. What remains due on the following note, April 1st, 1863, at 7 per cent. compound interest?

$1,000. CLEVELAND, January 1, 1858.

For value received, I promise to pay A. B. Smith & Co., or order, one thousand dollars on demand, with interest at 7 per cent.

J. D. FOSTER.

On the back of this note were receipted the following payments:

June 10, 1858,	received	$70
Sept. 25, 1859,	"	80
July 4, 1860,	"	100

Nov. 11, 1861,	"	....	30
June 5, 1862,	"	....	50

Ans. $1022.34.

DISCOUNT AND PRESENT WORTH.

Discount being of the same nature as interest, is, strictly speaking, the use of money before it is due. The term is applied, however, to a deduction of so much per cent. from the face of a bill, or the deducting of interest from a note before any interest has accrued. This is the practice followed in our Banks, and is therefore called Bank discount, in order to distinguish it from true discount.

The method of computing bank discount differs in no way from that of computing simple interest, but the method of finding *true discount* is quite different, *e. g.*, a debt of $107, due one year hence, is considered to be worth $100 now, for the reason that $100 let out at interest now, at 7 per cent., would amount to $107 at the end of a year.

In calculating interest, the sum on which interest is to be paid is known, but in computing discount we have to find *what sum* must be placed at interest so that *that sum*, together with its interest, will amount to the given principal. The sum thus found is called the "Present Worth."

We have already seen that $1.00 is the present worth of $1.07 due one year hence, at 7 per cent., therefore, to get the present worth of any sum due one year hence, at 7 per cent., it is only necessary to find how many times $1.07 is contained in the given sum, and we have the present worth; hence

To find the present worth of any sum, and the discount for any time, at any rate per cent., we have the following

RULE.

Divide the given sum by the amount of $1 *for the given time and rate, and the quotient will be the present worth.*

From the given sum subtract the present worth, and the remainder will be the discount.

EXERCISES.

1. What is the present worth of $224, due 2 years hence, at 6 per cent.? Ans. $200.

2. What is the discount on \$670, due 1 year and 8 months hence, at 7 per cent.? Ans. \$70.

3. What is the discount on \$501, due 1 year and 5 months hence, at 8 per cent.? Ans. \$51.

4. What is the present value of a debt of \$678.75, due 3 years and 7 months hence, at $7\frac{1}{2}$ per cent.? Ans. \$534.97$\frac{1}{2}$.

5. What is the discount on \$88.16, due 1 year, 8 months, and 12 days hence, at 6 per cent.? Ans. \$8.16.

6. If the discount on \$1060, for 1 year, at 6 per cent., is \$60; what is the discount on the same sum for one-half the time?

Ans. \$30.87.

7. How much cash will discharge a debt of \$145.50, due 2 years, 6 months and 12 days hence, at 6 per cent.? Ans. \$126.30.

8. If I am offered a certain quantity of goods for \$2500 cash, or for \$2821.50, on 9 months credit; which is the best offer, and by how much? Ans. Cash by \$200.

9. What is the difference between the interest and discount of \$46.16, due at the end of 2 years, 6 months, and 24 days, at 6 per cent.? Ans. 95 cents.

10. A merchant sold goods to the amount of \$1500, one-half to be paid in 6 months, and the balance in 9 months; how much cash ought he to receive for them after deducting $1\frac{1}{2}$ per cent. a month?

Ans. \$1331.25.

11. Suppose a merchant contracts a debt of \$24000, to be paid in four instalments, as follows: one-fifth in 4 months; one-fourth in 9 months; one-sixth in 1 year and 2 months, and the rest in 1 year and 7 months; how much cash must he give at once to discharge the debt, money being worth 6 per cent.? Ans. 22587.65.

12. Bought goods to the amount of \$840, on 9 months credit; how much money would discharge the debt at the time of purchasing the goods, interest being 8 per cent.? Ans. \$792.45.

13. A bookseller marks two prices in a book, one for ready money, and the other for one year's credit, allowing discount at 5 per cent. If the credit price be marked \$9.80; what ought to be the price marked for cash? Ans. \$9.33.

14. A man having a horse for sale, offered it for \$225, cash; or, \$230 at 9 months credit; the buyer chose the latter; did the seller lose or make by his bargain, and how much, supposing money to be worth 7 per cent.? Ans. He lost \$6.47.

15. A. B. Smith owes John Manning as follows:—\$365.87, to

be paid December 19th, 1863; $161.15, to be paid July 16th, 1864; $112.50, to be paid June 23rd, 1862; $96.81, to be paid April 19th, 1866, allowing discount at 6 per cent.; how much cash should Manning receive as an equivalent, January 1st, 1862?

Ans. $653.40.

16. I buy a bill of goods amounting to $2500 on six months' credit, and can get 5 per cent. off by paying cash; how much would I gain by paying the bill now, provided I have to borrow the money, and pay 6 per cent. a year for it? Ans. $53.75.

BANKS AND BANKING.

General Principles of Banking.—Banks are commonly divided into the two great classes of banks of deposit and banks of issue. This, however, appears at first sight to be rather an imperfect classification, inasmuch as almost all banks of deposit are at the same time banks of issue, and almost all banks of issue also banks of deposit. But there is in reality no ambiguity; for by banks of deposit are meant banks for the custody and employment of the money deposited with them or entrusted to their care by their customers, or by the public; while by banks of issue are meant banks which, besides employing or issuing the money entrusted to them by others, issue money of their own, or notes payable on demand. The Bank of England is principally a bank of issue; but it, as well as the other banks in the different parts of the empire that issue notes, is also a great bank of deposit. The private banking companies of London, and the various provincial banks, that do not issue notes of their own, are strictly banks of deposit. Banking business may be conducted indifferently by individuals, by private companies, or by joint stock companies or associations.

Utility and Functions of Banks of Deposit.—Banks of this class execute all that is properly understood by banking business; and their establishment has contributed in no ordinary degree to give security and facility to commercial transactions. They afford, when properly conducted, safe and convenient places of deposit for the money that would otherwise have to be kept, at a considerable risk, in private houses. They also prevent, in a great measure, the necessity of carrying money from place to place to make payments, and enable them to be made in the most convenient and least expensive manner.

The objects of banking.—Correct sentiments beget correct conduct. A banker ought, therefore, to apprehend correctly, the objects of banking. They consist in making pecuniary gains for the stockholders by legal operations. The business is eminently beneficial to society; but some bankers have deemed the good of society so much more worthy of regard than the private good of stockholders, that they have supposed all loans should be dispensed with direct reference to the beneficial effect of the loans on society, irrespective, in some degree, of the pecuniary interests of the dispensing bank. Such a banker will lend to builders, that houses or ships may be multiplied; to manufacturers, that useful fabrics may be increased; and to merchants, that goods may be seasonably replenished. He deems himself, *ex-officio*, the patron of all interests that concern his neighbourhood, and regulates his loans to these interests by the urgency of their necessities, rather than by the pecuniary profits of the operations to the bank, or the ability of the bank to sustain such demands. The late Bank of the United States is a remarkable illustration of these errors. Its manager seemed to believe that his dutes comprehended the equalization of foreign and domestic exchanges, the regulation of the price of cotton, the upholding of State credit, and the control, in some particulars, of Congress and the President—all vicious perversions of banking to an imagined paramount end.

When we perform well the direct duties of our station, we need not curiously trouble ourselves to effect, indirectly, some remote duty. Results belong to Providence, and by the natural catenation of events (a system admirably adapted to our restricted foresight), a man can usually in no way so efficiently promote the general welfare, as by vigilantly guarding the peculiar interests committed to his care. If, for instance, his bank is situated in a region dependent for its prosperity in the business of lumbering, the dealers in lumber will naturally constitute his most profitable customers; hence, in promoting his own interest out of their wants, he will, legitimately, benefit them as well as himself, and benefit them more permanently than by a vicious subordination of his interests to theirs.

Men will not engage permanently in any business that is not pecuniarily beneficial to them personally; hence, a banker becomes recreant to even the manufacturing and other interests that he would protect, if he so manage his bank as to make its stockholders unwilling to continue the employment of their capital in banking. This principle, also, is illustrated by the late United States Bank, for the stupendous temporary injuries which its mismanagement inflicted on society, are a smaller evil than the permanent barrier its mismanagement has probably produced against the creation of any similar institution.

Bank of England Notes Legal Tender.—According to the law as it stood previously to 1834, all descriptions of notes were legally payable at the pleasure of the holder in coin of the standard weight and purity. But the policy of such a regulation was very questionable; and we regard the enactment of the Stats. 3 & 4, Will. 4, c. 99, which makes Bank of England notes legal tender, everywhere except at the Bank and its branches, for all sums above £5, as a great improvement.

Savings Banks have been in use in Europe over fifty years, and in Canada and the United States, almost as long. They are established for the purpose of receiving from people in moderate circumstances, small sums of money on interest. In England the deposits are held by the Government, and invested in the three per cent. funds. In New England, New York and other States, the deposits are generally loaned on bond and mortgage at six or seven per cent. interest.

Friendly Societies.—Friendly Societies are associations, mostly in England, of persons chiefly in the humblest classes for the purpose of making provision by mutual contribution against those contingencies in human life, the occurrence of which can be calculated by way of average. The principal objects contemplated by such societies are the following: The insurance of a sum of money to be paid on the birth of a member's child, or on the death of a member or any of his family; the maintenance of members in old age and widowhood; the administration of relief to members incapacitated for labor by sickness or accident; and the endowment of members or their nominees. Friendly Societies are, therefore, associations for mutual assurance, but are distingushed from assurance societies, properly so called, by the circumstance that the sums of money which they insure are comparatively small.

BANK DISCOUNT.

The Bank Discount of a note is the simple interest on the sum for which it is given from the time it is *discounted* to the time it becomes due, including three days of grace.

Suppose, for example, in getting a note of $200 discounted at a bank I am charged $12 for discount, which being deducted, I receive but $188, so that I pay interest on $12 which I did not receive. From this it is clear that I am paying a higher rate of interest in discounting a note at a bank, than I would pay were I to borrow money at the same rate. As bank discount is the same as interest, we derive the following

RULE.

Find the interest on the sum specified in the note at the given rate, and for the given time, including three days of grace, and this will be the BANK DISCOUNT.

Subtract the discount from the face of the note, and the remainder will be the PROCEEDS OR PRESENT WORTH.

EXERCISES

1. What is the bank discount on a note, given for 60 days, for $350, at 6 per cent.?* Ans. $3,67.

2. What is the bank discount on a note of $495, for 2 months, at 5 per cent.? Ans. 4.33.

3. What is the present value of a note of $7840 discounted at a bank for 4 months and 15 days, at 6 per cent.? Ans. $7659.68.

4. How much money should be received on a note for $125, payable at the end of 1 year, 3 months, and 15 days, if discounted at a bank at 8 per cent.? Ans. $112.

5. A note, dated December 3rd, 1860, for $160.40, and having 6 months to run, was discounted at a bank, April 3rd, 1861, at 6 per cent.; how long had it to run, and what were the proceeds? Ans. 64 days; proceeds $158.71.

6. On the first day of January, 1866, I received a note for $2405 at 60 days, and on the 12th of the same month had it discounted at a bank at 7 per cent.; how much did I realize upon it. Ans. $237.61.

7. A merchant sold 240 bales of cotton, each weighing 280 pounds, for $12\frac{1}{2}$ cents per pound, which cost him, the same day, 10 cents per pound; he received in payment a good note, for 4 months' time, which he discounted immediately at a bank at 7 per cent.; what will be his profits? Ans. $1479.10:

8. I hold a note against Clemes, Rice & Co., to the amount of $327.40 dated April 11th, 1866, having six months to run after date, and drawing interest at the rate of 6 per cent. per annum. What are the proceeds if discounted at the Girard Bank on the 10th of August, at $7\frac{3}{10}$ per cent.? Ans. $332.99.

NOTE. When a note drawing interest, is discounted at a bank, the interest is calculated on the face of the note from its date to the time of maturity, and added to the face of the note, and this amount discounted for the length of time the note has still to run.

9. What will be the discount on the following note if discounted at the City Bank on the 17th of Nouember, at 6 per cent. (360 days to a year),

* Throughout all the exercises, unless otherwise specified, the year is to be considered as consisting of 365 days. Since it is customary in business when a fraction of a cent occurs in and result to reject it. if less than half a cent, and if not less, to call it a cent, we have adopted this principal throughout the book

$527.$\frac{91}{100}$. OBERLIN, Oct. 4, 1866.

Ninety days after date for value received, we promise to pay to the order of Smith, Warren & Co., five hundred twenty-seven and $\frac{91}{100}$ dollars at the City Bank, Oberlin, with interest at eight per cent. THOMPSON & BURNS.

10. What will be the discount at $7\frac{3}{10}$ per cent. on a note for $227.41, drawing interest at 8 per cent., dated May 1st, 1865, at 1 year after date, if discounted on March 7th, 1866?

11. What amount of money will I receive on the following note, if discounted at the First National Bank of Detroit on June 21st, at 9 per cent.?

$473.80. DETROIT, May 17, 1866.

Three months after date I promise to pay to the order of J. R. Sing & Co., four hundred and seventy-three and $\frac{80}{100}$ Dollars, at the First National Bank, Detroit, for value received with interest at $7\frac{3}{10}$ per cent. RICHARD DUNN.

12. What must I pay for the following note on August 15th, 1866, so as to make at the rate of 30 per cent. interest per annum on the money I pay for it? Ans. $708.54.

$746.75. ADRIAN, January 19, 1866.

One year from date, for value received, we promise to pay James Ames, or order, seven hundred and forty-six $\frac{75}{100}$ dollars, at the Commercial Bank, Adrian, with interest at $7\frac{3}{10}$ per cent. per annum. WILSON & CUMMINGS.

13. A holds a note against B to the amount of $478.92, dated May 10th, 1865 at 1 year after date drawing $7\frac{3}{10}$ per cent. interest. I purchase this note from A. on August 18th, paying for it such a sum that will allow me 20 per cent. interest on my money. What shall I pay for it?

14. I got my note for $2000 discounted at a bank, May 20, 1862, for 2 months, and immediately invested the sum received in flour. June 7, 1862, I sold half the flour at 10 per cent. less than cost, and put the money on interest at 9 per cent. August 13, 1862, I sold the remainder of the flour at 18 per cent. advance, and expended the money for cloth at $1 per yard; 12 days after I sold the cloth at 1.16\frac{2}{3}$ per yard, receiving half the pay in cash, which I lent on interest at $7\frac{1}{2}$ per cent. and a note for the other half, to be on inter-

est from October 4, 1862, at $6\frac{3}{4}$ per cent. When my note at the bank became due I renewed it for 5 months, and when this note became due I renewed it for 2 months, and when this note became due I renewed it for such a time that it became due July 20, 1863, at which time I collected the amount due me, and paid my note at the bank. Required the loss or gain by the transaction.

It is sometimes necessary to know the amount for which a note must be given, in order that it shall produce a given sum when discounted at a bank.

EXAMPLE.

1. Suppose we require to obtain $236.22 from a bank, and that we are to give our note, due in two months; for what amount must we draw the note, supposing that money is worth 9 per cent.?

SOLUTION.

From the nature of this example we can readily perceive that such a sum must be put on the face of the note, that when discounted the proceeds will be exactly $236.22. If we were to take a *one dollar note* and discount it at a bank for the given time, and at the given rate, the proceeds would be .98425. Hence, for *every dollar* we put upon the face of the note we receive .98425, and to receive $236.22 we would have to put as many dollars on the face of the note as are represented by the number of times that .98425 is contained in $236.22, which is 240. Therefore, we must put $240 on the face of a note due at the end of two months to produce $236.22 when discounted at a bank at 9 per cent. From this we deduce the following

RULE.

Deduct the bank discount on $1, *for the given time and rate, from* $1, *and divide the desired amount by the remainder. The quotient will be the face of the note required.*

2. For what sum must a note be given, having 4 months to run, that shall produce $1950, if discounted at a bank at 7 per cent.?

Ans. $1997.78.

3. What must be the face of a note, so that when discounted for 5 months and 21 days, at 7 per cent., it will produce $57.97, cash?

Ans. $60.

4. Suppose your note for 6 months is discounted at a bank at 6 per cent., and $484.75 placed to your credit, what must have been the face of the note? Ans. $500.

5. A merchant bought a quantity of goods for $600. For what sum must he write his note, to be discounted at a bank for 6 months, at 6 per cent.? Ans. $618.88.

6. A farmer bought a farm for $5000 cash, and having only one-half of the sum on hand, he wishes to obtain the balance from the bank. For what sum must he give his note, to be discounted for 9 months, at 6 per cent.? Ans. $2619.17.

7. If a merchant wishes to obtain $550 of a bank, for what sum must he give his note, payable in 60 days, allowing it to be discounted at ½ per cent. per month? Ans. $555.75.

8. I sold A. Mills, merchandize valued at $918.16, for which he was to pay me cash, but being disappointed in receiving money expected, he gave me his endorsed note at 90 days, for such an amount that when discounted at the bank at 7 per cent. it would produce the price of the merchandize. What was the face of the note?

9. I am owing R. Harrington on account, now due, $168.45; he also holds a note against me for $210, due in 34 days, including days of grace; he allows a discount of 8 per cent. on the note, and if I give him my note at 60 days for an amount that will be sufficient if discounted at 6 per cent., to produce the amount of account and note. What will be the face of new note?

10. Samuel Johnson has been owing me $274.48 for 84 days. I charge him interest at 6 per cent. per annum for this time, and he gives me his note at 90 days for such an amount that when discounted at the Girard Bank, at 8 per cent., the proceeds will equal the amount now due. What is the face of the note?

From the many dealings business men have, in regard to discount and interest, it is frequently required to know what rate of interest corresponds to a given rate of bank discount.

EXAMPLE.

1. What rate of interest is paid when a note, payable in 362 days, is discounted at 10 per cent.?

SOLUTION.

If we discount $1 for the given time, and at the given rate, the proceeds will be .90, or 90 cents. Hence, the discount being 10 cents, we are paying 10 cents for the use of 90 cents. Now, if we pay 10 cents for the use of 90, for the use of 1 cent we must pay $\frac{1}{90}$ of 10 cents, or $\frac{1}{9}$ of a cent, and for $1, or 100 cents, we must pay 100 times $\frac{1}{9}$ of a cent, or $\frac{100}{9}$=.11$\frac{1}{9}$, and for $100, 11\frac{1}{9}$, or 11$\frac{1}{9}$ per cent. Therefore, to find the rate of interest corresponding to a given rate of bank discount, we deduce the following

RULE.

Divide the given rate per cent., expressed decimally, or the rate per unit, by the number denoting the proceeds of $1 *for the given time and rate. The quotient will be the rate of interest required.*

EXERCISES.

2. What rate of interest is paid when a note, payable in 60 days, is discounted at 7 per cent.? Ans. 7$\frac{21}{247}$.

3. What rate of interest is paid when a note, payable in 3 months, is discounted at 6 per cent.? Ans. 6$\frac{186}{1969}$.

4. A note, payable in 6 months, is discounted at 1 per cent. a month; what rate of interest is paid? Ans. 12$\frac{244}{313}$.

5. What rate of interest is paid, when a note of $200, payable in 70 days, is discounted at $\frac{3}{4}$ per cent. a month? Ans. 9$\frac{81}{491}$.

6. When a note of $45, payable in 65 days, is discounted at 7 per cent., to what rate of interest does the bank discount correspond? Ans. 7$\frac{833}{9006}$.

7. A bank, by discounting a note at 6 per cent., receives for its money a discount equivalent to 6$\frac{1}{2}$ per cent. interest; how long must the note have been discounted before it was due? Ans. 1 yr., 3 mos., 12d.

COMMISSION.

COMMISSION is the term applied to money paid to an agent to remunerate him for his trouble in buying, selling, valuing, or for forwarding merchandise or other property.

The goods sent to a commission merchant or agent, to be sold on account and risk of another, are termed a *consignment*.

The person to whom these goods are consigned is called the *consignee or correspondent.*

The term shipment is sometimes used instead of consignment.

EXAMPLE.

A commission merchant sells for me goods worth $1200, and charges 4 per cent.; what have I to pay him?

SOLUTION.

4 per cent. of $1200 is equal to $1200×.04=$48. Hence I would have to pay $48, and from this we deduce the following

RULE.

Find the percentage on the given sum at the given rate, which will be the commission.

EXERCISES.

1. Consigned to A.K.Boomer, Esq., Syracuse, by the Troy, N.Y., foundry, agricultural implements which are sold for $1875.75; what is the agent's commission at 2½ per cent.? Ans. $46.89.

2. Bought in Boston 12 chests of tea, containing 64 lbs. each, at $1.12½ per lb., on a commission of 1¾ per cent.; what was my commission? Ans. $15.12.

3. My Toledo correspondent has bought for me 2768 lbs. of bacon, at 12½ cts. a pound; what is his commission at 3¼ per cent.? $11.25.

4. Bought a carriage and pair of horses, per the order of S. Williams, Portland; paid for the horses $240, and charged 4½ per cent., and paid for the carriage $160, and charged 1½ per cent.; how much did I earn? Ans. $13.20.

5. A commission agent in a Southern State bought cotton worth $2284 for an English manufacturer, and charged 5½ per cent.; what is his commission? Ans. $125.62.

6. On another occasion the manufacturer gave the commission merchant $165.78, for purchasing for him cotton worth $3684; what was the rate per cent? Ans. 4½

7. An English commission merchant buys for a Portland house, £576 10s. 0d. worth of provisions, and charges 4½ per cent.; what is his commission? Ans. £25 18s. 10⅕d.

8. A New York provision merchant instructs a Belfast (Ireland) commission merchant to purchase for him £534 4s. 0d. worth of

bacon and hams, and offers him $7\frac{1}{4}$ per cent.; what does the agent get? Ans. £38 14s. 7d.

9. A book agent in Cincinatti, sells $487.50 worth of books for Day & Co., of Montreal, and receives $72.05 for his trouble; at what rate per cent. was he paid? Ans. 15 nearly.

10. An agent sells 84 sewing machines at $25 each, and his commission amounts to $262.60; what is the rate? Ans. $12\frac{1}{2}$.

When a sum has to be sent to a commission agent, such that it will be equal both to the sum to be invested, and the agent's commission, it is plain, as already noted, that this is merely a case of percentage. It is the same as the first part of case IV., and we will have the corresponding

RULE.

Divide the given amount by 1, *increased by the given rate per unit, and the quotient will be the sum to be invested; subtract this from the given amount, and the remainder will be the commission.*

EXAMPLE.

If I send $1890 to a commission merchant, and instruct him to buy merchandise with what is left after his commission at 5 per cent. is deducted; what will be the sum invested, and the agent's commission?

SOLUTION.

It is plain that for every dollar of the proposed investment I must remit 105 cents, 100 towards the investment, and 5 towards the commission, and hence the number of dollars which can be invested from the sum remitted will be the same as the number of times that 1.05 is contained in 1890. Now, $1890÷1.05 gives $1800, the sum to be invested, and this subtracted from $1890, leaves $90, the commission to which the agent is entitled.

EXERCISES.

1. Remitted to A. B., St. Pauls, $988 to purchase flour for me with the balance that remains after deducting his commission at 4 per cent.; required the purchase money and percentage?

Ans. $950 and $38.

2. Received a commission to buy wheat with $779, less by my commission at $2\frac{1}{2}$ per cent.; required the price of the wheat and my commission. Ans. $760, and $19.

3. Remitted to my correspondent to Augusta $266.76, to pay for lumber which he purchased for me, and to pay his own commission at 4 per cent.; what was the price of the lumber, and what the commission? Ans. $256.50, and $10.26.

4. John Jones, Newmarket, commissions W. Orr, Portland, to procure for him a quantity of fine flour, and remits $917.61; how much flour can he have, after allowing $4\frac{3}{4}$ per cent., and what will the commission amount to? Ans. $876, and $41.61.

5. John Stalker, London, commissions J. Fleming New York, to purchase for him as much butter as he can procure for the balance between $779.52, and his own commission at $1\frac{1}{2}$ per cent.; how many pounds butter did he get at 25 cents per lb.; what the whole price, and what was the commission? Ans. 3072 lbs., $768, and $11.52.

6. Dr. Gallipot is about to remove to England, and sends to a London cabinet maker $4005.45 towards getting his house furnished, he is charged $3\frac{1}{2}$ per cent. over and above the price of the furniture, for time and labour, what does the furniture cost? Ans. $3870.

7. Graham Bros., of Newbury, send to R. White, Charleston, bacon and hams worth $1560, they charge $5\frac{1}{2}$ per cent. commission, and the charge for lading is $75.15; how much does R. White owe them? Ans. $1720.95.

8. P. Robson, commission merchant, Albany, buys for T. Black & Co., Baltimore, groceries, the price of which, together with their commission at 4 per cent. comes to $475.02; what was the price of the goods, and what was the amount of the commission?

Ans. $456.75, and $18.27.

BROKERAGE.

Brokerage is a per centage paid to an agent for negociating bills, collecting accounts, exchanging money, buying and selling shares and stocks, and all similar transactions. Such an agent is called a Broker. A smaller percentage is usually allowed to a broker than to a commission merchant, because the work he has to do requires less time and labour. Like commission, brokerage is merely a particular case of percentage, and hence the

RULE.

To find the brokerage on any sum, find the percentage on the given sum at the given rate, which will be the brokerage

1. A broker in Buffalo has bought for me $1275 worth of Erie R. R. stock; what will be the brokerage at $2\frac{1}{8}$ per cent.

Ans. $27\frac{09}{100}$.

2. I pay a collector of accounts 2 per cent. for collecting $118.50; how much does it cost me? Ans. $2.37.

3. I pay a broker $1\frac{7}{8}$ per cent. for selling $2716.75 government stock; how much do I give him? Ans. $50.94, nearly.

4. Advised R. P., broker, to collect two bills amounting to $897, he has collected $\frac{2}{3}$ of it, and I have given him $1\frac{1}{2}$ per cent. on the amount collected; how much have I paid him? Ans. $8.97.

5. A. B. sent me $756 to purchase flour for him. I have charged $2\frac{1}{4}$ per cent. commission on the whole sum, and purchased flour with the remainder; what is my commission, and how much do I vest in flour for A. B.? Ans. $738.99, and $17.01.

6. The school taxes on all the sections of a country amount to $1180, and collectors get $2\frac{5}{8}$ per cent.; how much remains available for school purposes? Ans. $1149.03.

7. Instructed a broker in Syracuse to sell for me 200 shares of N. Y. C. R. R. stock, at $114\frac{1}{8}$; what will be my proceeds, broker's commission being $\frac{7}{8}$ per cent.

8. I am charged $\frac{1}{4}$ per cent. by a broker in Raleigh, for negociating a draft for $750; what are the proceeds coming to me?

Ans. $$748.12\frac{1}{2}$.

9. Bought G. W. R. shares to the amount of $578, and paid my broker $2\frac{1}{4}$ per cent.; how much did I give him? Ans. $13.01.

10. Gave D. F. $3\frac{1}{3}$ per cent. for collecting accounts for me to the amount of $639; how much did I give him? Ans. $21.30.

To find the sum that can be invested when the given amount includes both the brokerage and the investment.

For example, if I wish a broker to invest for me $700, and his charge is 2 per cent., I must obviously remit to him $714, as $14 is 2 per cent. on $700; conversely, if I send him $714, and instruct him to invest for me that sum, *minus* his own percentage, he will have to calculate how much he will have remaining to invest after deducting his own charge. Now, since his percentage is $2 on every $100, he should get from me $102 for every $100 he is to invest, and therefore the sum he can invest will be the 102nd part of what I remit, *i. e.*, $714÷1.02=$700. Hence the

RULE.

Divide the given amount by one, increased by the given rate per unit of brokerage, and the quotient will be the sum to be invested; subtract this from the given amount, and the remainder will be the brokerage.

EXERCISES.

1. A broker receives $574, with instructions to invest what remains after deducting brokerage at $2\frac{1}{2}$ per cent., in R. R. shares; how much has he to invest? Ans. $560.

2. The assessment on a certain district, together with the percentage for collection at $2\frac{1}{4}$ per cent., is $1717.80; what is the amount of the assessment, and what the expense of collection?
Ans. $1680, and $37.80.

3. A tax amounting to $3276.52, including collector's fees at 4 per cent., is levied on a certain town; what is the amount of the tax, and how much is the collector entitled to?
Ans. $3150.50, and $126.02.

4. A gentleman once invested in U. S. government bonds, a certain sum which, with the broker's fee at $1\frac{3}{4}$ per cent., amounted to $18,315; what was the amount of the investment? Ans. $18,000.

5. A Portland broker negociates a draft for $1218 for a Hamilton merchant, at $1\frac{1}{2}$ per cent.; what are the proceeds?
Ans. $1199.73.

6. A broker, after deducting his charge at $1\frac{1}{4}$ per cent., invests the balance of $2450.25 for his employer in bank stock; how much does he invest? Ans. $2420.

7. My broker invests for me in oil well shares, at $83 each, what remains after deducting his fee at $\frac{1}{2}$ per cent. from $8341.50; how much does he invest, and how many shares does he purchase?
Ans. $8300, and 100 shares.

8. A broker's charge is $285, at $1\frac{1}{2}$ per cent., on a certain sum invested; what is the sum?—(See Percentage, Case II.)
Ans. $19000.

9. A broker sells stocks for me, and the sum which is realized, together with the brokerage at 4 per cent., amounts to $910; what is the sum procured, and what the brokerage? Ans. $875 and $35.

1. My agent in Richmond has purchased cotton for me to the amount of $1785.80 and charges me a commission of $\frac{7}{8}$ per cent.; how much have I to remit him to pay for the cotton and commission. Ans. 1801.42\frac{1}{2}$.

2. I have received from a correspondent in Troy $4783.11, with instructions to invest the same in Five-twenties at 105$\frac{1}{2}$, first deducting my commission of $\frac{3}{4}$ per cent. What is the commission, and what amount of Five-twenties can I purchase?

Ans. Commission $35.61; invested in Five-twenties, $4500.

3. A collector receives $20 for collecting $900; at what per cent. is he paid? Ans. 2$\frac{2}{9}$.

4. A purchased per the order of Andrew Campbell & Co., Nashville, Tenn., 14872 lbs. C. C. bacon at 13$\frac{1}{4}$ cts. per lb., charging a commission of 1$\frac{1}{2}$ per cent. A wishes to draw on them for reimbursement; what must be the face of the draft if it cost $\frac{1}{2}$ per cent. to get it cashed, and what is the commission on purchase?

Ans. Face of dft. $2010.15; Commission $29.56.

5. A broker invests for me $1750, and I pay him for his trouble $43.75, at what rate per cent. do I pay him? Ans. 2$\frac{1}{2}$.

6. An Auctioneer valued the furniture of a deceased gentleman, and charging 4 per cent., he was paid $53.86; what was the value of the furniture? Ans. $1346.50.

7. I sent to Taylor & Morrison, Com. merchants, New York, 250 firkins butter, containing on an average 56 lbs. each, at 15 cts. per lb. They sold at an advance of 10 per cent.; freight, &c., deducted $10.45, commission 2$\frac{1}{2}$ per cent. They have remitted me a sight draft for net proceeds, which they purchased at $\frac{3}{8}$ per cent. premium, charging $\frac{1}{4}$ per cent. commission on face of draft. What amount of draft did I receive, and what amount of commission charged?

8. A certain district pays $800 school taxes, the collector gets $38 for collecting; what per centage does he get? Ans. 4$\frac{3}{4}$.

9. B. instructed a broker to sell for him 100 shares of the N. Y. C. R. R. at 112$\frac{1}{2}$, how much would the broker's commission be at $\frac{3}{4}$ per cent.

10. An accountant is entrusted to make schedules of the debts and assets of a bankrupt; he charges only 2$\frac{1}{2}$ per cent. on the debts, on the principle that he will have little trouble in getting the accounts due by the bankrupt sent in; but as he knows very well that he will have trouble in getting correct statements sent in of accounts due to the bankrupt, he stipulates for 5$\frac{1}{2}$ per cent. on these; how much does he get altogether, the debts being $2786, and the assets $618?

Ans. $103.64.

INSURANCE.

INSURANCE is an engagement by which one party is bound, in consideration of receiving a certain sum, to indemnify another for something in case it should in any way be lost. The party undertaking the risk is seldom, if ever, an individual, but a joint stock company, represented by an agent or agents, and doing business under the title of an "*Insurance Company*," or "*Assurance Company*," such as the "Globe Insurance Company," the "Mutual Insurance Company."

Some companies are formed on the principle that each individual shareholder is insured, and shares in the profits, and bears his portion of the losses. Such a company is usually called a *Mutual Insurance Company*.

The sum paid to the party taking the risk is called the *Premium of Insurance*, or simply the *Premium*.

The document binding the parties to the contract, is called the *Policy of Insurance*, or simply the *Policy*.

The party that undertakes to indemnify is called the *Insurer*, or *underwriter* after he has written his name at the foot of the policy.

The person or party guaranteed is called the *Insured*.

As there are many different kinds of things that may be at stake or risked, so there are different kinds of insurance which may be classified under three heads.

Fire Insurance, including all cases on land where property is exposed to the risk of being destroyed by fire, such as dwelling houses, stores and factories.

Marine Insurance.—This includes all insurances on ships and cargoes. Such an insurance may be made on the ship alone, and in that case it is sometimes called *hull insurance*, and sometimes *bottomry*, the ship's bottom representing the whole ship, just as we say fifty sail for fifty ships. The insurance may be made on the cargo alone, and is then usually called *Cargo Insurance*. It may be made on both ship and cargo, in which case the general term *Marine Insurance* will be applicable. This kind, as the name implies, insures against all accidents by sea.

Life Insurance.—This is an agreement between two parties, that in case the one insured should die within a certain stated time, the other shall, in consideration of having received a stipulated sum annually, pay to the lawful heir of the deceased, or some one mentioned in his will, or some other party entitled thereto, the amount recorded in the policy.

For instance, a man may, on the occasion of his marriage, insure his life for a certain sum, so that should he die within a certain time, his widow or children shall be paid that sum by the other party. Again, a father may insure the life of his child, so that in case of the child's death within a specified time, he shall be paid the sum agreed upon, or that the child, if it lives to a certain age, shall be entitled to that sum. One person may insure the life of another. Supposing that A owes B a certain sum, there is the risk that A may die before he is able to pay B; another party engages, for a certain yearly sum, to pay B in case A should fail to do so during his life time.

In some instances, insurances are effected to gain a support in case of sickness. Such a contract is called a *Health Insurance.* Insurances are now also effected for compensation in case of railway accidents. These we may call *Railway Accident Insurances.*

A policy is often transferred from one party to another, especially as collateral security for debt or some analogous obligation. If the payments agreed upon are not regularly kept up, the policy lapses, that is, becomes null and void, so that the holder of it forfeits not only his claim to the sum insured, but also the instalments previously paid. In many companies a person can insure in such a way as to be entitled to have a share of the profits.

The date at which the system of insurance began cannot be clearly ascertained; but, whatever its date, its origin seems to have been protection against the perils of the sea. We know that it was practised, in a certain way, by the ancient Greeks and Romans. If a Roman merchant sent a cargo to a distant port, he made a contract with some one engaged in such business, that he would advance a certain sum, to be repaid with interest, if the vessel reached her destination in safety, but should the vessel or cargo, or both be lost, the lender was to bear the loss. This was termed *respondentia,* (a respondence) a term corresponding pretty nearly to the English word repayment. It was lawful to charge interest in such cases, above the legal interest in ordinary cases, on account of the greatness of the risk. The lender of the money usually sent an agent of his own on board the vessel to look after the cargo, and receive the repayment on the safe delivery of the goods. This agent corresponded pretty nearly to our more modern *supercargo.* As the art of navigation advanced, and the securities afforded by law became more stringent, and also facilities of communication increased, this system gradually gave way, and has eventually been supplanted by communications by post, and telegraphic messages to agents at the ports of destination.

With regard to the equitableness of insurances, and their utility in promoting commercial exterprise, we may remark that they make the interest of every merchant, the interest of every other. To show this, we may compare an *insurance office* to a *club*. Suppose the merchants of a town to form a club, and establish a fund, out of which every member, if a loser, was to be indemnified, it is plain that no loss would fall on the individual, except his share as a member of the club. Even so the insurance system causes that each speculator, by insuring his own stake, contributes so much to the funds of a company, which is bound to indemnify each loser. On the other hand, the insurer or insuring company, gains in this way, that the profits accruing from cases where no loss is sustained, far exceed the cases where loss is sustained, and the trifling expense of insuring is of no moment to the insured, in comparison with the damage of a disastrous voyage, or consuming conflagration. By the insurance system, loss is virtually distributed over a large community, and therefore falls heavily on no individual, from which we draw our conclusion, that it is equivalent to a *mutual mercantile indemnification club.*

We must now show the rules of the *club*, and principles on which its calculations are made.

The principal thing to be taken into account, in all insurances, is the amount of risk. For example, a store, where nothing but iron is kept, would be considered *safe;* a factory, where fire is used, would be accounted *hazardous*, and one where inflammable substances are used would be designated *extra hazardous*, and the rates would be higher in proportion to the increased risks. As, however, the degrees of risk are so very varied, only a rough scale can be made, and hence the estimate is nothing more than a calculation of probabilities. In life insurances, the rates are regulated chiefly by the age, and general health of the individual, and also by the general health of the family relations. Connected with this is the calculation of the average length of human life.

Almost all the calculations in insurance come under two heads. FIRST, to find the premium of insurance on a given amount, and at a given rate; and, SECONDLY, to find how much must be insured at a given rate, so that in case of loss, both the principal and premium may be recovered.

As the premium is reckoned as so much by the hundred, insurance is merely a particular case of percentage. Hence to find the premium of insurance on any given amount, at a given rate per cent., we deduce the following

RULE.

*Multiply the given amount by the rate per unit.**

EXAMPLES.

1. To find the cost of insuring a block of buildings valued at \$2688, at 6 per cent.? Here we have .06 for the rate per unit, and \$2688×.06=\$161.28, the answer.

2. What will be the cost of insuring a cargo worth \$3679, at 3 per cent.? The rate per unit is .03, and \$3679×.03=\$110.37, the answer.

3. A gentleman employed a broker to insure his residence and outhouses, valued at \$2760, the rate being 8 per cent., and the broker's charge 1½ per cent,; how much had he to pay? The cost of insurance is \$2760×.08=\$220.80, and the brokerage \$41.40, which added to \$220.80, will give \$262.20, the answer.

EXERCISES.

What will be the premium of insurance on goods worth \$1280, at 5½ per cent.? Ans. \$70.40.

2. A ship and cargo, valued at \$85,000, is insured at 2¼ per cent.; what is the premium? Ans. \$1912.50.

3. A ship worth \$35,000, is insured at 1½ per cent., and her cargo, worth \$55,000, at 2½ per cent.; what is the whole cost? Ans. \$1900.00.

4. What will be the cost of insuring a building valued at \$58,000, at 2½ per cent.? Ans. \$1450.00.

---

* It is plain that the rate can be found, if the amount and premium are given, and the amount can be found if the rate and premium are given. In the case of insuring property, a professional surveyor is often employed to value it, and likewise in the case of life insurance, a medical certificate is required, and in each case the fee must be paid by the person insured. As 100, the basis of percentage, is a constant quantity, when any two of the other quantities are given, the third can be found.

5. What must I pay to insure a house valued at $898.50, at $\frac{3}{4}$ per cent.?

6. A village store was valued at $1180; the proprietor insured it for six years; the rate for the first year was $3\frac{1}{4}$ per cent., with a reduction of $\frac{1}{4}$ each succeeding year; the stock maintained an average value of $1568, and was insured each of the six years, at $2\frac{1}{4}$ per cent.; how much did the proprietor pay for insurance during the six years? Ans. $397.53.

7. A store and yard were valued at $1280, and insured at $1\frac{1}{8}$ per cent.; the policy and surveyor's fee came to $2.25; what was the whole cost of insuring? Ans. $16.65.

8. W. Smith, Port Huron, requests R. Tomlinson, Toronto, to insure for him a building valued at $976; R. Tomlinson effects the insurance at $4\frac{3}{8}$ per cent., and charges $\frac{3}{8}$ per cent commission; how much has W. Smith to remit to R. Tomlinson, the latter having paid the premium? Ans. $46.36.

9. The cost of insuring a factory, valued at $25,000, is $125; what is the rate per cent.? Ans. $\frac{1}{2}$.

10. A $1\frac{1}{4}$ per cent. insuring my dwelling house cost me $50; what is the value of the house? Ans. $4000.00.

To find how much must be insured for, so that in case of loss, both principal and premium may be recovered.

Here it is obvious that the sum insured for must exceed the value of the property in the same ratio that 100 exceeds the rate.

EXAMPLE.

To find what sum must be insured for on property worth $600, at 4 per cent., to secure both property and premium, we have as $100—4=$96 : $100 : : $600 : F. P.$=\frac{600\times100}{96}=$$625, the sum required. Taking the rate per unit we find $\frac{100-4}{100}=\frac{96}{100}=.96$. This gives the

RULE.

Divide the value of the property by 1, *diminished by the rate per unit, and the quotient will be the sum required.*

EXAMPLES.

1. A foundry is valued at $874: for what sum at 8 per cent. must it be insured to secure both the value of the property and the premium? One *minus* the rate or 1.00—.08=.92, and $874÷.92 =$950, the answer.

The premises of a gunsmith, who sells gunpowder, are valued at $2618.85: for how much, at 15 per cent., must they be insured in order to recover the value of the property and also the premium of insurance? Subtract .15, the rate per unit, from 1, and the remainder is .85 and $2618.85÷.85 gives $3081, the sum required.

EXERCISES

1. A chemist's laboratory and appurtenances are valuea ac $26,250, for what sum should he insure them at 6¼ per cent., to secure both property and premium? $28,000.

2. A New York merchant sent goods worth $1,186 by water conveyance to Chicago; he insured them from New York to Buffalo at 1¼ per cent., and from Buffalo to Chicago at 2½ per cent., and in both cases so as to secure the premium as well as the cargo; how much did the insurance cost him? Ans. $45.42.

3. A person owned a flour mill, valued at $1846.05, which he insured at 1¼ per cent. He also owned a flax mill, valued at $846.30, which he insured at 2½ per cent., and in both cases at such a sum as to secure both property and premium. Which cost him most, and how much more?

Ans. The flour mill cost him $1.67 more than the other.

4. Collins & Co., of Philadelphia, ordered a quantity of pork from G. S. Coates & Son, Cincinnati, which amounts to $2423.10. They insure it to Pittsburg at ½ per cent., and from Pittsburg to Philadelphia at 3 per cent., and in all cases so as to secure both the price and premium. How much does the whole insurance come to? Ans. $87.12.

5. In order to secure both the value of goods shipped and the premium, at 1¾ per cent., an insurance is effected on $1526.72. What is the value of the goods? Ans. $1500.00.

6. The Mechanics' Institute is valued at $18,000; it is insured at 1¼ per cent., so that in case of fire, the property and premium may both be recovered. For how mnch is it insured?

Ans. $18,227.85.

7. How much must be insured on a cargo worth $40,000, at ½ per cent., to secure both the value of the cargo and the cost of insurance? Ans. $40,201.00.

8. The Rossin House, King-street, Toronto, is valued at, say, $150,000, and is insured at 1¾ per cent, so that in case of another conflagration, both the value of the property and the premium of insurance may be recovered. For how much must it be insured? Ans. $152,671.76, nearly.

9. A jail and court-house, adjoining chemical works, and therefore deemed hazardous, will not be insured under 2½ per cent. How much will secure both property and premium, the valuation being $17,550.00? Ans. $18,000.00.

10. A cotton mill is insured for $12,000, at 4 per cent., to secure both premium and property. What is the value of the property?

11. What sum must be insured on a vessel and cargo valued at $40,000, at 5½ per cent., in order to secure both the premium and property? Ans. $42,328.04.

12. How much must be insured on property worth $70,000, at 4½ per cent., to secure both premium and property, a commission of ¾ per cent. having been charged? Ans. $73,848.17.

LIFE INSURANCE.

A LIFE INSURANCE may be effected either for a term of years or for the whole period of life. The former is called a *Temporary Insurance*, and binds the insurer to pay the amount to the legal heir or legatee or creditor, if the insured should die within the specified time. The latter is called a *Life Insurance*, because it is demandable at death, no matter how long the insured may live.

The rate per annum that the insured is to pay is reckoned from tables constructed on a calculation of the average duration of life beyond different ages. This calculation is made from statistical returns called BILLS OF MORTALITY, and the result is called THE EXPECTATION OF LIFE.

The annual premium is fixed at such a rate as would, at the end of the expectation of life, amount to the sum insured. From tables of the expectation of life other tables are constructed, showing the premium on $100 for one year, calculated on the supposition that it is to be paid annually in advance.

LIFE INSURANCE TABLE.

Age next Birthday.	1 year.	7 years.	For Life.	Age next Birthday.	1 year.	7 years.	For Life.
15	.83	.85	1.44	38	1.19	1.28	2.75
16	.84	.86	1.47	39	1.22	1.31	2.85
17	.85	.87	1.51	40	1.24	1.36	2.95
18	.86	.88	1.54	41	1.27	1.41	3.07
19	.87	.90	1.58	42	1.31	1.47	3.19
20	.88	.91	1.62	43	1.35	1.54	3.32
21	.89	.92	1.66	44	1.40	1.62	3.45
22	.90	.93	1.70	45	1.47	1.71	3.60
23	.91	.95	1.74	46	1.54	1.80	3.75
24	.92	.96	1.79	47	1.62	1.90	3.92
25	.93	.98	1.84	48	1.71	2.02	4.09
26	.95	.99	1.89	49	1.81	2.14	4.27
27	.96	1.01	1.94	50	1.91	2.28	4.46
28	.98	1.03	2.00	51	2.03	2.42	4.67
29	.99	1.05	2.06	52	2.15	2.59	4.89
30	1.01	1.07	2.12	53	2.29	2.76	5.12
31	1.03	1.09	2.18	54	2.44	2.95	5.36
32	1.05	1.11	2.25	55	2.60	3.15	5.62
33	1.07	1.14	2.32	56	2.78	3.38	5.89
34	1.09	1.16	2.40	57	2.96	3.62	6.19
35	1.11	1.19	2.48	58	3.17	3.87	6.50
36	1.14	1.21	2.56	59	3.39	4.17	6.83
37	1.16	1.24	2.65	60	3.64	4.50	7.18

EXAMPLES.

Supposing a young man, on coming of age, wishes to effect an insurance for $3000 *for the whole period of his life.* To find the annual premium which he must pay, we look for 21 in the left hand column, and opposite that, in the column headed FOR LIFE, we find the number 1.66, which is the premium for one year on $100, and $\frac{1.66}{100}$=.0166 is the premium on $1 for 1 year, and hence $3000×.0166=$49.80, is the whole annual premium.

If the insurance is to last *for seven years only*, we find under that heading .92, and $\frac{.92}{100}$=.092, and $3000×.092=$27.60, the annual premium.

If the insurance is to be *for one year only*, we find .89 under that head, and $3000×.089=$26.70, the premium.

From these explanations we can now derive a rule for finding the annual premium, when the age of the individual and the sum to be insured for are known.

RULE.

Find the age in the left hand column of the table, and opposite this in the vertical column for the given period will be found the premium on $100 *for one year, and this divided by* 100 *will give the premium on* $1 *for one year, and the given sum multiplied by this will be the whole annual premium.*

EXERCISES.

1. What will be the annual premium for insuring a person's life, who is 18 years old, for $1000 for 7 years? Ans. $8.80.

2. What amount of annual premium must be paid by A. B. Smith, who wishes to insure his life for 7 years for $2000, his age being 25 years? Ans. $19.60.

3. John Jones, 35 years of age, wishes to effect an insurance for life for $1500. What amount of annual premium must he pay? Ans. $37.20.

4. A gentleman in Chicago, 32 years of age, being about to start for Australia, and wishing to provide for his family in case of his death, obtains an insurance for seven years for $3000. What amount of annual premium must he pay? Ans. $33.30.

5. Amos Fairplay, 48 years of age, being bound on a dangerous voyage, and wishing to provide for the support of his widowed mother, in case of accident to himself, insures his life for 1 year for $2500. What amount of premium must he pay? Ans. $42.75.

6. A gentleman, 50 years of age, gets his life insured for $3000, by paying an annual premium of $4.46 on each $100 insured; if he should die at the age of 75 years, how much less will be the amount of insurance than the payments, allowing the latter to be without interest? Ans. $345.

7. A gentleman, 45 years of age, gets his life insured for $5000, for which he pays an annual premium of $180, and dies at the age of 50 years. Suppose we reckon simple interest at 7 per cent. on his payments, what is gained by the insurance? Ans. $3911.

PROFIT AND LOSS.

In the language of arithmetic, the expression *Profit and Loss* is usually applied to something gained or something lost in mercantile transactions, and the most important rule relating to it directs how to find at what increased rate above the cost price goods must be sold to produce a fair remuneration for time, labour and expenditure; or, in case of loss by unforeseen circumstanees, to estimate the amount of that loss as a guide in future transactions.

There are other cases, however, which we shall consider in detail.

CASE I.

When the prime cost and selling price are known, to find the gain or loss.

RULE.

Find, by the rule of practice, the price at the difference between the prime cost and selling price, which will be the gain or loss according as the selling price is greater or less than the prime cost; or,

Find the price at each rate, and take the difference.

EXAMPLES.

To find what is gained by selling 4 cwt. of sugar, which cost 12½ cents per lb., at 15 cents per lb.

Here the difference between the two prices is 2½ cents per lb., and 400 lbs., at 2½ cents per lb., will give $10. Also, 400 lbs. at 15 cents per lb.=$60, and at 12½ cents=$50, and $60—$50=$10.

Again, if 120 lbs. of tobacco be bought at 92 cts. per lb., and, being damaged, is sold at 75 cents per lb., the loss will be a loss of 17 cents in the pound, and 120 lbs., at 17 cents per lb., is $20.40; or, 120 lbs., at 92 cents, will come to $110.40, and at 75 cents, to $90, and $110.40—$90=$20.40.

EXERCISES.

1. If 224 lbs. of tea be bought at 60 cents per lb., and sold at 95 cents per lb.; how much is gained? Ans. $78.40.

2. A grocer bought 24 barrels of flour, at $5.80 per barrel, and sold 12 barrels of it at $6.10 per barrel, 9 barrels at $6.20 per barrel, and the rest at $6.25; how much did he gain? Ans. $8.55.

3. If a person is obliged to sell 216 yards of flannel, which cost him $86.40, at 37½ cents per yard; how much does he lose?

Ans. $5.40.

4. If a dealer buys 78 bushels of potatoes, at $62\frac{1}{2}$ cents per bushel, and retails them at $87\frac{1}{2}$ cents per bushel; how much does he gain? Ans. $19.50.

5. A wine merchant bought 374 gallons of wine, at $3.20 per gallon, and sold it at $3.35 per gallon; how much did he gain? Ans. $56.10.

CASE II.

To find at what price any article must be sold, to gain a certain rate per cent., the cost price, and the gain or loss per cent. being known.

RULE.

Multiply the cost price by 1 *plus the gain, or* 1 *minus the loss.*

EXAMPLE.

If a quantity of linen be bought for 75 cents a yard; at what price must it be sold to gain 16 per cent.?

Since 16 per cent. is 16 cents for every dollar, each dollar in the cost price would bring $1.16 in the selling price, so that we have $\$1.16 \times .75 = .87$, or 87 cents.

EXERCISES.

1. Railroad shares being purchased for $2500, and sold at a gain of 20 per cent.; for what amount were they sold? Ans. $3000.

2. A property having been bought for $2000 was sold at a gain of 10 per cent. For what was it sold? Ans. $2200.

3. A horse was bought for $50, but, proving lame, was sold at a loss of 15 per cent. At what price was he sold? Ans. $42.50.

4. Bought a horse for $897 and sold it at a loss of 11 per cent; for what sum was it sold? Ans. $798.33.

5. A merchant buys dry goods for $1562, and sells them at a profit of 22 per cent. For what were they sold? Ans. $1905.64.

CASE III.

To find the cost when the selling price and the gain per cent. are known.

RULE.

Divide the selling price by 1 *plus the gain, or* 1 *minus the loss.*

To find what was the first cost of a quantity of flour which produced 8 per cent. profit by being sold for $127.44.

Since the gain is 8 per cent. of the cost, it follows that each dollar laid out has brought in a return of $1.08, and therefore the cost must have been as many dollars as the number of times that 1.08 is contained in 127.44, which is 118, and therefore the first cost must have been $118.

EXERCISES.

1. If flaxseed is sold at $17.40 per bushel, and 13 per cent. lost, what was the first cost? Ans. $20.00.

2. A dealer bought 116 hogs for $580, and sold them at a gain of 25 per cent.; at what price did he sell each on an average?

3. If 13 sheep be sold for $52.65, and 25 per cent. gained on the first cost, how much was paid for each at first? Ans. $3.24.

4. If $16\frac{3}{4}$ per cent. be lost on the sale of linen at $1.25, what was the first cost? Ans. $1.50.

5. If a quantity of glass be sold for $4, and 10 per cent. gained, for what sum was it bought? Ans. $3.64, nearly.

CASE IV.

To find the gain or loss per cent. when the first cost and selling price are known.

RULE.

Divide the gain or loss by the first cost.

EXAMPLE.

If a web of linen be bought for $20 and sold for $25, what is the gain per cent?

Here $5 are gained on $20, and $20 is $\frac{1}{5}$ of $100, therefore $25 will be gained on $100, *i. e.*, 25 per cent.

EXERCISES.

1. If a quantity of goods be bought for $318.50, and sold for $299.39, how much per cent. is lost? Ans. 6 per cent.

2. If two houses are bought, the one for $150 and the other for $250; and the first sold again for $100 and the latter for $350, what per cent. is gained on the whole? Ans. $12\frac{1}{2}$.

A grocer buys butter at 24 cents per lb. and sells it at 30 cents per lb., what does he gain per cent? Ans. 25.

4. If a cattle dealer buys 20 cows, at an average price of $20, and pays 50 cents for the freight of each per railroad, what per cent. does he gain by selling them at $25.62½ each? Ans. 25.

5. A tobacconist bought a quantity of tobacco for $75, but a part of it being lost, he sold the remainder for $60: what per cent. did he lose? Ans. 20.

CASE V.

Given the gain or loss per cent. resulting from the sale of goods at *one* price, to find the gain or loss per cent. by selling the same at *another* price.

RULE.

Find by case III. *the first cost, and then by case* IV. *the gain or loss per cent. on that cost at the second selling price.*

EXAMPLE.

If a farmer sells his hogs at $5 each, and realizes 25 per cent.; what per cent. would he realize by selling them at $7 each.

We find by case III., that the cost was $4, and then by case IV. what the gain per cent. would be on the seeond supposition, that is $3÷4=.75, or 75 per cent.

EXERCISES.

1. If a grocer sells rum at 90 cents per bottle, and gains 20 per cent.; what per cent. would he gain by selling it at $1.00 per bottle? Ans. 33⅓.

2. If a hatter sells hats at $1.25 each, and loses 25 per cent.; what per cent. would he lose by selling them at $1.60 each? Ans. 4.

3. If a storekeeper sells cloth at $1.25, and loses 15 per cent.; would he gain or lose, and how much, by selling at $1.65? Ans. He would gain 12 per cent. nearly.

4. A milliner sold bonnets at $1.25, and thereby lost 25 per cent.; would she have gained or lost by selling them at $1.10? Ans. She would have lost 16 per cent.

5. A merchant sold a lot of goods for $480, and lost 20 per cent.; would he have gained or lost by selling them for $720, and how much? Ans. He would have gained 20 per cent.

6. A quantity of grain was sold for $90, which was 10 per cent. less than the cost; what would have been the gain per cent. if it had been sold for $150? Ans. 50.

7. A grocer sold tea at 45 cents per pound, and thereby gained $12\frac{1}{2}$ per cent.; what would he have gained per cent. if he had sold the tea at 54 cents per pound? Ans. 35.

8. A farmer sold corn at 65 cents per bushel, and gained 5 per cent.; what per cent. would he have gained if he had sold the corn at 70 cents per bushel? Ans. $13\frac{1}{13}$.

MISCELLANEOUS EXERCISES.

1. If I buy goods amounting to $465, and sell them at a gain of 15 per cent.; what are my profits?

2. Suppose I buy $400\frac{1}{5}$ barrels of flour, at $16.75 a barrel, and sell it at an advance of $\frac{3}{8}$ per cent.; how much do I gain? Ans. $25.14.

3. If I buy 220 bushels of wheat, at $1.15 per bushel, and wish to gain 15 per cent. in selling it; what must I ask a bushel?

4. A grocer bought molasses for 24 cents a gallon, which he sold for 30 cents; what was his gain per cent.? Ans. 25.

5. A man bought a horse for $150, and a chaise for $250, and sold the chaise for $350, and the horse for 100; what was his gain per cent.? Ans. $12\frac{1}{2}$.

6. A gentleman sold a horse for $180, and thereby gained 20 per cent.; how much did the horse cost him? Ans. $150.

7. In one year the principal and interest of a certain note amounted to $810, at 8 per cent.; what was the face of the note? Ans. $750.

8. A carpenter built a house for $990, which was 10 per cent. less than what it was worth; how much should he have received for it so as to have made 40 per cent.? Ans. $1540.

9. A broker bought stocks at $96 per share, and sold them at $102 per share; what was his gain per cent.? Ans. $6\frac{1}{4}$.

10. A merchant sold sugar at $6\frac{1}{2}$ cents a pound, which was 10 per cent. less than it cost him; what was the cost price? Ans. $7\frac{2}{9}$ cents per pound.

11. A merchant sold broadcloth at $4.75 per yard, and gained $12\frac{1}{2}$ per cent.; what would he have gained per cent. if he had sold it at $5.25 per yard? Ans. $24\frac{13}{38}$.

12. I sold a horse for $75, and by so doing, I lost 25 per cent.; whereas, I ought to have gained 30 per cent.; how much was he sold for under his real value? Ans. $55.

13. A watch which cost me $30 I have sold for $35, on a credit of 8 months; what did I gain by my bargain, allowing money to be worth 6 per cent.? Ans. $3.65.

14. Bought 84 yards of broadcloth, at $5.00 per yard; what must be my asking price in order to fall 10 per cent., and still make 10 per cent. on the cost? Ans. 6.11\frac{1}{9}$.

15. A farmer sold land at 5 cents per foot, and gained 25 per cent. more than it cost him; what would have been his gain or loss per cent. if he had sold it at 3$\frac{1}{2}$ cents per foot?

Ans. 12$\frac{1}{2}$ per cent. loss.

16. What must I ask per yard for cloth that cost $3.52, so that I may fall 8 per cent., and still make 15 per cent., allowing 12 per cent. of sales to be in bad debts? Ans. $5.

17. A merchant sold two bales of cotton at $240 each; for one he received 60 per cent. more than its cost, and for the other 60 per cent. less than its cost. Did he gain or lose by the operation, and how much? Ans. loss $270.

18. Bought 2688 yards of cloth at $2.16 per yard, and sold one-fourth of it at $2.54 per yard; one-third of it at $2.75 per yard, and the remainder at $2,90 per yard. Find the whole gain, and the gain per cent. Ans. $1612.80 and 27$\frac{883}{1121}$ per cent.

19. A flour merchant bought the following lots:—

118 barrels at	$9.25	per barrel.
212 "	9.50	"
315 "	9.12$\frac{1}{2}$	"
400 "	10.00	"

The expenses amounted to $29.50, besides insurance at $\frac{1}{3}$ per cent. At what price must he sell it per barrel to gain 15 per cent?

Ans., $11.05.

20. Bought 100 sheep at $5 each; having resold them at once and received a note at six months for the amount; having got the note discounted at the Fourth National Bank, at six per cent., I found I had gained 20 per cent. by the transaction. What was the selling price of each sheep? Ans., $6.19.

STORAGE.

When a charge is made for the accommodation of having goods kept in store, it is called *storage.*

Accounts of storage contain the entries showing when the goods were received and when delivered, with the number, the description of the articles, the sum charged on each for a certain time, and the total amount charged for storage, which is generally determined by an average reckoned for some specified time, usually one month (30 days).

EXAMPLES.

1. What will be the cost of storing wheat at 3 cents per bushel per month, which was received and delivered as follows :—Received, August 3rd, 1865, 800 bushels; August 12th, 600 bushels. Delivered, August 9th, 250 bushels; September 12th, 350 bushels; September 15th, 400 bushels, and October 1st, the balance.

SOLUTION.

1865.		Bush.		Days.		Bush.
August 3.	Received......	800	×	6	=	4800 in store for one day.
" 9.	Delivered......	250				
	Balance.	550	×	3	=	1650 in store for one day.
" 12.	Received......	600				
	Balance	1150	×	31	=	35650 in store for one day.
Sept. 12.	Delivered......	350				
	Balance........	800	×	3	=	2400 in store for one day.
" 15.	Delivered.......	400				
	Balance........	400	×	16	=	6400 in store for one day.
Oct. 1.	Delivered.......	400				
	Total.................................					50900 in store for one day.

50,900 bushels in store for *one day* would be the same as $50900 \div 30 = 1696\frac{2}{3}$ bushels in store for *one month* of 30 *days,* and the storage of 1697 bushels for one month, at 3 cents per month, would equal $1697 \times .03 = \$50.91$.

It is customary, in business, when the number of articles upon which storage is to be charged, as found, contains a fraction *less than a half,* to reject the fraction; but if it is *more than a half,* to regard it as an entire article.

From the solution of the foregoing example, we deduce the following

RULE.

Multiply the number of bushels, barrels, or other articles, by the number of days they are in store, and divide the sum of the products by 30, *or the number of days in any term agreed upon. The quotient will give the number of bushels, barrels, or other articles on which storage is to be charged for that term.*

2. What will be the cost of storing salt at 3 cents a barrel per month, which was put in store and taken out as follows:—Put in, January 2, 1866, 450 barrels; January 3, 75 barrels; January 18, 300 barrels; January 27, 200 barrels; February 2, 75 barrels. Taken out, January 10, 60 barrels; January 30, 150 barrels; February 10, 190 barrels; February 20, 300 barrels; March 1, 250 barrels; and on March 12, the balance, 150 barrels? Ans. $39.44.

3. Received and delivered, on account of T. C. Musgrove, sundry bales of cotton, as follows:—Received January 1, 1866, 2310 bales; January 16, 120 bales; February 1, 300 bales. Delivered February 12, 1000 bales; March 1, 600 bales; April 3, 400 bales; April 10, 312 bales; May 10, 200 bales. Required the number of bales remaining in store on June 1, and the cost of storage up to that date, at the rate of 5 cents a bale per month.

Ans. 218 bales in store; $321.18 cost of storage.

4. W. T. Leeming & Co., Commission Merchants, Albany, in account with A. B. Smith & Co., Oswego, for storage of salt and gunpowder, received and delivered as follows:

Received, January 18, 1866, 400 kegs of gunpowder and 50 barrels of salt; January 25, 250 barrels of salt; February 4, 150 barrels of salt, and 50 kegs of gunpowder; February 15, 100 kegs of gunpowder; March 5, 64 kegs of gunpowder; April 15, 50 kegs of gunpowder, and 75 barrels of salt. Delivered, February 25, 15 kegs of gunpowder, and 40 barrels of salt; March 10, 150 kegs of gunpowder, and 285 barrels of salt; April 20, 200 kegs of gunpowder; April 125, 50 barrels of salt, and 200 kegs of gunpowder. Required the number of barrels of salt and kegs of gunpowder in store May 1, and the bill of storage up to that date. The rate of storage for salt being 3 cents a barrel per month, and for gunpowder 12 cents a keg per month.

Ans. In store, 50 barrels of salt and 99 kegs of gunpowder; bill of storage, $206.01.

GENERAL AVERAGE.

THIS is the term used to denote the contribution of all persons interested in a ship, freight, or cargo, towards the loss or damage incurred by any particular part of a ship, or cargo, for the preservation of the rest. This sacrifice of property is called *jettison*, from the goods being cast into the sea to save the vessel; although not only property destroyed in that way is the subject of general average, but also any damages or expenses voluntarily incurred for the good of all. For example, the expense of unloading the cargo that the ship may be repaired; masts or sails cut away and abandoned to save the ship.

The only articles exempt from contribution are provisions, wearing apparel of passengers, and wages of the seamen.

The owners contribute according to the clear value of the ship and freight at the end of the voyage, after deducting the wages of the crew and other expenses.

In New York $\frac{1}{2}$, and in other States $\frac{1}{3}$ of gross freight is sometimes deducted for seamen's wages; but as a general custom the exact amount is ascertained and deducted.

Goods that have been subject to jettison, and are lost, are valued, when the average is calculated at the place of the ship's destination, at the price they could have sold for there; but when the average is to be ascertained at the port of lading, the invoice price is the standard of value.

In making an account of the articles which are to contribute, the property lost or sacrificed must be included, and its owners must suffer the same proportionate loss as the rest. The losses to the different parties interested in the vessel, freight and cargo, are paid by their insurers.

When repairs have to be made to a ship—new sails, masts, or rigging, for example—one-third of the expense is deducted on account of *melioration*, or the improved condition of the ship by these repairs. When the ship is new, and on her first voyage, the full amount of the expense of repairs is allowed in computation of the loss.

EXAMPLE.

On the 26th June, 1865, the steamer *Cuba* left New York for Liverpool with a cargo, as follows:—Shipped by T. A. Collins, $7480; R. Evans & Co., $5365; H. C. Wright, $9218; W. Manning & Co., $11428; E. Carpenter, $7559. When off Sandy Hook a heavy gale was experienced, during which cargo to the value of $3498 was thrown overboard; of this $1123.40 belonged to R. Evans & Co., and the balance to E. Carpenter. The necessary repairs of the steamer cost $876, and the expenses in port, while getting repaired, were $253. The steamer was valued at $100,000; gross freight, $4310. The seamen's wages were $860. What was the loss per cent., and what was the loss of each contributory interest?

SOLUTION.

Loss for general benefit.		*Contributory interests.*	
Cargo thrown overboard,	$3498	Value of steamer..........	$100,000
Repairs to steamer less $\frac{1}{3}$	584	Invoice price of cargo....	41,050
Expenses in port..........	253	Fr'ght, less seamen's wages	3,460
Total loss............	$4335	Total contrib. int....	$144,500

$4335÷144,500=.03 loss per unit, or 3 per cent.

$100,000×.03=$3000.00, steamer's share of loss.
7,480×.03= 224.40, T. A. Collins' share of loss.
5,365×.03= 160.95, R. Evan & Co.'s share of loss.
9,218×.03= 276.54, H. C. Wright's share of loss.
11,428×.03= 342.84, W. Manning & Co.'s share of loss.
7,559×.03= 226.77, E. Carpenter's share of loss.
3,450×.03= 103.50, Freight's share of loss.

$4335.00, Total loss.

$3000.00—837.00=$2163.00, balance payable by steamer.
1123.40—160.95= $962.45, balance receivable by R. Evans & Co.
2374.60—226.77= 2147.83, balance receivable by E. Carpenter.

NOTE.—It is evident that since the steamer lost $837 ($584 by repairs, and $253 by expenses),—that the net amount required from the steamer will be $3000—837=$2163. R. Evans & Co. having lost by merchandize being thrown overboard $1123.46, a sum greater than their share of the general loss, so that there must be due them $1123.40 —160.95=$962.45; so also the amount of E. Carpenter's share of the general loss must be deducted from his individual loss in order to find the balance due him.

RULE.

Find the rate per unit of loss, by which multiply the value of each contributory interest, and the product will be the share of loss to be sustained by each.

EXERCISES.

1. The steamship *Ocean Queen* on her trip from Philadelphia to Liverpool, was crippled in a storm, in consequence of which the captain had to throw overboard a portion of the cargo, amounting in value to $4465.50, and the necessary repairs of the vessel cost $423. The contributory interests were as follows:—Vessel, $30,000; gross freight, $6225; cargo shipped by J. Jones & Co., $3650; by Henry Anderson, $6500; by George Millan, $2000; by J. Foster & Son, $550; by Brown Brothers, $5450; and by Wilson & Carter, $8500. Of the cargo thrown overboard, there belonged to Henry Anderson the value of $3000, and to Brown Brothers the remainder, $1465.50. The cost of detention in port in consequence of repairs, was $116.50; seaman's wages, $2075. How ought the loss to be shared among the contributory interests? Ans. 8 per cent.

2. The steamer *Persia* left Boston for Halifax, June 30th, loaded with 7210 bushels of spring wheat, shipped by J. M. Musgrove, and invoiced at 95 cents per bushel; 4815 bushels of corn, shipped by Thomas A Bryce & Co., and invoiced at 60 cents per bushel; 2180 barrels of flour, shipped by A. B. Smith & Co., and invoiced at $5.50 per barrel. When near Halifax, the steamer collided with the *Bay State*, and the captain found it necessary to throw overboard 1600 bushels of wheat, 1280 bushels of corn, and 720 barrels of flour. On estimating the proportionate loss, it was allowed that the wheat would have sold in Montreal at an advance of 10 per cent., the corn at an advanee of 15 per cent., and the flour for $5 per barrel. The contributory interests were:—Steamer, $95,000; cargo, $; gross freight, $2361.20. The cost of repairs to steamer was $2198.15; cost arising from detention during repairs, $318; seamen's wages, $1252.50. How much of the loss had each contributory interest to bear?

3. The steamer *Edith* left Baltimore for New Orleans with 7600 bushels of wheat, valued at $1.25 per bushel, shipped by Dunn, Lloyd & Co., and insured in the Hartford Insurance Company at $1\frac{3}{4}$ per cent., 9200 bushels of corn, valued at 75 cents per bushel,

shipped by J. W. Roe, and insured in the Ætna Insurance Company at $1\frac{3}{4}$ per cent.; 14,800 bushels of oats, valued at $37\frac{1}{2}$ cents per bushel, shipped by Morris, Wright & Co., and insured in the Mutual Insurance Company at $1\frac{1}{2}$ per cent.; 1,800 barrels of flour, valued at $5.25 per barrel, shipped by Smith & Worth, and insured in the Beaver Insurance Company at $1\frac{1}{4}$ per cent. In consequence of a violent gale in the Gulf of Mexico, it was found necessary to throw overboard the flour, 4,600 bushels of oats, and 3,150 bushels of wheat. The propeller was valued at $45,000, and insured in the Beaver Insurance Company for $12,000, at 2 per cent., and in the Western for $25,000, at $2\frac{1}{4}$ per cent. The gross freight was $4950; seamen's wages, $340, and repairs to the boat, $3953.75; what was the loss sustained by each of the contributory interests, the propeller being on her first trip?

TAXES AND CUSTOMS DUTIES.

A tax is a money payment levied upon the subjects of a State or the members of any community, for the support of the government.

A tax is either levied upon the property or the persons of individuals. When levied upon the person, it is called a *poll tax*.

It may be either *direct* or *indirect*. When direct, it is levied from the individuals, or the property in the hands of the ultimate owners. When indirect, it is in the nature of a *customs'* or *excise duty*, which is levied upon imports, or manufactures, before they reach the consumer, although in the end they are paid by the latter.

Customs' duties are paid by the importer of goods at the port of entry, where a *custom-house* is stationed, with government employees called *custom-house officers*, to collect these dues.

Excise duties are those levied upon articles manufactured in the country.

An invoice is a complete list of the particulars and prices of goods sent from one place to another.

A *Specific* duty is a certain sum paid on a ton, hundred weight, yard, gallon, &c., without regard to the cost of the article.

An *ad valorem* duty is a percentage levied on the actual cost, or fair market value of the goods in the country from which they are imported.

Gross weight is the weight of goods, upon which a specific duty is to be levied, before any allowances are deducted.

Net weight is the weight of the goods after all allowances are deducted.

Among the allowances made are the following:

Breakage—an allowance on fluids contained in bottles or breakable vessels.

Draft—the allowance for waste.

Leakage—an allowance for waste by leaking.

Tare and tret are the deductions made for the weight of the case or barrel which contains the goods.

When goods, invoiced at gold value, upon which duty is payable, are imported into this country from any foreign country, the custom house duties are payable in gold, for else manifest injustice might be done. If the duty were payable in greenbacks, it would be necessary, in order to obtain uniformity, either to increase or decrease the rate per cent. of duty, as greenbacks fluctuated in value, compared with gold (the invoice price of the goods), or else the goods imported would require to be reduced to their value in greenbacks at time of delivery. To avoid all this trouble and confusion, goods that are invoiced at their gold value, the duties are made payable in the same currency.

When goods are imported from any country which has a depreciated currency, a note is attached to the invoice, certifying the amount of depreciation. This is the duty of the Consul representing the country *to* which the goods are exported, and residing at the port *from* which they are exported.

EXAMPLES.

To find the specific duty on any quantity of goods.

Suppose an Albany Provision Merchant imports from Ireland 59 casks of butter, each weighing 68 lbs., and that 12 lbs. tare is allowed on each cask, and 2 cents per lb. duty on the net weight.

We find the gross is......................59×68=4012 lbs.
" tare is......................59×12= 708 lbs.

Hence the net weight is..............................3304 lbs
The duty is 2 cents per lb.............................. 2

The duty, therefore, is..............................$66.08

To find the *ad valorem* duty on any quantity of goods.

Suppose a Troy dry goods merchant to import from Montreal 436 yards of silk, at $1.75 per yard, and that 35 per cent. duty is charged on them.

Here we find the whole price by the rule of Practice to be $763, then the rest of the operation is a direct case of percentage, and therefore we multiply $763 by .35, which gives $267.05, the amount of duty on the whole.

Hence we have the following

RULE FOR SPECIFIC DUTY.

Subtract the tare, or other allowance, and multiply the remainder by the rate of duty per box, gallon, &c.

RULE FOR AD VALOREM DUTY.

Multiply the amount of the invoice by the rate per unit.

EXERCISES.

1. Find the specific duty on 5120 lbs. of sugar, the tare being 14 per cent., and the duty $2\frac{3}{4}$ cents per lb. Ans. $121.09.

2. What is the ad valorem duty on a quantity of silks, the amount of the invoice being $95,800, and the duty $62\frac{1}{2}$ per cent? Ans. $59,875.

3. At 30 per cent., what is the ad valorem duty on an importation of china worth $1260. ? Ans. $378.

3. What is the specific duty, at 10 cents per lb., on 45 chests of tea, each weighing 120 lbs., the tare being 10 per cent. ? Ans. $486.

5. What is the ad valorem duty on a shipment of fruit invoiced at $4560, the duty being 40 per cent.? Ans. $1824.

6. What is the specific duty on 950 bags of coffee, each weighing 200 lbs., the duty being 2 cents per lb., and the tare 2 per cent? Ans. $3724.

7. What is the ad valorem duty on 20 casks of wine, each containing 75 gallons, at 18 cents a gallon? Ans. $270.

8. A. B. shipped from Oswego 24 pipes of molasses, each containing 96 gallons; 2 per cent. was deducted for leakage, and 12 cents duty per gallon charged on the remainder; how much was the duty? Ans. $270.95.

9. Peter Smith & Co., Brooklin, import from Cadiz, 80 baskets of port wine, at 70 francs per basket; 42 baskets of sherry wine, at 35 francs per basket; 60 casks of champagne, containing 31 gallons each, at 4 francs per gallon. The waste of the wine in the casks was reckoned at a gallon each cask, and the allowance for breakage in the baskets was 5 per cent.; what was the duty at 30 per cent., $18\frac{3}{5}$ cents being taken as equal to 1 franc? Ans. $776.54.

10. J. Johnson & Co., of Boston, import from Liverpool 10 pieces of Brussels carpeting, 40 yards each, purchased at 5s. per yard, duty 24 per cent.; 200 yards of hair cloth, at 4s. per yard, duty 19 cwt.; 100 woollen blankets, at 2s. 6d., duty 16 per cent.; and shoe-lasting to the cost of £60, duty 4 per cent. Required the whole amount of duty, allowing the value of the pound sterling to be $4.84. Ans. $173.64.

11. John McMaster & Co., of Collingwood, Canada West., bought of A. M. Smith, of Buffalo, N. Y., goods invoiced at $5440.50, which should have passed through the custom-house during the first week in May, when the discount on American invoices was $43\frac{1}{4}$ per cent., but they were not passed until the fourth week in May, when the discount was $36\frac{3}{4}$ per cent. The duty in both cases being 20 per cent.; what was the loss sustained by McMaster & Co. on account of their goods being delayed? Ans. $70.60.

STOCKS AND BONDS.

CAPITAL is a term generally applied to the property accumulated by individuals, and invested in trade, manufactures, railroads, buildings, government securities, banking, &c. The capital of incorporated companies is generally termed its "capital stock," and is divided into shares; the persons owning one or more of these shares, being called stockholders. The shares in England, are usually £100, £50, or £10 each. In the United States they are generally $100, $50, or $10 each.

The management of incorporated companies is generally vested in officers and directors, as provided in the law or laws, who are elected by the stockholders or shareholders; each stockholder, in most cases, being entitled to as many votes as the number of shares he holds; but sometimes the holder of a few shares votes in a larger proportion than the holder of many.

The accumulating profits which are distributed among the stockholders, once or twice a year, are called "dividends," and when "declared," are a certain percentage of the par value of the shares. In mining, and some other companies, where the shares are only a few dollars each, the dividend is usually a fixed sum "per share." Certificates of stock are issued by every company, signed by the proper officers, indicating the number of shares each stockholder is entitled to, and as an evidence of ownership; these are transferable, and may be bought and sold like any other property. When the market value equals their nominal value they are said to be "*at par.*" When they sell for more than their nominal value, or face, they are said to be above par, or at a "premium"; when for less, they are below par, or at a "discount." Quotations of the market value are generally made by a percentage of their par value. Thus, a share which is $25 at par, and sells at $28, is quoted at twelve per cent. premium, or 112 per cent.

When states, cities, counties, railroad companies, and other corporations, borrow large amounts of money, for the prosecution of their objects, instead of giving common promissory notes, as with the mercantile community, they issue bonds, in denominations of convenient size, payable at a specified number of years, the interest usually payable semi-annually at some well known place. These are usually payable to "bearer," and sometimes to the "order" of the owner or holder. When issued by Governments or States, these bonds are frequently called Government stocks or State stocks, under authority of law. To these bonds are attached, what are called "*coupons,*" or certificates of interest, each of which is a due bill for the annual or semi-annual interest on the bond to which it is attached, representing the amount of the periodical dividend or interest; which coupons were usually cut off, and presented for payment as they become due.. These bonds and coupons are signed by the proper officers, and like certificates of capital stock, are negotiable by delivery. The loan is obtained by the sale of the bonds, with coupons attached, but they are sometimes negotiated at par. Their market value depends upon the degree of confidence felt by capitalists of their being paid at maturity, and the rate of interest compared with the rate in the market.

Treasury notes are issued by the United States Government, for the purpose of effecting temporary loans, and for the payment of contracts and salaries, which resemble bank notes, and are made payable without interest generally. Recently such notes have been issued bearing one year or three years' interest.

"Consols" is a term abbreviated from the expression "consolidated," the British Government having at various times borrowed money at different rates of interest and payable at different times, "consolidated" the debt or bonds thus issued, by issuing new stock, drawing interest at three per cent, per annum, payable semi-annually, and redeemable only at the option of the Government, becoming practically perpetual annuities. With the proceeds of this, the old stock was redeemed. The quotations of these three per cent. perpetual annuities, or "consols," indicate ordinarily the state of the money market, as they form a large portion of the British public debt.

"Mortgage Bonds" are frequently issued by owners of real property, with coupons attached, which render the bonds more saleable as well as more convenient for the collection of interest.

"Coupon Bonds," being negotiable by delivery, are payable to the holder; and in case of loss or theft, the amount cannot be recovered from the government or corporation issuing them, unless ample notice is given of the loss.

"Registered Bonds" are those payable only to the "order" of the holder or owner, and are more safe for investment.

By law, stockholders are liable for the whole debts of the corporation, in case of failure. In some States the law provides that they are liable only to an amount equal to their stock. In England the statute provides for "Limited" liability, by an Act passed in 1862 termed the "Limited Act."

CASE I.

The premium or discount being known, to find the market value of any amount of stock.

EXAMPLES.

If G. W. R. shares are at 7 per cent. *premium*, to find the value of 30 shares of $100.

Here it is plain that each $100 will bring $107, and that each $1 will bring $1.07, and as the par value is $3000, the advanced value will be 3000 times 1.07, which gives $3210, the market value, and $3210—$3000=$210, the gain.

Again, if the same are sold at a *discount* of 7 per cent., it is plain that each $100 would bring only $93, and therefore each $1 would bring only $0.93, and therefore as the par value is $3000, the depreciated value will be 3000 times .93, which gives $2790, and therefore the loss would be $3000—2790=210.

From this we derive the

RULE.

Multiply the par value by 1 *plus or minus tne rate per unit, according as the shares are at a premium or a discount.*

EXERCISES.

1. What is the market value of $450 stock, at $8\frac{1}{2}$ per cent. discount? Ans. $411.75.

2. What is the value of 29 shares of $50 each, when the shares are 11 per cent. below par? Ans. $1290.50.

3. A man purchased 60 shares of $5 each, from an oil well company, when the shares were at a discount of 8 per cent., and sold them when they were at a premium of 10 per cent; how much did he gain? Ans. $54.

4. A man purchased $10,000 stock when it was at an advance of 8 per cent., and sold when it was at a discount of 8 per cent.; how much did he lose? Ans. $1600.

5. If a man buys 15 shares of $100 each, when the shares are at a premium of 5 per cent., and sells when they have advanced to 12 per cent., how much does he gain? Ans. $105.

CASE II.

To find how much stock a given sum will purchase at a given premium or discount.

Let it be required to find how much stock can be purchased for $21,600 when at a *premium* of 8 per cent.

In this case it will require $108 to purchase $100 stock, and therefore $1.08 to purchase $1 stock, and hence the amount that can be purchased for $21600 will be represented by the number of times that $1.08 is contained in 21600, which gives $20000.

Again: Let it be required to find how much stock can be purchased for $5520, when at a discount of 8 per cent. When stocks are 8 per cent. below par, $92 will purchase $100 stock, and therefore $0.92 will purchase $1, and hence the amount that can be purchased for $5520 will be represented by the number of times that .92 is contained in 5520, which gives $6000 stock.

Hence we derive the

RULE.

Divide the given sum by 1 *plus or minus the rate per unit, according as the shares are at a premium or a discount.*

EXERCISES.

6. When stocks are at a premium of 12 per cent., how much can be purchased for $8064? Ans. $7200.

7. When stocks are at a discount of 9 per cent., how much can be bought for $3640? Ans. $4000.

8. When G. T. R. stock is at 18 per cent. below par, how much can be bought for $42,640. Ans. $52000.

9. When G. W. R. stock is at a premium of 9 per cent., how much will $4578 purchase? Ans. $4200.

10. When government stock is selling at $92\frac{1}{2}$, what amount of stock will $28,675 purchase, and to what will it amount with brokerage at $\frac{1}{4}$ per cent.? Ans. $31077.50.

CASE III.

The premium or discount being known, to find the par value.

To find the par value of $1,296, when stock is at a premium of 8 per cent.

At 8 per cent. premium, each $1 brings $1.08, hence the par value will be represented by the number of times 1.08 is contained in 1296, which gives $1200 for the par value.

To find the par value of $1104, when stock is at a discount of 8 per cent.

Each $1 will bring $0.92, and therefore the par value will be represented by the number of times that .92 is contained in 1104, which gives $1200, the par value. Hence the

RULE.

Divide the market value by 1 *plus or minus the rate per unit, according as the stocks are selling above or below par.*

EXERCISES.

11. What is the par value of $24420, when stock is 11 per cent. above par? Ans. $22000.

12. What is the par value of $10800, when stocks are at a discount of 4 per cent.? Ans. $11250.

13. When government stocks are at 6 per cent. premium; how much will $20246 purchase at par value? Ans. $19100.

14. The shares in a canal company are at 15 per cent. discount; how many shares of $100 will $11390 purchase? Ans. 134.

15. The shares of a British gas company were selling in 1848, at a discount of 12 per cent.; a speculator purchased a certain number of shares for £792; the value of the shares suddenly rose to par; how many shares did he purchase, and how much did he gain?

Ans. 9 shares; £108 gain.

CASE IV.

To find to what rate of interest a given dividend corresponds.

If a person receives a dividend of 12 per cent. on an investment made at 20 per cent. above par, the corresponding interest may be calculated thus:

As the stock was bought at 20 per cent., or .20 above par, $1.20 of market value corresponds to $1 of par value, and as every $1 of par value corresponds to 12 per cent. interest, or .12, it follows that the per cent. which was invested will be represented by the number of times that 1.20 is contained in .12, which is .10 or 10 per cent. Hence the

RULE.

*Divide the rate per unit of dividend by 1 plus or minus the rate per cent. premium or discount, according as the stocks are above or below par.**

EXERCISES.

16. If a dividend of 10 per cent. be declared on stock vested at 25 per cent. advance; what is the corresponding interest?

Ans. 8 per cent.

17. If a dividend of 4 per cent. be declared on stock invested at 12 per cent. below par, what is the corresponding interest?

Ans. $4\frac{6}{11}$.

18. If money invested at 24 per cent. yields a dividend of 15 per cent., what is the rate of interest? Ans. $12\frac{3}{31}$.

19. If railroad stock is invested at 18 per cent. above par, and a dividend of 6 per cent. be declared, what is the rate of interest?

Ans. $5\frac{5}{59}$.

20. If bank stock be invested at 15 per cent. below par, and a dividend of 10 per cent. declared, what is the rate of interest?

Ans. $11\frac{13}{17}$.

MISCELLANEOUS EXERCISES.

1. What must be paid for 20 shares of railway stock, at 5 per cent. premium, the shares being $100 each? Ans. $2100.

---

* To find at what price stock paying a given rate per cent. dividend can be purchased, so that the money invested shall produce a given rate of interest, *divide the rate per unit of dividend by the rate per unit of interest.*

2. What is the par value of bank stock worth \$8740, at a premium of 15 per cent.? Ans. \$7600.

3. Railway stock was bought at $15\frac{3}{4}$ below par, for \$1895.62$\frac{1}{2}$; how many shares were there, each share being \$150? Ans. 15 shares.

4. If 6 per cent. stock yields 8 per cent. on an investment, at what per cent. discount was it bought? Ans. 25.

5. If bank stock which pays 11 per cent. dividend, is 10 per cent. above par, what is the corresponding rate of interest on any investment? Ans. 10.

6. When 4 per cent. stocks were at $17\frac{7}{8}$ discount, A bought \$1000; how much did he pay, and how much did he gain by selling when stock had risen to $86\frac{1}{4}$? Ans. \$821.25, and \$41.25.

7. What will \$850 bank stock cost at a discount of $9\frac{3}{8}$ per cent., $\frac{1}{8}$ per cent. being charged for brokerage? Ans. \$771.38.

8. On the data of the last example, how much would be lost by selling out at $10\frac{1}{2}$ per cent.? Ans. \$10.03.

9. What income should I get by laying out \$1620 in the purchase of 3 per cent. stock at 81? Ans. \$60.

10. What sum must be invested in the 4 per cent. stocks at 84, to yield an income of \$280? Ans. \$5880.

11. What rate of interest will a person receive by investing in the $4\frac{1}{2}$ per cent. stocks at 90? Ans. 5 per cent.

12. A person transfers his capital from the $3\frac{1}{2}$ per cent. stocks at 77, to the 4 per cent. at 89; what is the increase or decrease per cent. in his income? Ans. Decrease 25.

13. A person sells out of the 3 per cent. stock at 96, and invests his money in railway 5 per cent. stock at par; how much per cent. is his income increased? Ans. 60.

14. What must be the market value of $5\frac{1}{2}$ per cent. stock, so that after deducting an income tax of 2 cents on the dollar, it may produce 5 per cent. interest? Ans. $107\frac{4}{5}$.

15. A gentleman invested \$7560 in the $3\frac{1}{2}$ per cent. stocks at $94\frac{1}{2}$, and on their rising to 95 sold out, and purchased G. T. R. 4 per cent. stock at par; what increase did he make in his annual income? Ans. \$24.

16. How much more may a person increase his annual income by lending \$3800, at 6 per cent., than by purchasing railway 5 per cent. stock at 95? Ans. \$28.

17. A person sells $4200 railway stock which pays 6 per cent. at 115, and invests one-third of the proceeds in the 3 per cent. consols at $80\frac{1}{2}$, and the balance in savings' bank stock, which pays 9 per cent. at par; what is the decrease or increase of his annual income? Ans. Increase $97.80.

18. A person having $10,000 consols, sells $5000 at $94\frac{7}{8}$, and on their rising to $98\frac{5}{8}$ he sells $5000 more; on their again rising he buys back the whole at 96; how much does he gain? Ans. $75.

19. The sum of $4004 was laid out in purchasing 3 per cent. stocks at $89\frac{3}{8}$, and a whole year's dividend having been received upon it, it was sold out, the whole increase of capital being $302.40; at what price was it sold out? Ans. $93\frac{1}{8}$.

20. Suppose a person to have been an original subscriber for 500 shares of $50 each, in the First National Bank, payable by instalments, as follows:—$\frac{1}{8}$ in three months, which he sold for $5\frac{1}{4}$ per cent. advance; $\frac{3}{8}$ in 6 months, which brought him $6\frac{3}{8}$ per cent. advance, and the balance in nine months, which he was compelled to sell at $8\frac{3}{4}$ per cent. discount; what did he gain by the whole transaction? Ans. $808.33.

PARTNERSHIP.

Partnership has been defined to be the result of a contract, under which two or more persons agree to combine property, or labour, for the purpose of a common undertaking, and the acquisition of a common profit.

A *dormant*, or *sleeping* partner, is one who shares in the concern, but does not appear to the world as such.

A *nominal* partner is one who lends his name and credit to a firm, without having any real interest in the profits.

All the partners may contribute equally to the business; or the capital may be contributed by some or one, and the skill and labour by the other. Or, unequal proportions may be furnished by each.

The contract need not be in writing, but all parties to be bound must assent to it, and it is usually contained in an instrument called "*Articles of Partnership.*" A dissolution can take place at any time by mutual consent.

A partnership *at will* is one in which there is no limited time affixed for its continuance, and the whole firm may be dissolved by any of its members at a moment's notice. A document is, however, generally drawn up and signed upon a dissolution, called a *settlement,* which contains a statement of the mode of adjustment of the accounts, and the apportionment of profits or losses.

EXAMPLE.

Two persons, A. and B., enter into partnership. A. invests \$300 and B. \$400. They gain during one year \$210; what is each man's share of the profit?

SOLUTION BY PROPORTION.

A.'s stock, \$300
B.'s " 400

Entire stock \$700 : 300 : : \$210 : \$90 A.'s gain.
" " 700 : 400 : : \$210 : 120 B.'s "

SOLUTION BY PERCENTAGE.

Since the entire amount invested is \$700, and the gain \$210, the gain on every \$1 of investment will be represented by the number of times that 700 is contained in \$210, which is .30 or 30 cents on the dollar. Now if each man's stock be multiplied by .30 it will represent his share of the gain thus:

\$300×.30=\$ 90 A.'s gain.
400×.30= 120 B.'s "

Entire stock....... 700 210 Entire gain.

Hence,—To find each partner's share of the profit or loss, when there is no reference to time, we have the following

RULE.

As the whole stock is to each partner's stock, so is the whole gain or loss to each partner's gain or loss; or, divide the whole gain or loss by the number denoting the entire stock, and the quotient will be the gain or loss on each dollar of stock; which multiplied by the number denoting each partner's share of the entire stock, will give his share of the entire gain or loss.

EXERCISES.

1. Three persons, A., B., and C., enter into partnership. A. advances \$500, B. \$550, and C. \$600; they gain by trade \$412.50. What is each partner's share of the profit?

Ans. A.'s \$125; B.'s \$137.50; C.'s \$150.

2, A, B, C and D purchase an oil well. A pays for 6 shares, B for 5, C for 7, and D for 8. Their net profits at the end of three months have amounted to $7800; what sum ought each to receive?

Ans. A, $1800; B, $1500; C, $2100; D, $2400.

3. A and B purchased a lot of land for $4500. A paid $\frac{1}{3}$ of the price, and B the remainder; they gained by the sale of it 20 per cent.; what was each man's share of the profit?

Ans. A, $300; B, $600.

4. A captain, mate, and 12 sailors, won a prize of $2240, of which the captain took 14 shares, the mate 6, and the remainder was equally divided among the sailors; how much did each receive?

Ans. The captain, $980; the mate, $420; each sailor, $70.

5. A and B invest equal sums in trade, and clear $220, of which A is to have 8 shares on account of transacting the business, and B only 3 shares; what is each man's gain, and what allowance is made A for his time? Ans. Each man's gain $60; A $100 for his time.

6. A, B, C and D enter into partnership with a joint capital of $4000, of which A furnishes $1000; B $800; C $1300, and D the balance; at the end of nine months their net profits amount to $1700; what is each partner's share of the gain, supposing B to receive $100 for extra services?

Ans. A, $400; B, $320; C, $520; D, $360.

7. Six persons, A, B, C, D, E and F, enter into partnership, and gain $7000, which is to be divided among them in the following manner:—A to have $\frac{1}{5}$; B, $\frac{1}{7}$; C, $\frac{1}{3}$ as much as A and B, and the remainder to be divided between D, E and F, in the proportion of 2, $2\frac{1}{2}$ and $3\frac{1}{2}$; how much does each partner receive?

Ans. A, $1400; B, $1000; C, $800; D, $950; E, $1187.50; F, $1662.50.

8. A, B and C enter into partnership with a joint stock of $30,000, of which A furnished an unknown sum; B furnished $1\frac{1}{2}$, and C $1\frac{1}{4}$ times as much. At the end of six months their profits were 25 per cent. of the investment; what was each man's share of the gain? Ans. A's, $2000; B's, $3000; and C's, $2500.

9. A, B, C and D trade in company with a joint capital of $3000; on dividing the profits, it is found that A's share is $120; B's, $255; C's, $225; and D's, $300; what was each partner's stock?

Ans. A's, $400; B's, $850; C's, $750; and D's, $1000.

10. Three labouring men, A, B and C, join together to reap a certain field of wheat, for which they agree to take the sum of

$19.84; A and B calculate that they can do $\frac{4}{5}$ of the work; A and C $\frac{3}{5}$; B and C $\frac{3}{5}$ of it; how much should each receive according to these estimates? Ans. A, $8.32; B, $7.04; and C, $4.48.

To find each partner's share of the gain or loss, when the capital is invested for different periods.

EXAMPLE.

Two merchants, A and B, enter into partnership. A invests $700 for 15 months, and B $800 for 12 months; they gain $603; what is each man's share of the profits?

SOLUTION.

$700×15=$10500
$800×12= 9600

20100 : 10500 : : $603 : $315 A's gain.
20100 : 9600 : : $603 : $288 B's gain.

The reason for multiplying each partner's stock by the time it was in trade, is evident from the consideration that $700 invested for 15 months would be equivalent to $700×15 equal to $10500 for one month, that is $10500 would yield, *in one month*, the same interest that $700 would *in fifteen months*. Likewise $800 invested for 12 months would be the same as $9600 for one month; hence the question becomes one of the previous case, that is, their investments are the same as if they had invested respectively $10500 and $9600 for equal times; hence the

RULE.

Multiply each man's stock by the time he continues it in trade; then say, as the sum of the products is to each particular product, so is the whole gain or loss to each man's share of the gain or loss.

EXERCISES.

11. A, B and C are associated in trade. A furnished $300 for 6 months; B, $350 for 7 months, and C, $400 for 8 months. Their profits amounted to $1490 at the time of dissolution; what was the profit belonging to each partner?

Ans. A, $360; B, $490; C, $640.

12. A, B and C contract to perform a certain piece of work; A employs 40 men for $4\frac{1}{2}$ months; B 45 men for $3\frac{1}{2}$ months, and C 50 men for $2\frac{1}{4}$ months. Their profits, after paying all expenses, are $850; how much of this belongs to each?

Ans. A, $340; B, $297.50; C, $212.50.

13. Four men, A, B, C and D, hired a pasture for $27.80; A puts in 18 sheep for 4 months; B, 24 for 3 months; C, 22 for 2 months; and D, 30 for 3 months; how much ought each to pay?

Ans. A and B each, $7.20; C, $4.40; D, $9.

14. On the first day of January A began business with a capital of $760, and on the first of February following he took in B, who invested $540; and on the first of June following they took in C, who put into the business $800. At the end of the year they found they had gained $872; how much of this was each man entitled to?

Ans. A, $384.93; B, $250.71; C, $236.36.

15. Three merchants, A, B and C, entered into partnership with a joint capital of $5875, A investing his stock for 6 months, B his for 8 months, and C his for 10 months; of the profits each partner took an equal share; how much of the capital did each invest?

Ans. A, $2500; B, $1875; C, $1500.

16. Two merchants, A and B, entered into partnership for two years; A at first furnished $800, and at the end of one year, $500 more; B furnished at first $1000, at the end of 6 months, $500 more, and after they had been in business one year, he was compelled to withdraw $600 At the expiration of the partnership their net profits were $2550; how much must A pay B who wishes to retire from the business? Ans. $2190.

17. Three persons, A, B and C, form a partnership for one year, commencing January 1st, 1865; A puts in $4000; B, $3000; and C, $2500; April 1st, A withdraws $500, and B withdraws $600; June 1st, C puts in $800 more; September 1st, A furnishes $700 more, and B $400 more. At the end of the year they find they have gained $1500; what is each partner's share of it?

Ans. A, $608.68; B, $423.31; C, $468.01.

18. John Adams commenced business January first, 1865, with a capital of $10000, and after some time formed a partnership with William Hickman, who contributed to the joint stock the sum of $2800 cash. In course of time they admitted into the firm Joseph Williams, with a stock worth $3600. On making a settlement January first, 1866, it was found that Adams had gained $2250;

Hickman, \$420; and Williams, \$405; how long had Hickman's and Williams' money been employed in the business, and what rate of interest per annum had each of the partners gained on their stock?

Ans. Hickman's 8 months; Williams' 6 months. Gain, $22\frac{1}{2}$ per cent. interest.

BANKRUPTCY.

When any person is unable to meet his liabilities, he makes an *assignment* of his property to some other person or persons, called *official assignee or assignees*, whose *office* it is to distribute the available property, after paying expenses, rateably among the creditors. An allowance for maintenance is generally made to the insolvent, but sometimes he is compelled to surrender all his estate, but only in case of manifest *fraud*, which the word *bankrupt* originally implied, though now it is used as nearly synonimous with insolvent. The property to be divided is called the *assets*. The shares of the property which are divided among creditors, are called *dividends*.

EXAMPLE.

A bankrupt owes A \$400; B. \$350, and C, \$600; his net assets amount to \$810 cash; how much is he able to pay on the \$1, and how much will each creditor receive?

SOLUTION.

$\$400+\$350+\$600=\$1350$, total liabilities. Now, if he has \$1350 to pay, and only \$810 to pay it with, he will only be able to pay $\$810\div1350=.60$ or 60 cents on the \$1. Therefore, A will receive $\$400\times.60=\$240$; B, $\$350\times.60=\$210$, and C, $\$600\times.60=\$360$. Hence the

RULE.

Divide the net assets by the number denoting the total amount of the debts, and the quotient will be the sum to be paid on each dollar, then multiply each man's claim by the sum paid on the dollar, and the product will be the amount he is to receive.

EXERCISES.

1. A becomes bankrupt. He owes B, $800; C, $500; D, $1100, and E, $600. The assets amount to $1110; how much can he pay on the dollar, and how much does each creditor receive?

Ans. He can pay 37 cents on the dollar, and B receives $296; C, $185; D, $407; and E, $222.

2. A house becomes bankrupt; its liabilities are $17940; its assets are $8970; what is the dividend, and what is the shase of the chief creditor to whom $1282 are due?

Ans. The dividend is 50 cents on the dollar, and the principal creditor gets $641.

3. A shipbuilder becomes bankrupt, and his liabilities are $303000; the premises, building and stock are worth $220000, and he has in cash and notes $12875; the creditors allow him $3000 for maintenance of his family; the costs are $3\frac{1}{2}$ per cent. of the amount available for the creditors; what is the dividend, and how much does a creditor get to whom $1360.60 are due?

Ans. The dividend is 75 cents on the dollar, and the creditor specified gets $1020.

4. Foster & Co. fail. They owe in Alhany, $22000; in Baltimore, $18000; in Philadelphia, $17100; in Charleston, $16000; in Boston, $4400, and in Newark, $4200. Their assets are: house property, $14000; farms, $2200; cash in bank, $4400; railway stock, $4200; sundry sums due to them, $20135; what is the dividend, and how much goes to each city?

Ans. Dividend, 55 cents on the dollar; to be paid in Albany, $12100; in Baltimore, $9900; in Philadelphia, $9405; in Charleston, $8800, in Boston, $2420; in Newark, $2310.

5. The firm of Reuben Ring & Nephews becomes bankrupt. It owes to Buchanan & Ramsay, $1080; to Kinneburgh & McNabb, $850; to Collier Bros., $1720; to David Bryce & Son, $1580; to Sinclair & Boyd, $970. The assets are: house and store, valued at $848; merchandise in stock, $420; sundry debts, $220. What can the estate pay, and what is the share of each creditor?

Ans. The estate pays 24 cents on the dollar, and the payments are: to Buchanan & Ramsay, $259.20; to Kinneburgh & McNabb, $204; to Collier Bros., $412.80; to David Bryce & Son, $379.20; to Sinclair & Boyd, $231.80.

EQUATION OF PAYMENTS.

Equation of Payments is the process of finding the average or mean time at which the payment of several sums, due at different times, may all be made at one time, so that neither the debtor nor creditor shall be at any loss.

The date to be found is called the *equated time.*

The mode of finding equated time almost universally adopted is very simple, though, as we shall show in the sequel, not altogether correct. It is known as *the mercantile rule.*

Let us observe, in the first place, that the standard by which men of business reckon the advantage that accrues to them from receiving money before the time fixed for its payment, and the loss they sustain by the payment being deferred beyond the appointed time, is the interest of money for each such period. Thus, if $50 be a year overdue, the loss is $3, at 6 per cent.; and, if $50 be paid a year in advance of the time agreed upon, the gain to the payee is $3, at the same rate. In the former case, the person receiving the money charges the payer $3 interest for the inconvenience of lying out of his money, but, in the latter case, he deducts $3 from the debt, for the advantage of having the money in hand. If, on the 1st May, A gives B two notes, one for $50, at a term of three months, and the other for $80, at a term of seven months, the first will be legally due on the 1st August, and the 2nd on the 1st December; but A is not able to meet the first at August, and it is held over till the 1st November, when A finds himself in a position to pay both at once. The first is then three months over-due, and accordingly B claims interest for that time, which, at 6 per cent., is 75 cents, but as A tenders payment of the whole debt at once, and the second note will not be due for another month, A claims a deduction of one month's interest, which, at the same rate, is 40 cents, and accordingly A, in addition to the debt, pays B 35 cents.

Let us now suppose another case. A owes B $130, as before, and he gives B two notes—one for $50, on 1st May, at 3 months, and another, on the 6th May, for $80, at 8 months. The first falls due on 1st August, and the other on the 6th January, but A and B agree to settle at such a time that neither shall have interest to pay, but that A shall simply have to pay the principal. Supposing that a settlement is made on 6th November, we find that the 1st note is

3 months and 6 days over due, and the interest on it for that period is 80 cents, while the second will not be due for 2 months, and the interest on it for that period is also 80 cents; consequently, the interest that A should pay, and that which B should allow being equal, they balance each other, and the principal only has to be paid.

There are, then, three methods for the payment of several debts, or a debt to be paid by instalments. The first is to pay each instalment as it becomes due. This needs no elucidation, nor is it often practised, except in the case of small debts, due by persons of contracted means.

The second is what has been illustrated above by the first example, viz., that interest is added for overdue money, and deducted for sums paid in advance of the stipulated time.

The third has been illustrated by the second example, viz., to fix on such a time that the interests on the overdue and underdue sums shall be equal, so that the debtor has only to give the principal to the creditor. If, in this last case, the time should come out as a mixed number, the fraction must be taken as another day, or thrown off, making the payment fall due a day earlier. The principle on which all such settlements are made is, that the interest of any sum paid *in advance* of a stipulated time is equivalent to the interest of the same sum *overdue* for a like time.

With these explanations we are now ready to investigate a rule for the Equation of Payments. For this purpose let us suppose a case. R. Evans owes J. Jones $200, which he undertakes to pay by two instalments of $100 each, (basis of interest 6 per cent.,) the first payment to be made at once, and the second at the expiration of two years. But the first payment is not made till the end of the first year, at which time R. E. tenders payment of the whole amount. For the accommodation of having the first payment deferred for one year he is to pay $6, *i. e.*, $106 in all, and in return for making the second payment a year before it is due, he claims a discount at the same rate, which gives $6. He has therefore, by the mercantile rule, to pay $106+94=$200, so that the $6 in the latter case balances the $6 in the former. This takes one year as the equated time, and is the mode usually adopted on account of its simplicity, though not strictly accurate.

To find the equated time when there are several payments to be made at different dates.

If A owes B $300, payable at the end of 4 months; $500, payable at the end of 6 months, and $400, payable at the end of $10\frac{1}{2}$ months, to find at what time the whole may be paid, so that interest shall be chargeable to neither party. The interest of $300 for 4 months is the same as the interest of $1 for 1200 months; the interest of $500 for 6 months is the same as the interest of $1 for 3000 months, and the interest of $400 for $10\frac{1}{2}$ months is the same as the interest of $1 for 4200 months. The sum of all these is 8400 months, and the interest of the whole is the same as the interest of $1 for 8400 months, and if $1 requires 8400 months to produce a certain interest, the sum of all the principals will require only the $\frac{1}{1200}$ part of 8400 months to produce the same interest, and $8400 \div 1200 = 7$, and hence the equated time is 7 months.

RULE.

Multiply each payment by the time that must elapse before it becomes due, and divide the sum of these products by the sum of the payments.

EXAMPLE.

To find the equated time for the payment of three debts, the first for $45, due at the end of 6 months; the second for $70, due at the end of 11 months, and the third for $75, due at the end of 13 months.

$$\begin{array}{rr} \$45\times\ 6= & \$270 \\ 70\times 11= & 770 \\ 75\times 13= & 975 \\ \hline 190 & 2015 \end{array}$$

and $2015 \div 19 = 10\frac{23}{38}$, so that the equated time will be 10 months and 18 days, the small remaining fraction being rejected.

Let us suppose that nothing is paid until the end of the 13 months, and all paid at once, then the amount to be paid will be, at 6 per cent.,

For first debt overdue 7 months, $45+1.57½, interest for 7 months	$46.57½
For second debt overdue 2 months, $70+.70, interest for 2 months	70.70
For third debt just due, $75, no interest	75.00
	$192.27½

The work may often be somewhat shortened by counting the differences of time from the date at which the first payment becomes due, the mean time between the dates when the first and last become due being alone required.

If a person owes $1200 to be paid in four instalments, $100 in 3 months; $200 in 10 months; $300 in 15 months, and $600 in 18 months, then the excesses of time of the last three above the first are 7, 12 and 15 months, and the work will stand as below.

$$\begin{array}{ll} \$100 & \text{(no time.)} \\ 200\times 7 & =1400 \\ 300\times 12 & =3600 \\ 600\times 15 & =9000 \\ \hline 1200) & 14000(11\frac{2}{3} \end{array}$$

and $11\frac{2}{3}\times 3=14\frac{2}{3}$ months. This gives the

RULE.

Multiply each debt, except the one first due, by the difference between its term and the term of the first; divide the sum of the products by the sum of the debts, the quotient with the term of the first added to it will be the equated time.

Another method, which is often convenient, may be illustrated by the example already given, as the two operations will give the same result.

Interest on $300 for 4 months	=	$ 6.00
Interest on 500 for 6 "	=	15.00
Interest on 400 for $10\frac{1}{2}$ "	=	21.00
Interest on 1200 for 1 month	=	6)42.00(7 months as before.

RULE.

Find the interest on each instalment for the given time, and divide the sum of these by the interest of the whole debt for one month, and the quotient will be the equated time.

As the sum of the instalments is equal to the debt, the result will be the same for any rate of interest.

For the first instalment, $300, overdue 3 months, A has to pay	$4 50
For the second instalment, $500, overdue 1 month, A has to pay	2 50
	$7 00

For the third instalment, $400, not due for 3½ months, A has to get.. $7 00

so that the amounts of interest exactly balance, and the paying of the whole, at the end of 7 months, is precisely equivalent to the paying of each instalment as it falls due. The only difference that could arise is, that it might be inconvenient for the creditor to lie out of the first instalment for the three months. In all other respects the settlement is *strictly equitable,* according to the *understanding* that exists among business men. In the first place, the difference between this and what is called "the accurate rule," is insignificantly small; and, in the second place, the "mercantile rule" saves much time, and time is equivalent to so much capital in mercantile transactions. Independently, however, of any other consideration, we may remark that when the mode of reckoning is *conventionally understood,* it becomes perfectly equitable, because every merchant knows the terms on which he can do business with any other, just as bank discount becomes perfectly equitable, because every man, before going to a bank for the discounting of a note, knows perfectly well on what terms he can have it.

Much warm discussion has been indulged in on this subject; but, as we consider the discussion more subtle than profitable, we shall dismiss the subject in a few words. We shall adopt the usual case, that A owes B $200, one-half to be paid at the present time, and the remainder at the end of two years. It is perfectly obvious that, at the end of the first year, A should pay $106, that is, the principal, *plus* the interest agreed upon. Regarding the settlement of the second instalment, if A proffers payment of the whole at once, he is clearly entitled to claim a reduction for the unexpired term. Now, the question is, what ought the reduction to be. By the mercantile rule he should pay $94, but the true present worth of $100, due at the end of the year, would be $94.33\frac{51}{53}$, so that he would have to pay $106 on the instalment over due, and $94.33\frac{51}{53}$ on the one not due, making $200.33\frac{51}{53}$, whereas the object is to find at what time interest should be chargeable to neither party.

As a further illustration of the general rule, let us suppose that J. Smith owes R. Evans $1300, of which $700 are to be paid at the end of 3 months, $100 at the end of 4 months, and the balance at the end of 8 months, to find the equated time.

We shall suppose that J. Smith agrees to pay R. Evans the whole amount at the time the debt was contracted; then J. Smith would owe R. Evans $1300, *minus* the discount for the length of time the amount was paid before it became due, viz., three months, equalling the discount on $210 for 1 month; $100, less the discount for 4 months, equalling the discount on $400 for 1 month; $500, less the discount for 8 months, equalling the discount on $4000 for 1 month. This gives a total of $2100+$400+$4000=$6500, for 1 month.

Now, it is evident that if J. Smith wished to pay the whole amount at such a time that there should be no loss to either party, he must retain this amount for such a length of time as it will take this amount to equal the discount on $6500 for 1 month, which will be $\frac{1}{1300}$ of $6500, that is, for 5 months.

To prove that 5 months must be the equated time, we have recourse to the principles laid down under the head of Interest. If a settlement is not made until the expiration of 5 months from the time the debt was contracted, then J. Smith would owe R. Evans $700, *plus* the interest of that principal during the time it remained unpaid after becoming due, viz., two months, which would give an amount of $707. So also, $100, *plus* the interest for 1 month, would be $100.50, and $500, *minus* its discount for 3 months (the length of time paid before due), would give $7.50, leaving $492.50, and $707+$100.50+$492.50=$1300.

EXERCISES.

1. T. C. Musgrove owes H. W. Field $900, of which $300 are due in 4 months; $400 in 6 months, $200 in 9 months; what is the equated time for the payment of the whole amount? Ans. 6 months.

2. E. P. Hall & Co. have in their possession 5 notes drawn by G. W. Armstrong, all dated 1st January, 1865; the first is drawn at 4 months, for $45; the second at 8 months, for $120; the third at 10 months, for $75; the fourth at 11 months, for $60; and the fifth at 15 months, for $90; for what length of time must a single note be drawn, dated 1st May, 1865, so that it may fall due at the properly equated time? Ans. 6 months.

3. A merchant sold goods as follows, on a credit of 6 months:—May 10, a bill of $600; June 12, a bill of $450; September 20, a bill of $900; at what time will the whole become due?

Ans. January 16.

4. A merchant proposed to sell goods amounting to $4000 on 8 months' credit, but the purchaser preferred to pay $\frac{1}{2}$ in cash and $\frac{1}{4}$ in 3 months; what time should be allowed him for the payment of the remainder? Ans. 2 years, 5 months.

5. A gentleman left his son $1500, to be paid as follows: $\frac{1}{5}$ in 3 months, $\frac{1}{3}$ in 4 months, $\frac{1}{4}$ in 6 months, and the remainder in 8 months; at what time ought the whole to be paid at once?

Ans. 4 mos., 15 days.

6. A merchant bought goods amounting to $6000. He agrees to pay $500 in cash, $600 in six months, $1500 in 9 months, and the remainder in 10 months; at what time ought he to pay the whole in one payment? Ans. $8\frac{31}{60}$ months.

7. There is due to a merchant $800, one-sixth of which is to be paid in 2 months, one-third in 3 months, and the remainder in 6 months; but the debtor agrees to pay one-half in cash; how long may he retain the other half, so that neither party may sustain loss?

Ans. $8\frac{2}{3}$ months.

8. A merchant sold to W. L. Brown, Esq., goods to the amount of $3051, on a credit of 6 months, from September 25th, 1864. October 4th Brown paid $476; November 12th, $375; December 5th, $800; January 1st, 1865, $200. When, in equity, ought the merchant to receive the balance?

9. A having sold B goods to the amount of $1200, left it optional with him either to take them on 8 month's credit, or to pay one-half in cash, one-fifth in two months, one-sixth in four months, and the remainder at an equated time, to correspond with the terms first named; what was the time? Ans. 4 years, 4 mos.

10. A grocer sold 484 barrels of rosin, as follows:

February 6th, 35 barrels @ $3.12½, on 4 months' time.
March 12th, 38 barrels @ 3.00, on 4 months' time.
March 12th, 411 barrels @ 2.62½, on 4 months' time.

What is the equated time for the payment of the whole?

Ans. July 9th.

11. Bought of A. B. Smith & Co. 1650 barrels of flour, at different times, and on various terms of credit, as by the following statement; what is the equated time for the payment of the whole?

May 6th, 150 barrels, at $4.50, on 3 months' credit.
May 20th, 400 barrels, at 4.75, on 4 months' credit.
July 10th, 500 barrels, at 5.00, on 5 months' credit.
August 4th, 600 barrels, at 4.25, on 4 months' credit.

Ans. November 7th.

12. J. B. Smith & Co. bought of A. Hamilton & Son 576 barrels of rosin, as follows:

May 3rd, 62 barrels @ $2.50, on 6 months' credit.

May 10th, 100 barrels @ 2.50, on 6 months' credit.
May 18th, 10 barrels @ 2.50, as cash.
May 26th, 50 barrels @ 2.75, on 30 days' credit.
May 26th, 345 barrels @ 2.50, on six months' credit.
May 26th, 9 barrels @ 2.00, on six months' credit.

What is the equated time for the payment of the whole?

Ans. November 3rd.

13. Purchased goods of J. R. Worthington & Co., at different times, and on various terms of credit, as by the following statement:

March	1st, 1863, a bill of	$675.25,	on 3 months' credit.
July	4th, 1863, a bill of	376.18,	on 4 months' credit.
September	25th, 1863, a bill of	821.75,	on 2 months' credit.
October	1st, 1863, a bill of	961.25,	on 8 months' credit.
January	1st, 1864, a bill of	144.50,	on 3 months' credit.
February	10th, 1864, a bill of	811.30,	on 6 months' credit.
March	12th, 1864, a bill of	567.70,	on 5 months' credit.
April	15th, 1864, a bill of	369.80,	on 4 months' credit.

What is the equated time for the payment of the whole?

Ans. March 16th, 1864.

AVERAGING ACCOUNTS.

When one merchant trades with another, exchanging merchandise, or giving and receiving cash, the memorandum of the transactions is called an *Account Current*. If the goods be purchased at different dates, or for different terms of credit, and some are not due while others are overdue, the fixing on a time when all may be settled, so that no interest shall be chargeable to either party, is called *Averaging the Account*.

Since interest is the standard to which is referred the benefit of receiving money before it is due, so that in the meantime it can be used in trade, and also the damage of not getting it when due, it is fair and proper that interest should be charged on all sums overdue, and deducted from all not due. In illustration, let us suppose that A sells goods to B, March 2, on 4 months' credit, and again an equal amount on March 20, on 6 months' credit; the first will be due on July 2, and the second on September 20. Should B tender payment of the whole on June 2, he would be entitled to claim interest for one month on the first purchase, and for three months and eighteen days on the second. But if payment be delayed till August 2, A would be entitled to one month's interest on the first purchase, and B to the interest on the second for one month and eighteen days, so that there would be in favour of B, on the whole, a balance of interest for eighteen days. Again, supposing the settlement is not made till September 20, when all is due, no interest can be either charged or claimed on the second purchase, the term of credit having just then expired; but as the first debt is two months and eighteen days overdue, A is entitled to interest on it for that period. If neither is paid till after September 20, A has a right to claim interest on each for the period it has been overdue. But this regulates only one side of the account. In order to settle the other, let us suppose that B has, in the meantime, sold goods to A, it is obvious that B's claims on A must be settled on the very same principle, and that therefore the final result must be simply the finding of the balance. It is more usual, however, in accounts current, to fix on a time such that the interest due by A shall exactly balance that due by B. To illustrate this, let us suppose a case corresponding to a ledger account:

R. EVANS.

1865.	Dr.
July 21, To Merchandise on 2 months' credit...	$200
July 25, To Cash....................................	150
Aug. 24, To Merchandise on 4 months' credit...	100
Sept. 21, To Merchandise on 3 months' credit...	250
	$700

1865.	Cr.
August 1, By Cash................................	$100
August 20, By Merchandise at 22 days..........	110
Sept'r 30, By Cash	180
Balance..	310
	$700

To find in this case at what time the account may be settled so that interest shall be chargeable to neither party. Equating the time, as in equation of payments, we have the following operation:

DR.			CR.		
1865			1865.		
July 25......150× 0			August 1. ......100× 0		
Sept. 21.......200× 58=11600			Sept. 12........110×22= 2420		
Decr. 24.......250×152=38000			Sept. 30........180×71=12780		
Decr. 21.......100×149=14900				390	15200
	700	64500	15200÷390=39 days.		
64500÷700=92 days.			Due 39 days from August 1, viz., on September 9.		
Due 92 days from July 25, viz., on October 25.					

Time from September 9, to October 25=46 days.
Excess of debit above credit 700—390=310.
390×46=17940, and 17940÷310=58 days, nearly.

Counting 58 days forward, from October 25, will bring us to December 22, the time required for a settlement, with interest chargeable to neither party. Here the time is counted forward from the average date of the larger side which becomes due last, but had it become due first, we should have counted backward.

The first transaction on the debit side being two months' credit from July 21, is not to be taken into consideration till September 21. The second transaction, being a cash one, and therefore considered as so much due, will therefore mark the date from which all others shall be reckoned; and, since there is no interval of time, we write it without a multiplier. The next transaction has a term of credit extending to 152 days, and therefore we write 250×152= 11600.

The term of the next extends from September 21 to December 21, a period of 149 days, and we write 100×149=14900. The sum of the debits is $700, and the sum of the results obtained by multiplying each item by the number of days it has to run from July 25 is $64500. Then 64500÷700=92, the equated time in days for the debit side. Now, as already explained, the interest for $700 for 92 days will be the same as the interest of $64500 for 1 day. Hence, the debits are due 92 days from July 25, viz., on October 25.

In like manner, on the credit side, the first transaction being a cash one, we start from its date, August 1, and, as there is no interval, we have no multiplier. The second being merchandise, on 22 days' credit, we write 110×22=2420. The third is cash paid 71 days after August 1, and we write 180×71=12780.

Had the account been settled on September 9, the debits would have been paid 46 days before coming due, and the credit side would have gained and the debit side lost the interest for that time.

Again, we must consider how long it would take the balance, $310, to produce the same interest that $390 would produce in 46 days. It is obvious that whatever interest $390 gives in 46 days will require 46 times $390 for $1 to produce the same interest, that is, 390×46=17940 days, and it will require 17940÷310=58 days, for $310 to produce the same interest. If the settlement is made on October 25, the latest date, then the credit has been due 46 days, and therefore bearing interest; and in order that the debit side may be increased by an equal amount, the time must be extended beyond October 25, that is, it must be counted *forward.* For the same reason, if the greater side had become due first, then the balance must be considered as due at a *previous* date, and therefore we must count *backward.*

An account may be averaged from any date, but either the first or the last will be found the most convenient. The first due is generally used.

On the principles now explained may be founded the following

RULE.

Find the equated time when each side becomes due.

Multiply the amount of the smaller side by the number of days between the two average dates, and divide the product by the balance of the account.

The quotient thus obtained will be the time that the balance becomes due, counted from the average date of the larger side, **FORWARD** *when the amount of that side becomes due* **LAST**, *but* **BACKWARD** *when it becomes due* **FIRST**.

The *cash value* of a balance depends on the time of settlement. If the settlement be made *before* the balance is due, the interest for the unexpired time is to be *deducted;* but if the settlement is not made till *after* the balance is due, interest is to be *added* for the time it is overdue.

EXERCISES.

In J. H. Marsden's Ledger, we find the following accounts, which, on being equated, stand as follows; at what time should the respective balances commence to draw interest:

1. *Dr.* J. S. PECKHAM. *Cr.*
May 16th, 1865.........$724.45. | July 29th, 1865.........$486.80.
Ans. December 15th, 1864.

2. *Dr.* NELSON BOSTFORD. *Cr.*
November 19th, 1865 ......$635. | December 12th, 1865......$950.
Ans. January 27th, 1866.

3. *Dr.* JAMES CROW & CO. *Cr.*
February 24th, 1866....$512.25. | June 10th, 1865.........$309,70.
Ans. March 27th, 1867.

4. *Dr.* J. H. BURRITT & CO. *Cr.*
March 17th, 1866..........$145. | January 15th, 1866.....$695.60.
Ans. December 30th, 1865.

5. *Dr.* M. McDONALD. *Cr.*
August 27th, 1865..........$341. | November 7th, 1865.......$247.

6. *Dr.* JAMES I. MUSGROVE. *Cr.*
July 20th, 1866............$711. | April 14th, 1866..........$1260.
Ans. December 9th, 1865.

7. *Dr.* THOS. A. BRYCE & CO. *Cr.*
June 24th, 1864...........$1418. | September 7th, 1865......$2346.

8. *Dr.* E. R. CARPENTER. *Cr.*
December 2nd, 1865...$1040.80. | August 13th, 1865....$1112.40.

9. Required the time when the balance of the following account becomes subject to interest, allowing the merchandise to have been on 8 months' credit?

Dr. A. B. SMITH & CO. *Cr.*

1864.			1865.		
May 1,	To Mdse............	$300.00	Jan. 1,	By Cash....	$500.00
July 7,	" "	759.96	Feb. 18,	" Mdse. ..	481.75
Sep. 11,	" "	417.20	Mar. 19,	" Cash....	750.25
Nov. 25,	" "	287.70	April 1,	" Draft...	210.00
Dec. 20,	" "	571.10	May 25,	" Cash....	100.00

Ans. August 5, 1865.

10. When will the balance of the following account fall due, the merchandise items being on 6 months' credit?

Dr. J. K. WHITE. *Cr.*

1865.			1865.		
May 1,	To Mdse............	$312.40	June 14,	By Cash....	$200.00
May 23,	" "	85.70	July 30,	" Mdse....	185.90
June 12,	" Cash paid dft..	105.00	Aug. 10,	" Cash....	100.00
July 29,	" Mdse............	243.80	Aug. 21,	" Mdse....	58.00
Aug. 4,	" "	92.10	Sept. 28,	" "	45.10
Sept. 18,	" Cash............	50.00			

Ans. January 12, 1866.

11. When does the balance of the following account become subject to interest?

Dr. W. H. MUSGROVE. *Cr.*

1864.			1864.		
Aug. 10,	To Mdse 4 mos.	$285.30	Oct. 13,	By Cash.......	$400.00
Aug. 17,	" " 60 days	192.60	Oct. 26,	" "	150.00
Sept. 21,	" " 30 "	256.80	Dec. 15,	" Mdse 2 mos	345.80
Oct. 13,	" Cash p'd dft.	190.00	Dec. 30,	" " 4 "	230.40
Nov. 25,	" Mdse 6 mos.	432.20	1865.		
Nov. 30,	" " 90 days	215.25	Jan. 4,	" Cash.......	340.30
Dec. 18,	" " 2 mos.	68.90	Jan. 21,	" "	180.00
1865.					
Jan. 31,	" Cash.........	100.00			

12. In the following account, when did the balance become due, the merchandise articles being on 6 months' credit?

Dr. R. J. BRYCE in account with D. HICKS & Co. *Cr.*

1864.			1864.		
Jan. 4,	To Mdse............	$ 96.57	Jan. 30,	By Cash...	$240.00
Jan. 18,	" "	57.67	April 3,	" " ...	48.88
Feb. 4,	" Cash paid draft.	80.00	May 22,	" " ...	50.00
Feb. 4,	" Mdse............	38.96			
Feb. 9,	" Cash paid draft.	50.26			
Mar. 3,	" Mdse...........	154.46			
Mar. 24,	" "	42.30			
April 9,	" "	23.60			
May 15,	" "	28.46			
May 21,	" "	177.19			

Ans. December 22nd, 1864.

13. When, in equity, should the balance of the following account be payable?

Dr. J. McDonald & Co. *Cr.*

1865.			1864.		
Jan. 3,	To Cash....	$200	Sept. 20,	By Mdse, 6 mos..	$583.17
Jan. 31,	" "	300	Oct. 27,	" " 4 " ..	321.00
Feb. 8,	" "	75	Dec. 5,	" " 6 " ..	137.00
Feb. 21,	" "	100	1865.		
Mar. 10,	" "	350	Jan. 18,	" " 60 days.	98.75
Mar. 24,	" "	25	Feb. 26,	" " 6 mos..	53.98
Apr. 12,	" "	40	Apr. 15,	" " 4 " ..	634.00
June 1,	" "	80	June 12,	" " 2 " ..	97.23
June 20,	" "	125	Sept. 21,	" " 6 " ..	84.00
July 4,	" "	268	Dec. 29,	" " 6 " ..	132.14
Sept. 27,	" "	250			
Dec. 9,	" "	100			

Ans. October 10, 1866.

CASH BALANCE.

To find the true cash balance of an account, when each item draws interest.

EXAMPLE.

What is the balance of the following account on January 19th, 1866, a credit of three months being allowed on the merchandise, money being worth 6 per cent.?

Dr. Musgrove & Wright. *Cr.*

1865.			1865.		
Mar. 12,	To Merchandise....	$340.00	Apr. 20,	By Mdse...	$200.00
Apr. 21,	" " ...	150.00	May 4,	" Cash....	110.00
May 6,	" Cash paid draft	165.00	June 15,	" "	230.00
May 27,	" Mdse...........	215.00	Aug. 10,	" Mdse...	180.00
July 16,	" Cash	100.00	Sept. 23,	" Cash....	50.00
Sept. 10,	" Mdse...........	310.00	Nov. 12,	" " ...	50.00
Oct. 19,	" "	120.00	Dec. 15,	" " ...	100.00

SOLUTION.

Debits.			Credits.		
Due.			Due.		
June 12,	$340×221=	75140	July 20,	$200×183=	36600
July 21,	150×182=	27300	May 4,	110×260=	28600
May 6,	165×258=	42570	June 15,	230×218=	50140
Aug. 27,	215×145=	31175	Nov. 10,	180× 70=	12600
July 16,	100×187=	18700	Sept. 23,	50×118=	5900
Dec. 10,	310× 40=	12400	Nov. 12,	50× 68=	3400
Jan. 19,	120× 0=	0	Dec. 15,	100× 35=	3500
	$1400	6)207285		$920	6)140740
		$34.547			$23.456

The different items on the debit and credit sides of the account being on interest from the date on which it becomes due until the time of settlement, the total interest of all the debit items will be the same as the interest of $207285 for one day, or the interest of $1 for 207285 days, which is $34.547. So also, the total interest of all the credit items will be the same as the interest of $140740 for one day, or the interest of $1 for 140740 days, which is $23.456. Now, since each side of the account is to be increased by its interest, the cash balance will be represented by the number denoting the difference between the two sides of the account, after the interest is added; thus, $1400+$34.547=$1434.547, amount of debit side, and $920+$23.456=$943.456, amount of credit side, then $1434.547—$943.456=$491.09, cash balance.

SECOND METHOD.

Debits.					Credits.				
			Days.	Int.				Days.	Int.
Int. on	$340	for	221=	$12.523	Int. on	$200	for	183=	$6.100
"	150	"	182=	4.550	"	110	"	260=	4.766
"	165	"	258=	7.095	"	230	"	218=	8.356
"	215	"	145=	5.195	"	180	"	70=	2.100
"	100	"	187=	3.116	"	50	"	118=	.983
"	310	"	40=	2.066	"	50	"	68=	.566
"	120	"	0		"	100	"	35=	.583
	$1400			$34.545		$920			$23.454

Now, $34.545 debit interest—$23.454 credit interest=$11.09,

the balance of interest, and $1400, amount of debit items+$11.09 =$1411.09, and $1411.09—$920 amount of credit items=$491.09 the cash balance, which is the same as obtained by the first solution. Hence from the foregoing we deduce the following

RULE.

Multiply each item of debit and credit by the number of days intervening between its becoming due and the time of settlement. Then consider the sums of the products of the debit and credit items as so many dollars, and find the interest on each for one day, which will be the interest, respectively, of the debit and credit items.

Place the balance of interest on its own side of the account, and the difference then between the two sides will be the true balance; or,

Find the interest on each item from the date on which it becomes due to the time of settlement. The difference of the sums of interests, on the debit and credit sides of the account will represent the balance of interest, which is placed on its own side of the account, and the difference then between the two sides will be the true balance.

NOTE.—If any item should not come due until after the time of settlement, the side upon which it is, should be diminished, or the opposite side increased by the interest of such item from the time of settlement until due.

EXERCISES.

1. What will be the cash balance of the following account if settled on January 1, 1865, allowing interest at 8 per cent. on each item after it is due?

Dr. R. EVANS in account with JOHN JONES. *Cr.*

1864.			1864.		
June 11,	To Mdse, 4 mos.	$315.00	Apr. 15,	By Mdse, 3 mos.	$350.00
June 29,	" " 6 "	180.00	May 10,	" " 4 "	120.00
July 18,	" Cash p'd dft.	200.00	June 12,	" " 6 "	240.00
Aug. 25,	" Cash.........	75.00	June 30,	" Cash.........	100.00
Aug. 31,	" Mdse, 2 mos.	50.00	July 15,	" "	90.00
Sept. 3,	" " 1 "	100.00	July 27,	" "	80.00
Sept. 20,	" Cash.........	80.00	Aug. 6,	" Mdse, as cash	100.00
Oct. 14,	" "	150.00	Aug. 20,	" Cash.........	175.00
Oct. 19.	" Mdse, as cash	300.00	Aug. 30,	" Mdse, 3 mos.	75.00

Ans. $110.86.

2. A. B. Smith is in account and interest with J. K. Amos & Co., as follows:—Debtor, January 1, 1865, to merchandise, on 6 months,

$156.10; February 3, to cash paid draft, $100; March 20, to merchandise, on 4 months, $316.90; March 30, to merchandise, on 4 months, $162; May 15, to cash paid draft, $100; August 20, to merchandise, on 6 months, $213. Creditor, February 1, by cash, $120; March 20, by merchandise, on 4 months, $420.16; May 1, by merchandise, on 6 months, $300: July 1, by merchandise, on 4 months, $50; September 10, by merchandise, on 4 months, $99.84. Required, the true balance, if settled on December 1, 1865, interest being at 6 per cent.? Ans. $61.36.

3. Required the true balance, March 25, 1865, on the following account, each item drawing 7 per cent. interest from its date. A. B. Lyman in account and interest with John Russell & Co.:— Debtor, July 4, 1864, to merchandise, $200; September 8, to merchandise, $300; September 25, to merchandise, $250; October 1, to merchandise, $600; November 20, to merchandise, $400; December 12, to merchandise, $500; January 15, 1865, to merchandise, $100; March 11, to merchandise, $120. Creditor, July 20, 1864, by cash, $300; August 15, by cash, $350; September 1, by cash, $400; November 1, by cash, $320; December 6, by merchandise, $600; December 20, by cash, $100; February 1, 1865, by cash, $200; February 28, by merchandise, $150. Ans. $50.64.

ALLIGATION.

Alligation is the method of making calculations regarding the compounding of articles of different kinds or different values. It is a Latin word, which means *binding to*, or binding together.

It is usual to distinguish alligation as being of two kinds, *medial* and *alternate.*

ALLIGATION MEDIAL.

Alligation medial relates to the average value of articles compounded, when the actual quantities and rates are given.

EXAMPLE.

A miller mixes three kinds of grain: 10 bushels, at 40 cents a bushel; 15 bushels, at 50 cents a bushel; and 25 bushels, at 70 cents a bushel; it is required to find the value of the mixture.

10 bushels, at 40 cents a bushel, will be worth 400 cents.,
15 bushels, at 50 cents a bushel, will be worth 750 cents.,
25 bushels, at 70 cents a bushel, will be worth 1750 cents.,

giving a total of 50 bushels and 2900 cents, and hence the mixture is $2900 \div 50 = 58$ cents, the price of the mixture per bushel. Hence the

RULE.

Find the value of each of the articles, and divide the sum of their values by the number denoting the sum of the articles, and the quotient will be the price of the mixture.

EXERCISES.

1. A farmer mixes 20 bushels of wheat, worth $2.00 per bushel, with 40 bushels of oats, worth 50 cents per bushel; what is the price of one bushel of the mixture? Ans. $1.

2. A grocer mixes 10 pounds of tea, at 40 cents per pound; 20 pounds, at 45 cents per pound, and 30 pounds, at 50 cents per pound; what is a pound of this mixture worth? Ans. $46\frac{2}{3}$ cents.

3. A liquor merchant mixed together 40 gallons of wine, worth 80 cents a gallon; 25 gallons of brandy, worth 70 cents a gallon; and 15 gallons of wine, worth $1.50 a gallon; what was a gallon of this mixture worth? Ans. 90 cents.

4. A farmer mixed together 30 bushels of wheat, worth $1 per bushel; 72 bushels of rye, worth 60 cents per bushel; and 60 bushels of barley, worth 40 cents per bushel; what was the value of $2\frac{1}{2}$ bushels of the mixture? Ans. $1.50.

5. A goldsmith mixes together 4 pounds of gold, of 18 carats fine; 2 pounds, of 20 carats fine; 5 pounds, of 16 carats fine; and 3 pounds, of 22 carats fine; how many carats fine is one pound of the mixture? Ans. $18\frac{3}{7}$.

ALLIGATION ALTERNATE.

Alligation alternate is the method of finding how much of several ingredients, the quantity or value of which is known, must be combined to make a compound of a given value.

CASE I.

Given, the value of several ingredients, to make a compound of a given value.

EXAMPLE

How much sugar that is worth 6 cents, 10 cents, and 13 cents per pound, must be mixed together, so that the mixture may be worth 12 cents per pound?

SOLUTION.

		Gain.	Loss.
12 cents.	1 lb., at 6 cents, is a gain of 6 cents.		
	1 lb., at 10 cents, is a gain of 2 cents.	8	
	1 lb., at 13 cents, is a loss of 1 cent.		1
	7 lbs. more, at 13 cents, is a loss of......		7
		Gain 8	Loss 8

It is evident, in forming a mixture of sugar worth 6, 10 and 13 cents per pound so as to be worth 12 cents, that the gains obtained in putting in sugar of *less* value than the average price must exactly balance the losses sustained in putting in sugar of *greater* value than the average price. Hence in our example, sugar that is worth 6 cents per pound when put in the mixture will sell for 12, thereby giving a gain of 6 cents on every pound of this sugar put in the mixture. So also sugar that is worth 10 cents per pound, when in the mixture will bring 12, so that a gain of 2 cents is obtained on every pound of this sugar used in the compound. Again, sugar that is worth 13 cents per pound, on being put into the mixture will sell for only 12 cents, consequently a loss of 1 cent is sustained on every pound of this sugar used in forming the mixture. In this manner we find that in taking *one* pound of each of the different qualities of sugar there is a gain of 8 cents, and a loss of only 1 cent. Now, our losses must equal our gains, and therefore we have yet to lose 7 cents, and as there is only one quality of sugar in the mixture by which we can lose, it is plain that we must take as much more sugar at 13 cents as will make up the loss, and that will require 7 pounds. Therefore, to form a mixture of sugar worth 6, 10 and 13 cents per pound, so as to be worth 12 cents per pound, we will require 1 pound at 6 cents, 1 pound at 10 cents, and 1 pound at the 13 cents+7 pounds of the same, which must be taken to make the loss equal to the gain.

By making a mixture of any number of times these answers, it will be observed, that the compound will be correctly formed. Hence we can readily perceive that any number of answers may be obtained to all exercises of this kind. From what has been said we deduce the following

RULE.

Find how much is gained or lost by taking one of each kind of the proposed ingredients. Then take one or more of the ingredients, or such parts of them as will make the gains and losses equal.

EXERCISES.

1. A grocer wishes to mix together tea worth 80 cents, $1.20, $1.80 and $2.40 per pound, so as to make a mixture worth $1.60 per pound; how many pounds of each sort must he take?

Ans. 1 lb. at 80 cents; 1 lb. at $1.20; 2 lbs. at $1.80, and 1 lb. at $2.40.

2. How much corn, at 42 cents, 60 cents, 67 cents, and 78 cents per bushel, must be mixed together that the compound may be worth 64 cents per bushel?

Ans. 1 bush. at 42 cts.; 1 bush. at 60 cts.; 4 bush. at 67 cts.; and 1 bush. at 78 cts.

3. It is required to mix wine, worth 60 cents, 80 cents, and $1.20 per gallon, with water, that the mixture may be worth 75 cts. per gallon; how much of each sort must be taken?

Ans. 1 gal. of water; 1 gal. of wine at 60 cts.; 9 gal. at 80 cts.; and 1 gal at $1.20.

4. In what proportion must grain, valued at 50 cents, 56 cents, 62 cents, and 75 cents per bushel, be mixed together, that the compound may be 62 cents per bushel?

Give, at least, three answers, and prove the work to be correct.

5. A produce dealer mixed together corn, worth 75 cents per bushel; oats, worth 40 cents per bushel; rye, worth 65 cents per bushel, and wheat, worth $1 per bushel, so that the mixture was worth 80 cents per bushel; what quantity of each did he take?

Give four answers, and prove the work to be correctly done in each case.

CASE II.

When one or more of the ingredients are limited in quantity, to find the other ingredients.

EXAMPLE.

How much barley, at 40 cents; oats, at 30 cents, and corn, at 60 cents per bushel, must be mixed with 20 bushels of rye. at 85 cents per bushel, so that the mixture may be worth 60 cents per bushel ?

SOLUTION.

Bush.	Cents.		Gain.	Loss.
1	at 40,	gives..................	.20	...
1	at 30,	gives..................	.30	...
1	at 60,	gives..................	.00	.00
20	at 85,	gives..................	...	5.00
			.50	5.00
9	at 40,	gives..................	1.80	...
9	at 30,	gives..................	2.70	...
			$5.00	$5.00

By taking 1 bushel of barley, at 40 cents, 1 bushel of oats at 30 cents, and 1 bushel of corn at 60, in connection with 20 bushels of rye at 85 cents per bushel, we observe that our gains amount to 50 cents and our losses to $5.00. Now, to make the gains equal the losses, we have to take 9 bushels more at 40 cents, and 9 bushels more at 30 cents. This gives us for the answer 1 bushel+9=10 bushels of barley, 1 bushel+9=10 bushels of oats, and 1 bushel of corn. From this we deduce the

RULE.

Find how much is gained or lost, by taking one of each of the proposed ingredients, in connection with the ingredient which is limited, and if the gain and loss be not equal, take such of the proposed ingredients, or such parts of them, as will make the gain and loss equal.

EXERCISES.

6. How much gold, of 16 and 18 carats fine, must be mixed with 90 ounces, of 22 carats fine, that the compound may be 20 carats fine ?

Ans. 41 ounces of 16 carats fine, and 8 of 18 carats fine.

7. A grocer mixes teas worth $1.20, $1, and 60 cents per pound, with 20 pounds, at 40 cents per pound ; how much of each sort must he take to make the composition worth 80 cents per pound?

8. How much barley, at 50 cents per bushel, and at 60 cents per bushel. must be mixed with ten bushels of pease, worth 80 cents

per bushel, and 6 bushels of rye, worth 85 cents per bushel, to make a mixture worth 75 cents per bushel?

Ans. 3 bushels, at 50 cents; $2\frac{1}{3}$ bushels, at 60 cents.

9. How many pounds of sugar, at 8, 14, and 13 cents per pound, must be mixed with 3 pounds, worth $9\frac{1}{4}$ cents per pound; 4 pounds, worth $10\frac{1}{2}$ cents per pound; and 6 pounds, worth $13\frac{1}{2}$ cents per pound, so that the mixture may be worth $12\frac{1}{2}$ cents per pound?

Ans. 1 lb., at 8 cts.; 9 lbs., at 14 cts.; and $5\frac{1}{2}$ lbs., at 13 cts

CASE III.

To find the quantity of each ingredient, when the sum of the ingredients and the average price are given.

EXAMPLE.

A grocer has sugar worth 8, 10, 12 and 14 cents per pound, and he wishes to make a mixture of 240 pounds, worth 11 cents per pound; how much of each sort must he take?

SOLUTION.

	Gain.	Loss.
1 lb., at 8 cents, gives....................	3	.
1 lb., at 10 cents, gives....................	1	.
1 lb., at 12 cents, gives....................	.	1
1 lb., at 14 cents, gives....................	.	3
4 lbs.	4	4

240 lbs.÷4=60 lbs. of each sort.

By taking 60 lbs. of each sort we have the required quantity, and it will be observed that the gains will exactly balance the losses, consequently the work is correct. Hence the

RULE.

Find the least quantity of each ingredient by CASE I., *Then divide the given amount by the sum of the ingredients already found, and multiply the quotient by the quantities found for the proportional quantities.*

10. What quantity of three different kinds of raisins, worth 15 cents, 18 cents, and 25 cents per pound, must be mixed together to fill a box containing 680 lbs., and to be worth 20 cents per pound?

Ans. 200 lbs., at 15 cents; 200 lbs., at 18 cents; and 280 lbs., at 25 cents.

16

11. How much sugar, at 6 cents, 8 cents, 10 cents, and 12 cents per pound, must be mixed together, so as to form a compound of 200 pounds, worth 9 cents per pound ? Ans. 50 lbs. of each.

12. How much water must be mixed with wine, worth 80 cents per gallon, so as to fill a vessel of 90 gallons, which may be offered at 50 cents per gallon ? Ans. $56\frac{2}{8}$ gals. wine, and $33\frac{6}{8}$ gals. water.

13. A wine merchant has wines worth $1, $1.25, $1.50, $1.75, and $2. per gallon, and he wishes to form a compound to fill a 150 gallon cask that will sell at $1.40 per gallon; how many gallons of each sort must he take ? Ans. 54 of $1, and 24 of each of the others.

14. A grocer has sugars worth 8 cents, 10 cents 12 cents, and 20 cents per pound; with these he wishes to fill a hogshead that would contain 200 pounds; how much of each kind must he take, so that the mixture may be worth 15 cents per pound?

Ans. $33\frac{1}{3}$ lbs. of 8, 10, and 12 cents, and 100 lbs. of 20 cents.

15. A grocer requires to mix 240 pounds of different kinds of raisins, worth 8 cents, 12 cents, 18 cents, and 24 cents per lb., so that the mixture shall be worth 10 cents per pound; how much must be taken of each kind?

Ans. 192 lbs. of 8 cents, and 16 lbs. of each of the other kinds.

MONEY; ITS NATURE AND VALUE.

MONEY is the medium through which the incomes of the different members of the community are distributed to them, and the measure by which they estimate their possessions.

The precious metals have, amongst almost all nations, been the standard of value from the earliest time. Except in the very rudest state of society, men have felt the necessity of having some article, of more or less intrinsic value, that can at any time be exchanged for different commodities. No other substances were so suitable for this purpose as gold and silver. They are easily divisible, portable, and among the least imperishable of all substances. The work of dividing the precious metals, and marking or coining them, is generally undertaken by the Government of the country.

Money is a commodity, and its value is determined, like that of other commodities, by demand and supply, and cost of production. When there is a large supply of money it becomes cheap; in other words, more of it is required to purchase other articles. If all the money in circulation were doubled, prices would be doubled. The usefulness of money depends a great deal upon the rapidity of its circulation. A ten-dollar bill that changes hands ten times in a month, purchases, during that time, a hundred dollars' worth of goods. A small amount of money, kept in rapid circulation, does the same work as a far larger sum used more gradually: Therefore, whatever may be the quantity of money in a country, only that part of it will effect prices which goes into circulation, and is actually exchanged for goods.

Money hoarded, or kept in reserve by individuals, does not act upon prices. An increase in the circulating medium, conformable in duration and extent to a temporary activity in business, does not raise prices, it merely prevents the fall that would otherwise ensue from its temporary scarcity.

PAPER CURRENCY.

PAPER CURRENCY may be of two kinds—convertible and inconvertible. When it is issued to represent gold, and can at any time be exchanged for gold, it is called convertible. When it is issued by the sovereign power in a State, and is made to pass for money, by merely calling it money, and from the fact that it is received in payment of taxes, and made a legal tender, it is known as an inconvertible currency. Nothing more is needful to make a person accept anything as money, than the persuasion that it will be taken from him on the same terms by others. That alone would ensure its currency, but would not regulate its value. This evidently cannot depend, as in the case of gold and silver, upon the cost of production, for that is very trifling. It depends, then, upon the supply or the quantity in circulation. While the issue of inconvertible currency is limited to something under the amount of bullion in circulation, it will on the whole maintain a par value. But as soon as gold and silver are driven out of circulation by the flood of inconvertible currency, prices begin to rise, and get higher with every additional issue. Among other commodities the price of gold and silver articles will rise, and the coinage will rise in value as mere bullion. The paper currency will then become proportionably depreciated, as compared with the metallic currency of other countries. It would be quite impossible for these results to follow the issue of convertible paper for which gold could at any time be obtained.

All variations in the value of the circulating medium are mischievous; they disturb existing contracts and expectations, and the liability to such disturbing influences renders every pecuniary engagement of long date entirely precarious.

A convertible paper currency is, in many respects, beneficial. It is a more convenient medium of circulation. It is clearly a gain to the issuers, who, until the notes are returned for payment, obtain the use of them as if they were a real capital, and that, without any loss to the community.

THE CURRENCY OF CANADA.

In Canada there are two kinds of currency; the one is called the old or Halifax currency, reckoned in pounds, shillings, pence and fractions of a penny; the other is reckoned by dollars and cents as already explained under the head of Decimal Coinage. The equivalent in gold of the pound currency is 101.321 grains Troy weight of the standard of fineness prescribed by law for the gold coins of the united kingdom of Great Britain and Ireland. The only gold coins now in circulation in Britain are the sovereign, value one pound, or twenty shillings sterling; and the half sovereign, ten shillings. The dollar is one-fourth of the pound currency, and the pound sterling is equal to \$4.86$\frac{2}{3}$. In the year 1786, the congress of the United States adopted the decimal currency, the dollar being the unit, and the system was introduced into Canada in 1858. By the term *legal tender* is meant the proffer of payment of an account in the currency of any country as established by law. Copper is a legal tender in Canada to the amount of one shilling or twenty cents, and silver to the amount of ten dollars. The British sovereign of lawful weight passes current, and is a legal tender to any amount paid in that coin. There is a silver currency proper to Canada, though United States' coins are most in circulation. The gold eagle of the United States, coined before July 1, 1834, is a legal tender for \$10.66$\frac{2}{3}$ of the coin current in this province. The same coin issued after that is a legal tender for \$10.

EXCHANGE.

It often becomes necessary to send money from one town or country to another for various purposes, generally in payment for goods. The usual mode of making and receiving payments between distant places is by bills of exchange. A merchant in Liverpool. whom we shall call A. B., has received a consignment of flour from C. D., of Chicago; and another man, E. F., in Liverpool, has shipped a quantity of cloth, in value equal to the flour, to G. H. in Chicago. There arises, in this transaction, an indebtedness to Chicago for the flour, as well as an indebtedness from Chicago for the cloth. It is evidently unnecessary that A. B., in Liverpool, should send money to C. D. in Chicago, and that G. H., in Chicago, should send an equal sum to E. F. in Liverpool. The one debt may be applied in payment of the other, and by this plan the expense and risk attending the double transmission of the money may be saved. C. D. draws on A. B. for the amount which he owes to him; and G. H. having an equal amount *to pay* in Liverpool, buys this bill from C. D., and sends it to E. F., who, at the maturity of the bill, presents it to A. B. for payment. In this way the debt due from Chicago to Liverpool, and the debt due from Liverpool to Chicago are both paid without any coin passing from one place to the other.

An arrangement of this kind can always be made when the debts due between the different places are equal in amount. But if there is a greater sum due from one place than from the other, the debts cannot be simply written off against one another. Indeed, when a person desires to make a remittance to a foreign country, he does not make a personal search for some one who has money to receive from that country, and ask him for a bill of exchange. There are exchange brokers and bankers whose business this is. They buy bills from those who have money to receive, and sell bills to those who have money to pay. A person going to a broker to buy a bill may very likely receive one that has been bought the same day from a merchant. If the broker has not on hand any exchange that he has bought, he will often give a bill on his own foreign correspondent; and to place his correspondent in funds to meet it, he will remit to him all the exchange which he has bought and not re-sold.

When brokers find that they are asked for more bills than are offered to them, they do not absolutely refuse to give them. To enable their correspondents to meet the bills at maturity, as they have no exchange to send, they have to remit funds in gold and silver. There are the expenses of freight and insurance upon the specie, besides the occupation of a certain amount of capital involved in this; and an increased price, or premium, is charged upon the exchange to cover all.

The reverse of this happens when brokers find that more bills are offered to them than they can sell or find use for. Exchange on the foreign country then falls to a discount, and can be purchased at a lower rate by those who require to make payments.

There are other influences that disturb the exchange between different countries. Expectations of receiving large payments from a foreign country will have one effect, and the fear of having to make larger payments will have the opposite effect.

AMERICAN EXCHANGE

Exchange between Canada and the United States, especially the northern, is a matter of every day occurrence on account of the proximity of the two countries, and the incessant intercourse between them, both of a social and commercial character. The exigencies of the Northern States arising from the late war, compelled them to issue, to an enormous extent, an inconvertible paper currency, known by the name of "Greenbacks." As the value of these depended mainly on the stability of the government and the issue of the war, public confidence wavered, and in consequence, the value of this issue sunk materially. This caused a gradual rise in the value of gold until it reached the enormous premium of nearly two hundred per cent., or a quotation of nearly three hundred per cent., that is, it took nearly three hundred dollars in Greenbacks to purchase one hundred dollars in gold. It is to be hoped and expected, however, that as peace is now restored, matters will soon find their former level.

It has been deemed essential that this should be distinctly explained, as it has brought about a necessity for a constant calculation of the relative values of gold and greenbacks, and has generated an extensive business in that species of exchange.

When the term "American currency" is used in the following exercises it is understood to be Greenbacks.

CASE I.

To find the value of $1, American currency, when gold is at a premium.

EXAMPLE.

When gold is quoted at 140, or 40 per cent. premium, what is the value of $1, American currency?

SOLUTION.

Since gold is at a premium of 40 per cent., it requires 140 cents of American funds to equal in value $1, or 100 cents in gold. Hence the value of $1, American money, will be represented by the number of times 140 is contained in 100, which is .71$\frac{3}{7}$ or 71$\frac{3}{7}$ cents. Hence to find the value of $1 of any depreciated currency reckoned in dollars and cents, we deduce the following

RULE.

Divide 100 *cents by* 100 *plus the rate of premium on gold, and the quotient will be the value of* $1.

Subtract this from $1, *and the remainder will be the rate of discount on the given currency.*

CASE II.

To find the value of any given sum of American currency when gold is at a premium.

EXAMPLES.

What is the value of $280, American money, when gold is quoted at 140, or 40 per cent. premium?

SOLUTION.

We find by Case I. the value of $1 to be 71$\frac{3}{7}$ cents. Now, it is evident that if 71$\frac{3}{7}$ cents be the value of $1, the value of $280 will be 280 times 71$\frac{3}{7}$ cents, which is $200, or $280÷1.40=28000÷140=$200. Hence we have the following

RULE.

Multiply the value of $1 *by the number denoting the given amount of American money, and the product will be the gold value; or,*

Divide the given sum of American money by 100 (*the number of cents in* $1,) *plus the premium, and the quotient will be the value in gold.*

CASE III.

To find the premium on gold when American money is quoted at a certain rate per cent. discount.

EXAMPLE.

When the discount on American money is 40 per cent., what is the premium on gold ?

SOLUTION.

If American money is at a discount of 40 per cent., the discount on $1 would be 40 cents, and consequently the value of $1 would be equal to $1.00—40 cents, equal to 60 cents. Now, if 60 cents in gold be worth $1 in American currency, $1 or 100 cents in gold would be worth 100 times $\frac{1}{60}$ of $1, which is 1.66\frac{2}{3}$, from which if we subtract $1, the remainder will be the premium. Therefore, if American currency be at a discount of 40 per cent., the premium on gold would be 66$\frac{2}{3}$ per cent. Hence we deduce the following

RULE.

Divide 100 *cents by the number denoting the gold value of* $1, *American currency, and the quotient will be the value, in American currency, of* $1 *in gold, from which subtract* $1, *and the remainder will be the premium.*

CASE IV.

To find the value in American currency of any given amount of gold.

EXAMPLE.

What is the value of $200 of gold, in American currency, gold being quoted at 150 ?

SOLUTION.

When gold is quoted at 150, it requires 150 cents, in American currency, to equal in value $1 in gold. Now, if $1 in gold be worth $1.50 in American currency, $200 will be worth 200 times $1.50, which is $300. Hence the

RULE.

Multiply the value of $1 by the number denoting the amount of gold to be changed, and the product will be the value in American currency; or

To the given sum add the premium on itself at the given rate, and the result will be the value in American currency.

EXERCISES.

1 If American currency is at a discount of 50 per cent., what is the value of $450? Ans. $225.

2. The quotation of gold is 140, what is the discount on American currency? Ans. $28\frac{4}{7}$ per cent.

3. A person exchanged $750, American money, at a discount of 35 per cent. for gold; how much did he receive? Ans. $427.50.

4. Purchased a draft on Montreal, Canada East, for $1500 at a premium of $64\frac{7}{8}$ per cent.; what did it cost me? Ans.

5. If American currency is quoted at $33\frac{1}{3}$ per cent. discount; what is the premium on gold? Ans. 50 per cent.

6. Purchased a suit of clothes in Toronto, Canada West, for $35, but on paying for the same in American funds, the tailor charged me 32 per cent. discount; how much had I to pay him? Ans. $51.47.

7. What would be the difference between the quotations of gold, if greenbacks were selling at 40 and 60 per cent. discount? Ans. $83\frac{1}{3}$ per cent.

8. P. Y. Smith borrowed from C. R. King, $27 in gold, and wished to repay him in American currency, at a discount of 38 per cent.; how much did it require? Ans. $43.55.

9. J. E. Pekham bought of Sidney Leonard a horse and cutter for $315.50, American currency, but only having $200 of this sum, he paid the balance in gold, at a premium of 65 per cent.; how much did it require? Ans. $70.

10. A cattle drover purchased of a farmer a yoke of oxen valued at $135 in gold, but paid him $112 in American currency, at a discount of $27\frac{1}{2}$ per cent.; how much gold did it require to pay the balance? Ans. $53.80.

11. W. H. Hounsfield & Co., of Toronto, Canada West, purchased in New York City, merchandise amounting in value to $4798.40, on 3 months' credit, premium on gold being $79\frac{3}{8}$ per cent. At the

expiration of the three months they purchased a draft on Adams, Kimball and Moore, of New York, for the amount due, at a discount of 57¾ per cent.; what was the gain by exchange? Ans. $647.75.

12. A makes an exchange of a horse for a carriage with B; the horse being valued at $127.50, in gold, and the carriage at $210, American currency. Gold being at a premium of 65 per cent.; what was the difference, and by whom payable?

Ans. B pays A 23 cents in gold, or 37 cents in greenbacks.

13. A merchant takes $63 in American silver to a broker, and wishes to obtain for the same greenbacks which are selling at a discount of 30 per cent. The broker takes the silver at 3½ per cent. discount; what amount of American currency does the merchant receive? Ans. $86.85.

14. I bought the following goods, as per invoice, from John McDonald & Co., of Montreal, Canada East, on a credit of 3 months:

1120½ yards	Canadian Tweed at..............	95 cents per yard.
2190 "	long-wool red flannel at...........	60 " " "
3400 "	" white flannel at.........	55 " " "

Paid custom house duties, 30 per cent.; also paid for freight, $37.40. Gold at time of purchase was at a premium of 63¾ per cent.; what shall I mark each piece at per yard to make a net gain of 20 per cent. on full cost?

Ans. C. tweed, $2.44; red flannel, $1.54; white flannel, $1.41.

15. A merchant left Toronto, Canada West, for New York City to purchase his stock of spring goods, taking with him to defray expenses $95 in gold. After purchasing his ticket to the Suspension Bridge for $2.40, he expended the balance in greenbacks, which were at a discount of 41½ per cent. When in New York he drew from this amount $23.85 to "square" an old account then past due. On arriving home he found that he still had in greenbacks $16.40, which he disposed of at a discount of 43¾ per cent., receiving in payment American silver at a discount of 3½ per cent., which he passed off at 2½ per cent. discount for gold. What were his expenses in gold; the actual amount in greenbacks paid for expenses, and the amount of silver received?

Ans. Total expenses in gold, $71.76; expenses in greenbacks, $118.04; silver received, $9.53.

EXCHANGE WITH GREAT BRITAIN.

In Britain money is reckoned by pounds, shillings and pence, and fractions of a penny, and is called *Sterling money*, the gold sovereign or the pound sterling, consisting of 22 parts gold and 2 alloy, being the standard, and the shilling, one-twentieth part of the pound, a silver coin of 37 parts silver and 3 copper, and the penny, one-twelfth part of the shilling, a copper coin, the ingredients and size of which have frequently been altered.

The comparative value of the gold sovereign in the United States previous to the year 1834 was $\$4.44\frac{4}{9}$, but by Act of Congress passed in that year it was made a legal tender at the rate of $94\frac{8}{10}$ cents per pennyweight, because the old standard was less than the intrinsic value and also because the commercial value, though fluctuating, was always considerably higher. Hence, the full weight of the sovereign being 5 dwts. 3.274 grs., it was made equivalent to 4 dollars and $86\frac{2}{3}$ cents. The increase in the standard value was, therefore, equal to $9\frac{1}{2}$ per cent. of its nominal value.

The real par of exchange between two countries is that by which an ounce of gold in one country can be replaced by an ounce of gold of equal fineness in the other country.

If the course of exchange at New York on London were $108\frac{1}{2}$ per cent.; and the par of exchange between England and America $109\frac{1}{2}$ per cent., it follows that the exchange is 100 per cent. against England; but the quoted exchange at New York being for bills at 60 days sight, the interest must be deducted from the above difference.

The general form for the quotation of exchange with England is: 108, $108\frac{1}{2}$, 109, $109\frac{1}{2}$ &c., which indicates that it is at 8, $8\frac{1}{2}$, 9, or $9\frac{1}{2}$ per cent. premium on its nominal value.

EXAMPLE.

What amount of decimal money will be required to purchase a draft on London for £648 17s. 6d. ?—exchange 108.

The old par value or nominal value is $\$4.44\frac{4}{9}=\frac{40}{9}=\frac{1}{9}$ of $40 by reducing to an improper fraction. Now, the quotation is 108, or 8 per cent. above the nominal value, we find the premium on $40 at 8 per cent., which is $3.20, which added to $40 will give $43.20, and $43.20÷9=$4.80 to be remitted for every pound sterling, and therefore £648 17s. 6d. multiplied by 4.80 or 4.8 will be the value in our money. 17s. 6d.=.875 of a pound, and the operation is as follows:

```
  £648,875
       4.8
  --------
   5191000
  2595500
  --------
 $3114.6000
```

RULE.

To $40 add the premium on itself at the quoted rate, multiply the sum by the number representing the amount of sterling money, and divide the result by 9, the quotient will be the equivalent of the sterling money in dollars and cents.

NOTE.—If there be shillings, pence, &c., in the sterling money, they are to be reduced to the decimal of £1.

To find the value of decimal money in sterling money, at any given rate above par.

Let it be required to find the value of $465 in sterling money, at 8 per cent above its nominal value. Here we have exactly the converse of the last problem, and therefore, having found the value of £1 sterling, we divide the given sum instead of multiplying; thus the premium on $40, at 8 per cent., is $3.20, which added to $40 makes $43.20, and 43.20÷9=4.80, and $465÷4.80=£96.17.6.

RULE.

Divide the given sum by the number denoting the value of one pound sterling at the given rate above par, and if there be a decimal remaining reduce it to shillings and pence.

EXERCISES.

1. When sterling exchange is quoted at 108, what is the value of £1? Ans. $4.80.

2. If £1 sterling be worth $\$4.84\frac{4}{9}$, what is the premium of exchange between London and America. Ans. 9 per cent.

3. At 10 per cent. above its nominal value, what is the worth of £50 sterling, in decimal currency? Ans. $244.44.

4. When sterling exchange is quoted at $9\frac{1}{4}$ per cent. premium, what is the value of $1000? Ans. £205 18s. $11\frac{3}{4}$d.

5. At 12 per cent. above its nominal value, what will a bill for £1800 cost in dollars and cents? Ans. $8960.

6. A merchant sold a bill of exchange on London for £7000, at an advance of 11 per cent; what did he receive for it more than its real value? Ans. $\$466.66\frac{2}{3}$.

7. Bought a bill on London for £1266 15s. at $9\frac{1}{2}$ per cent. premium; what shall I have to pay for it? Ans. $6164.85.

8. A merchant sells a bill on London for £4000, at 8 per cent. above its nominal value, instead of importing specie at an expense of 2 per cent.; what does he save? Ans. $\$122.66\frac{2}{3}$.

9. A merchant in Kingston paid $7300 for a draft of £1500 on Liverpool; at what per cent. of premium was it purchased?

Ans. $9\frac{1}{2}$.

10. Exchange on London can be purchased in Detroit at $108\frac{1}{2}$; in New York at $108\frac{1}{4}$. At which place would it be the most advantageous to purchase a bill for £358 14s. 9d., supposing the N.Y. broker charges $\frac{1}{4}$ per cent. commission for investing and gold drafts on New York are at a premium of $\frac{3}{8}$ per cent.

Ans., Detroit by $6.82.

11. A broker sold a bill of exchange for £2000, on commission, at 10 per cent. above its nominal value receiving a commission of $\frac{1}{10}$ per cent. on the real value, and 5 per cent. on what he obtained for the bill above its real value; what was his commission?

Ans. $\$11.95\frac{5}{9}$.

12. I owe A. N. McDonald & Co., of Liverpool, $7218, net proceeds of sales of merchandise effected for them, which I am to remit them in a bill of exchange on London for such amount as will close the transaction, less $\frac{1}{4}$ per cent. on the face of the bill for my commission for investing. Bills on London are at 8 per cent. premium. Required the amount of the bill, in sterling money, to be remitted.

Ans. £1500.

TABLE OF FOREIGN MONEYS.

Cities and Countries.	Denominations of Money.	Value.
London, Liverpool, &c.	12 pence=1 shilling; 20 shillings =1 pound.....................=	4.86\frac{2}{3}$
Paris, Havre, &c........	100 centimes=1 franc...........=	.18$\frac{3}{5}$
Amsterdam, Hague, &c.	100 cents=1 guilder or florin...=	.40
Bremen	5 swares=1 grote; 72 grotes=1 *rix dollar*.......................=	.78$\frac{3}{4}$
Hamburg, Lubec, &c...	12 pfennings=1 schilling; 16s.= 1 *mark banco*.................=	.35
Berlin, Dantzic..........	12 pfennings=1 groschen; 30 gro. =1 thaler.........................=	.69
Belgium..................	100 centimes=1 franc...........=	.18$\frac{3}{5}$
St. Petersburg..........	100 kopecks=1 ruble............=	.75
Stockholm	12 rundstycks=16 skillings; 48s. =1 *rix dollar specie* ....=	1.06
Copenhagen.............	16 skillings=1 mark; 6 m.=1 *rix dollar*..........................=	1.05
Vienna, Trieste, &c....	60 kreutzers=1 florin...........=	.48$\frac{1}{2}$
Naples	10 grani=1 carlino; 10 car.=1 *ducat*...........................=	.80
Venice, Milan, &c......	100 centesimi=1 *lira*...........=	.16
Florence, Leghorn, &c.	100 centesimi=1 *lira*...........=	.16
Genoa, Turin, &c......	100 centesimi=1 *lira*...........=	.18$\frac{3}{5}$
Sicily.....................	20 grani=1 taro; 30 tari=1 oz.=	2.40
Portugal.................	1000 reas=1 millrea............=	1.12
Spain.....................	34 maravedis=1 *real vellon*=	.05
	68 maravedis=1 *real plate*..=	.10
Constantinople	100 aspers=1 *piaster*.... ....=	.05
British India...........	12 pice=1 anna; 16 annas=1 *rupee*..............................=	.44$\frac{1}{2}$
Canton...................	100 candarines=1 mace; 10 m.= 1 *tael*...........................=	1.48
Mexico	8 rials=1 *dollar*.................=	1.00
Monte Video............	100 centesimas=1 rial; 8 rials=1 *dollar*...........................=	.83$\frac{3}{10}$
Brazil....................	1000 reas=1 *milrea*............=	.82$\frac{4}{5}$
Cuba......................	8 reals plate or 20 reals vellon=1 *dollar*..........................=	1.00
Turkey...................	100 aspers=1 *piaster*..........=	.05
United States...........	10 mills=1 cent; 10 cents=1 dime; 10 dimes=1 *dollar*....=	variable.
New Brunswick......... Nova Scotia............ Newfoundland.........	4 farthings=1 penny; 12 pence =1 shilling; 20 shillings=1 pound.*..................=	4.00

* The Government of New Brunswick now issues postage stamps in the decimal currency, but so for as we have been able to ascertain, the currency of

ARBITRATION OF EXCHANGE.

Arbitration of Exchange is the method of finding the rate of exchange between two countries through the intervention of one or more other countries. The object of this is to ascertain what is the most advantageous channel through which to remit money to a foreign country.

Three things have here to be considered. *First*, what is the most secure channel; *secondly*, what is the least expensive, and *thirdly*, the comparative value of the currencies of the different countries. Regarding the two first considerations no general rule can be given, as there must necessarily be a continual fluctuation arising from political and other causes. We are therefore compelled to confine our calculation to the third, viz., the comparative value of the coin current of different countries.

For this purpose we shall investigate a rule, and append tables.

Let us suppose an English merchant in London wishes to remit money to Paris, and finds that owing to certain international relations, he can best do it through Hamburg and Amsterdam, and that the exchange of London on Hamburg is 13½ marcs per pound sterling; that of Hamburg on Amsterdam, 40 marcs for 36¼ florins, and that of Amsterdam on Paris, 56¾ florins for 120 francs, and thus the question is to find the rate of exchange between London and Paris.

SOLUTION:

We write down the equivalents in ranks, the equivalent of the first term being placed to the right of it, and the other pairs below them in a similar order. Hence the first term of any pair will be of the same kind as the second term of the preceding pair. As the answer is to be the equivalent of the first term, the first term in the last rank corresponds to the third term of an analogy, and is therefore a multiplier, it must be placed below the second rank. The

these three Provinces is, as usual, in pounds, shillings and pence. It is to be hoped that when the Confederation of the British Provinces takes place, the decimal currency will be speedily adopted in the Lower Provinces, and that the efforts now being made in Britain to adapt the same currency will prove successful.

terms being thus arranged, we divide the product of the second rank by that of the first, and the quotient will be the equivalent, as exhibited below:

£1 sterling = $13\frac{1}{2}$ marcs.
40 marcs = $36\frac{1}{4}$ florins.
$56\frac{3}{4}$ florins = 120 francs
£1 stg.

As it is most convenient to express the fractions decimally, we have

$$\frac{13.5 \times 36.25 \times 120 \times 1}{1 \times 40 \times 56.75} = 25.87 \text{ francs.}$$

The foregoing explanations may be condensed into the form of a

RULE.

Write down the first term, and its equivalent to the right of it, and the other pairs in the same order, the odd term being placed under the second rank, and then divide the product of the second rank by the product of the first, the quotient will be the required equivalent.

NOTE.—The true principle on which this operation is founded, is that each pair consists of the antecedent and consequent which are to each other in the ratio of equality IN POINT OF INTRINSIC VALUE, though not in regard to THE NUMBERS BY WHICH THEY ARE EXPRESSED, and therefore the required term and its equivalent must have the same relation to each other, that is, they will be an antecedent and a consequent in the ratio of equality as regards their *value*, but not as regards the *numbers* by which they are expressed.

EXERCISES.

1. If the exchange of London on Paris is 28 francs per pound sterling, and that of America on Paris 18 cents per franc; what is the rate of exchange of America on London, through Paris?

Ans. $5.04 per £ sterling.

2. If exchange between New York and London is at 8 per cent. premium, and between London and Paris $25\frac{1}{4}$ francs per pound sterling; what sum in New York is equal to 7000 francs in Paris?

3. When exchange between Portland and Hamburg is at 34 cents per mark banco, and between Hamburg and St. Petersburg is 2 marks, 8 schillings per ruble; how much must be paid in St. Petersburg for a draft on Portland for $650?

Ans. 764 rubles, $70\frac{10}{17}$ kopecks.

4. If a merchant buys a bill in London, drawn on Paris, at the rate of 25.87 francs per pound sterling, and if this bill be sold in Amsterdam at 120 francs for $56\frac{3}{4}$ florins, and the proceeds be invested in a bill on Hamburg, at the rate of $36\frac{1}{4}$ florins for 40 marcs; what is the rate of exahange between London and Hamburg, or what is £1 sterling worth in Hamburg? Ans. 13.449+marcs.

5. A merchant of St. Louis wishes to pay a debt of $5000 in New York; the direct exchange is $1\frac{1}{2}$ per cent. in favour of New York, but on New Orleans it is $\frac{1}{2}$ per cent. discount, and between New Orleans and New York at a $\frac{1}{4}$ per cent. premium; how much would be saved by the circular exchange compared with the direct? Ans. $87.56.

6. A merchant in Detroit wishes to remit to J. B. Gladstone & Co., of London, £3600 sterling. Exchange on London, in Detroit, is at a premium of 10 per cent. Exchange on London can be obtained at New York for 9 per cent. premium. If Detroit bills on New York are at a discount of $\frac{1}{4}$ per cent., and the merchant remits a draft to New York, and pays his agent $\frac{1}{2}$ per cent. for investing it in bills on London; what will he gain over the direct exchange? Ans. $123.80.

7. A merchant in London remits to Amsterdam £1000, at the rate of 18 pence per guilder, directing his correspondent at Amsterdam to remit the same to Paris at 2 francs, 10 centimes per guilder, less $\frac{1}{2}$ per cent. for his commission; but the exchange between Amsterdam and Paris happened to be, at the time the order was received, at 2 francs, 20 centimes per guilder. The merchant at London, not apprised of this, drew upon Paris at 25 francs per pound sterling. Did he gain or lose, and how much per cent.? Ans. $16\frac{56}{75}$ per cent. gain.

MIXED EXERCISES IN EXCHANGE.

1. When gold is quoted at 150 per cent. premium; what is the reason greenbacks are not at a discount of 50 per cent.?

2. Bar gold in London is 77s. 9d. per ounce standard; required, the arbitrated rate of exchange produced by its import to this country for coinage, at the rate of $232\frac{1}{6}$ grains of fine gold for the eagle of 10 dollars.

3. What sum in decimal money must I pay for a bill on London of £76 14s. 1d., exchange being $9\frac{1}{2}$ per cent. premium, and the broker's commission for negotiating the bill being $\frac{1}{2}$ per cent.?

4. A merchant shipped 2560 barrels of flour to his agent in Liverpool, who sold it at £1 8s. 6d. per barrel, and charged 2 per cent. commission; what was the net amount of the flour in decimal money, allowing exchange to be at a premium of 8 per cent.?

Ans. $17160.19.

5. What is the cost of a 30 days' bill on Montreal, at $\frac{1}{2}$ per cent. premium, the face of the bill being $1500? Ans. $1507.50.

6. What must be the face of a 60 days' draft on New Orleans to yield $1641.75, when sold at a discount of $\frac{1}{2}$ per cent.?

Ans. $1650.

7. What is the cost of a 30 days' bill on Chicago, at $\frac{3}{8}$ per cent. premium, and interest off at 6 per cent.; the face of the bill being $9256.40?* Ans. $9240.20.

8. A merchant paid $14400.12 for a bill on Havre for $79000 francs; how much was exchange below par? Ans. 2 per cent.

9. I have in possession the net proceeds of a sale of cotton amounting to $3765, which my correspondent desires me to remit to him in New Orleans; exchange on New Orleans is at a discount of $2\frac{1}{2}$ per cent., and I invest the whole in a draft at that rate, which I remit to him; what is the face of the draft? Ans. $3861.54.

10. The proceeds of a sale of goods, consigned to me from Bremen, is $2764.67, on which I am to charge a commission of 10 per cent., and remit the balance to my consignor in such a way as shall be most advantageous to him. Exchange on Paris can be had at 92 cents per 5 francs, and in Paris exchange on Bremen is 17 francs to 4 thalers. Exchange on Liverpool can be had a 9 per cent. premium, and in Liverpool exchange on Bremen is 6 thalers to the pound sterling. Direct exchange is $80\frac{1}{4}$ cents per thaler. Which course will be the best, allowing $\frac{1}{2}$ per cent. brokerage to correspondents both in Liverpool and Paris? Ans. By way of Paris.

11. A, of Buffalo, sent articles to the World's Fair in London, which were afterwards sold by B, of London, on A's account, net proceeds £1266 15s. sterling. B was instructed to invest this amount in bills on New York, and remit to A, which was accordingly done. B charged $\frac{1}{4}$ per cent. brokerage on the face of the bills for investing, and purchased the bills at 7 per cent. discount. Required

*When there is interest to be computed, it must be reckoned on the face of the bill or draft. When other than the value or cost of the bill is to be found, proceed as in percentage.

the amount of the bill A must receive in dollars and cents to close the transaction. Ans. $6037.53 nearly.

12. A merchant in Boston having to remit £434 15s. to Liverpool, wishes to know which is the most profitable, to buy a set of exchange on Liverpool at $10\frac{1}{2}$ per cent. premium, or send it by way of France; exchange on the latter place being $19\frac{3}{4}$ cents per franc, and exchange on Liverpool can be bought in France at the rate of $24\frac{1}{2}$ francs per pound sterling, and he has to pay his correspondent in France $\frac{3}{4}$ of 1 per cent. for purchasing the bill on Liverpool.

Ans. By way of France, $15.69.

13. John DcDonald & Co., of Toronto, Canada West, wish to remit to a creditor in London £1241 15s. 9d. Exchange on London can be bought in Toronto at $109\frac{3}{4}$, but Exchange on London can be purchased in New York for gold at $108\frac{1}{2}$. In New York it takes $1.85 greenbacks to equal $1 in gold. The broker in New York charges $\frac{3}{4}$ per cent. on the greenback value for investing. If Exchange on New York is at 47 per cent. discount, at which place would it be the most advantageous to purchase, and how much gain, and if the remittance be made by way of New York, what would be the face of the draft?

Ans. New York by $141.72; face of draft, $11161.21.

14. Find the arbitrated rate of exchange between London and Amsterdam when the exchange of London on Madrid is 37 pence for one dollar of plate, and that of Amsterdam on Madrid is 100 florins, 75 cents, for 40 ducats of plate.

15. Hughes Bros. & Co., purchase of E. Chaffey & Co., a sterling bill at 60 days on Gladstone & Hart, of London, for £3956 10s. They remit this bill to James Alder, in London, where it is accepted by Gladstone & Hart, and falls due on the 20th November, at which time it is protested causing an expense of £2 19s. Gladstone & Hart having failed, E. Chaffey & Co.'s agent in London pays James Alder on the 20th November, £2000 on account. How much must E. Chaffey & Co., pay to Hughes, Brothers & Co., on the 24th December, to cover the amount still due in London, allowing interest at the rate of 10 per cent. from November 20th, to the maturity of a 60 days' bill at date of 24th December, and $\frac{1}{4}$ of 1 per cent. commission for their trouble in negociating a new bill? Ans. $9815.91.

INVOLUTION.

Involution is the process of finding a given power of a given number.

We have noted already, under the head of multiplication, that the product of any number of equal factors is called the second, third, fourth, &c., power of the number, according as the factor is taken two, three, four, &c., times. Thus: $9=3\times3$ is the second power of 3; $27=3\times3\times3$ is the third power of three; $81=3\times3\times3\times3$ is the fourth power of 3. These are often written thus: 3^2, 3^3, 3^4, &c. The small figures, 2, 3, 4, indicate the number of factors, and therefore each is called the *index* or *exponent* of the power. Hence to find any required power of a given quantity, we have the

RULE.

Multiply the quantity continually by itself until it has been used as a factor as often as there are units in the index.

Since the first multiplication exhausts two factors, the number of operations will be *one* less than the number of factors.

Involution, then, is nothing more than multiplication, and for any power above the second, it is a case of continual multiplication. For the sake of uniformity the original quantity is called the *first power*, and also the root in relation to higher powers. Again, if we multiply 3×3 by $3\times3\times3$, we have five factors, or $3\times3\times3\times3\times3$, but this being an inconvenient form, it is written briefly 3^5, the 5 indicating the number of times that 3 is to be repeated as a factor. Hence, since 3×3 is written 3^2, and $3\times3\times3$ is written 3^3, it follows that $3^2\times3^3=3^5$, and therefore we may multiply quantities so expressed by *adding their indices*, and so also we may divide such quantities by *subtracting the index of the divisor from that of the dividend.* For example $3^3\div3^2=3$ or 3^1. If we divide 3^1 by 3^1 by subtracting the index of the divisor from that of the dividend, we obtain 3^0, but 3 or 3^1 divided by 3 or 3^1 is equal to 1, and therefore any quantity with an index *zero* is equal to unity.

When high powers are to be found, the operation may be shortened in the following manner:—Let it be required to find the sixteenth power of 2. We first find the second power of 2, which is 4, then $4\times4=16$, which is the fourth power, and $16\times16=256$, the eighth power, and $256\times256=65536$, the sixteenth power. If we wished to find the nineteenth power, we should only have to multiply the last result by 8, which is the third power of 2, for $2^{16}\times2^{3}=2^{19}$.

EXERCISES.

1. Find the second power of 697. Ans. 485809.
2. What is the third power of 854? Ans. 622835864.
3. What is the second power of 4.367? Ans. 19.070689.
4. Find the fourth power of 75. Ans. 31640625.
5. What is the sixth power of 1.12? Ans. 1.9738+.
6. What is the second power $.\dot{7}$, correct to six places? Ans. .060893+.
7. What is the fifth power of 4? Ans. 1024.
8. Find the third power of $.\dot{3}$ to three places? Ans. .036963.
9. What is the third power of $\frac{7}{9}$? Ans. $\frac{343}{729}$.
10. What is the fifteenth power of 1.04?* Ans. 1.800943.
11. Raise 1.05 to the thirty-first power. Ans. 4.538039.
12. What is the eighth power of $\frac{3}{5}$? Ans. $\frac{6561}{390625}$.
13. What is the second power of $4\frac{7}{8}$? Ans. $23\frac{49}{64}$.
14. Expand the expression 6^5. Ans. .7776.
15. What is the second power of $5\frac{1}{2}$? Ans. $\frac{121}{4}=30\frac{1}{4}$.
16. What part of 8^3 is 2^6? Ans. $\frac{1}{8}$.
17. What is the difference between 5^6 and 4^6? Ans. 11529.
18. Expand $3^5\times2^4$. Ans. 3888.
19. Express, with a single index, $47^3\times47^5\times47^6$? Ans. 47^{14}.
20. How many acres are in a square lot, each side of which is 135 rods? Ans. 113 acres, 3 roods, 25 rods.
21. What is the sixth power of .1? Ans. .000001.
22. What is the fourth power of .03? Ans. .00000081.
23. What is the fifth power of 1.05? Ans. .1.2762815625.
24. What is the third power of .001? Ans. .000000001.
25. What is the second power of $.\dot{0}04\dot{4}$? Ans. .00001836.

The second power of any number ending with the digit 5 may be readily found by taking all the figures except the 5, and multi-

* This exercise will be most readily worked by finding the sixteenth power, and dividing by 1.04. So in the next exercise, find the thirty-second power, and divide by 1.05. A still more easy mode of working such questions will be found under the head of logarithms.

plying that by itself, increased by a unit, and annexing 25 to the result.

Thus, to find the second power of 15, cut off the 5, and 1 remains, and this increased by 1 gives 2, and $2\times1=2$, and 25 annexed will give 225, the second power of 15. So also,

2,5	3,5	6,5	10,5	21,5	57,5
3	4	7	11	22	58
625	1225	4225	11025	46225	330625

EXERCISES ON THIS METHOD.

26. What is the second power of 135? Ans. 18225.
27. What is the second power of 205? Ans. 42025.
28. What is the second power of 335? Ans. 112225.
29. What is the second power of 455? Ans. 207025.
30. What is the second power of 585? Ans. 342225.
31. What is the second power of 795? Ans. 632025.

NOTE.—The square root of any quantity ending in 9, must end in either 3 or 7.

No second power can end in 8, 7, 3 or 2.

The second root of any quantity ending in 6, must end in 4 or 6.

The second root of any quantity ending in 5, must end also in 5.

The second root of any quantity ending in 4, must end either in 8 or 2.

The second root of any quantity ending in 1, must end either in 1 or 9.

The second root of any quantity ending in 0, must also end in 0.

EVOLUTION.

The root of any quantity is a number such that when repeated, as a factor, the specified number of times, will produce that quantity. Thus, 3 repeated twice as a factor gives 9, and therefore 3 is called the *second root* of 9, while 3 taken *three times* as a factor will give 27, and therefore 3 is called the *third root* of 27, and so also it is called the *fourth root* of 81.

There are two ways of indicating this. First, by the mark $\sqrt{}$ which is merely a modified form of the letter r, the initial letter of the English word root, and the Latin word *radix* (root). When no mark is attached, the simple quantity or *first root* is indicated. When the *second root* is meant, the mark $\sqrt{}$ alone is placed before the quantity, but if the third, fourth, &c., roots are to be indicated, the figures 3, 4, &c., are written in the angular space. Thus: $3=\sqrt{9}=\sqrt[3]{27}=\sqrt[4]{81}=\sqrt[5]{243}$, &c., &c. The other method is to write the index as a fraction. Thus, $9^{\frac{1}{2}}$ means the second root of the first power of 9, *i. e.* 3. So also, $27^{\frac{1}{3}}$ is the third root of the first power of 27. In the same manner $64^{\frac{2}{3}}$ means the third root of the second power of 64, or the second power of the third root of 64. Now the third root of 64 is 4, and the second power of 4 is 16, or the second power of 64 is 4096, and the third root of 4096 is 16, so that both views give the same result.

Evolution is the process of finding any required root of a given quantity.

SECOND OR SQUARE ROOT.

Extracting the square or second root of any number, is the finding of a number which, when multiplied by itself, will produce that number.

To find the second root, or square root of any quantity.

By inspecting the table of second powers, it will be found that the second power of any whole number less than 10, consists of either *one* or *two* digits; the second power of any number greater than 9, and less than 100, will in like manner be found to consist of *three* or *four* digits; and, universally, the second power of any number will consist of either *twice* the number of digits, or *one less than twice* the number of digits that the root itself consists of. Hence, if we begin at the units' figure, and mark off the given number in periods of two figures each, we shall find that the number of digits contained in the root will be the same as the number of periods. If the number of digits is even, each period will consist of two figures, but if the number of digits be odd, the last period to the left will consist of only one figure.

Let it now be required to find the second root of 144. We know by the rule of involution that 144 is the second power of 12. Now 12 may be resolved into *one ten* and *two units*, or 10+2, and 10+2 multiplied by itself, as in the margin, gives 100+40+4, and since 100 is the second power of 10, and 4 the second power of 2, and 40 is twice the product of 10 and 2, we conclude that the second power of any number thus resolved is equal to the sum of the second powers of the parts, *plus* twice the product of the parts. Hence to find the second root of 144, let us resolve it into the three parts 100+40+4, and we find that the second root of the first part is 10, and since 40 is twice the product of the parts, 40 divided by twice 10 or 20 will give the other part 2, and 10+2=12, the second root of 144. We should find the same result by resolving 12 into 11+1, or 9+3, or 8+4, or 7+5, or 6+6, but the most convenient mode is to resolve into the tens and the units.

```
10+2
10+2
--------
100+20
     20+4
----------
100+40+4
```

In the same manner, if it be required to find the second root of 1369, we have by resolution 900+420+49, of which 900 is the second power of 30, and 30×2=60, and 420÷60=7, the second part of the root, and 30+7=37, the whole root.

Again, let it be required to find the second root of 15129. This may be resolved as below:

10000 is the second power of 100.
400 is the second power of 20.
9 is the second power of 3.
4000 is twice the product of 20 and 100.
600 is twice the product of 100 and 3.
120 is twice the product of 20 and 3.

15129 is the sum of all, and hence 1 is the root of the hundreds, 2 the root of the tens, and 3 the root of the units.

Generalizing these investigations, we find that the second power of a number consisting of *units alone* is the product of that number by itself; that the second power of a number consisting of *tens and units* is the second power of the *tens*, *plus* the second power of the units, *plus* twice the product of the tens and units; that the second power of a number, consisting of hundreds, tens and units, is the sum of the squares of the hundreds, the tens, and the units, *plus* twice the product of each pair. Now since the complement of the full second power, to the sum of the second powers of the parts, is twice the product of the parts, it follows that, when the first figure of the root has been found, it must be doubled before used as a divisor to find the second term, and for the same reason each figure, when found, must be doubled to give correctly the next divisor. Hence the

RULE.

Beginning at the units' figure, mark off the whole line in periods of two figures each; find the greatest power contained in the left hand period, and subtract it from that period; to the remainder annex the next period; for a new dividend, place the figure thus obtained as a quotient, and its double as a divisor, and find how often that quantity is contained in the second partial dividend, omitting the last figure; annex the figure thus found to both divisor and quotient, multiply and subtract as in common division, and to the remainder annex the next period; double the last obtained figure of the divisor, and proceed as before till all the periods are exhausted,—if there be a remainder, annex to it two ciphers, and the figure thence obtained will be a decimal, as will every figure thereafter obtained.

EXAMPLES.

1. To find the second root of 797449.

First, commencing with the units' figure, we divide the line into periods, viz., 49, 74 and 79,—we then note that the greatest square contained in 79 is 64,—this we subtract from 79, and find 15 remaining, to which we annex the next period 74, and place 8, the second root of 64, in the quotient, and its double 16 as a divisor, and try how often 16 is contained in 157, which we find to be 9 times; placing the 9 in both divisor and quotient, we multiply and subtract as in common division, and find a remainder of 53, to which we annex the last period 49, and proceeding as before, we find 3, the last figure of the root, without remainder, and now we have the complete root 893.

8	797449	893
	64	
169	1574	
1783	1521	
	5349	
	5349	

2. This operation may be illustrated as follows:

To find the second root of 273529.

500	273529	500+20+3=523
500×2=1000+20, or	250000	
1020	23529	
1000+2×20+3=1043	20400	
	3129	
	3129	

3. To find the second root of 153687.

Here we obtain, by the same process as in the last example, the whole number 392, with a remainder of 23, which can produce only a fraction.

```
3       | 153687| 392.029+
        |  9    |
        |-------|
69      |  636  |
782     |  621  |
        |-------|
        |  1587 |
78402   |  1564 |
        |----------
784049  |    230000
             156804
             -------
              7319600
              7056441
              -------
               263159
```

We now annex two ciphers, placing the decimal point after the root already found, but as the divisor is not contained in this new dividend, we place a cipher in both quotient and divisor, and annex two ciphers more to the dividend, and by continuing this process we find the decimal part of the root, and the whole root is 392.029+.

EXERCISES.

1. What is the second root of 279841? Ans. 529.
2. What is the second root of 74684164? Ans. 8642.
3. What is the second root of 459684? Ans. 678.
4. What is the second root of 785? Ans. 28.01785+.
5. What is the second root of 1728? Ans. 41.569219+.
6. What is the second root of 666? Ans. 25.8069+.
7. What is the second root of 123456789? Ans. 11111.11106+.
8. What is the second root of 5 to three places? Ans. 2.236.
9. What is the side of a square whose area is 19044 square feet? Ans. 138 feet.
10. What is the length of each side of a square field containing 893025 square rods? Ans. 945 linear rods.

The second root of a fraction is found by extracting the roots of its terms, for $\frac{16}{25}=\frac{4}{5}\times\frac{4}{5}$ and therefore $\sqrt{\frac{16}{25}}=\sqrt{\frac{4}{5}\times\frac{4}{5}}=\frac{4}{5}$. So also, $\sqrt{\frac{49}{81}}=\frac{7}{9}$. Again, since $\sqrt{\frac{81}{100}}=\frac{9}{10}=.09$, and $.3\times.3=.09$, the second root of .09 is .3. This follows from the rules laid down for the multiplication of decimals.

To find the second root of a decimal or of a whole number and a decimal:

Point off periods of two figures each from the decimal point towards the right and left, adding a cipher, or a repetend, if the number of figures be odd.

From what has been said, it is plain that every period, except the first on the left, must consist of two digits, and every decimal presupposes something going before, for .5 indicates the half of some unit under consideration, and .5 is equivalent to .50, *and not to* .05, from which it is obvious that the second root of .5 is not the root of .05, but of .50, and therefore the second root of .5 is not .2+, as the beginner would naturally suppose, but .7+, for .2+ is the approximate root of .05.

ADDITIONAL EXERCISES.

11. What is the second root of .7 to five places of decimals? Ans. .83666.
12. Find the second root of .07 to six places. Ans. 264575.
13. What is the second root of .05? Ans. .2236+.
14. What is the second root of $.\dot{7}$? Ans. .8819+.
15. Find the second root of $.\dot{5}$. Ans. .74535+.
16. What is the second root of .1? Ans. .3162277+.
17. What is the second root of $.\dot{1}$? Ans. $.\dot{3}$.
18. What is the second root of 1.375? Ans. 1.1726, &c.*
19. What is the second root of .375? Ans. 61237, &c.*
20. What is the second root of 6.4? Ans. 2.52982+.
21. Find to four decimal places $\sqrt{3\frac{3}{20}}$. Ans. 1.7748.
22. Find $\sqrt{2}$ to four decimal places. Ans. 1.4142.
23. Find the value of $\sqrt{3271.4207}$. Ans. 57.196+.
24. Find the second root of .005 to five places. Ans. 07071.
25. Find the square root of 4.372594. Ans. 2.09107+.
26. What is the second root of .01? Ans. .1.
27. What is the second root of .001? Ans. 03162+.
28. What is the square root of .0001? Ans. .01.
29. What is the second root of .000001? Ans. .001.
30. What is the second root of 19.0968?

* The young student would naturally expect that the decimal figures of $\sqrt{1.375}$ and $\sqrt{.375}$ would be the same, but it is not so. If it were so, $\sqrt{1}+\sqrt{.375}$ would be equal to $\sqrt{1.375}$. That such is not the case, may be shown by a very simple example. $\sqrt{16}+\sqrt{9}=4+3=7$, but $\sqrt{16+9}=\sqrt{25}=5$. Let it be carefully observed, therefore, that *the sum of the second roots is not the same as the second root of the sum.*

OPERATION

4	$\dot{1}9.09\dot{6}\dot{8}$	4.37 trial.
83	16	4.36 true.
	309	
Trial 867	249	
	6068	
Too great by 1	6069	
True 866	6068	
	5196	
	872	

Here we find the remainder, 872, is greater than the divisor, 866, which seems inconsistent with ordinary rules; but it must be observed that we are not seeking an exact root, but only the closest possible approximation to it. If the given quantity had been 19.0969, we should have found an exact root 4.37. The remainder 872 being greater than the divisor, shows that the last figure of the root is too small by $\frac{99}{100}$, whereas 7 would be too great by $\frac{1}{100}$, and that 866 is not a correct divisor but an approximate one, and that the true root lies between 4.36 and 4.37.

When the root of any quantity can be found exactly, it is called a *perfect power* or *rational quantity*, but if the root cannot be found exactly, the quantity is called *irrational* or *surd*.

A number may be rational in regard to one root, and irrational in regard to another. Thus, 64 is rational as regards $\sqrt{64}=8$, $\sqrt[3]{64}=4$ and $\sqrt[6]{64}=2$, but it is irrational regarding any other root expressed by a whole number. But 64, with the fractional index $\frac{2}{3}$, *i. e.*, $64^{\frac{2}{3}}$, is rational, because it has an even root as already shown. We may call $64^{\frac{2}{3}}$ either the second power of the third root of 64, or the third root of the second power. In the former view, the third root of 64 is 4, and the second power of 4 is 16, and according to the second view, 64^2 is 4096, and the third root of 4096 is 16, the same as before. $\sqrt[4]{81}=3$ is rational, and $\sqrt{81}=9$ is rational, but 81 is not rational regarding any other root; while $\sqrt{25}$ is rational only regarding the second root, and $\sqrt[3]{8}=2$ only regarding the third root.

The second root of an even square may be readily found by resolving the number into its prime factors, and taking each of these factors once,—the product will be the root. Thus, 441 is $3\times3\times7\times7$ and each factor taken once is $3\times7=21$, the second root. Here let it be observed, that if we used each factor *twice* we should obtain the *second power*, but if we use each factor half the number of times that it occurs, we shall have the second root of that power. 64 is $2\times2\times2\times2\times2\times2=2^6$, *i. e.*, 2 repeated six times as a factor gives the number 64, and therefore half the number of these factors will give the second root of 64, or $2\times2\times2=8$, and $2\times2\times2$ multiplied by $2\times2\times2=8\times8=64$.

As this cannot be considered more than a trial method, though often expeditious, we would observe that the smallest possible divisors should be used in every case, and that if the number cannot be thus resolved into factors, it has no even root, and must be carried out into a line of decimals, or those decimals may be reduced to common fractions.

THIRD ROOT OR CUBE ROOT.

As extracting the second root of any quantity is the finding of what two equal factors will produce that quantity, so extracting the third root is the finding of what *three* equal factors will produce the quantity.

By inspecting the table of third powers, it will be seen that no third power has more than three digits for each digit of the first power, nor fewer than two less than three times the number of digits. Hence, if the given quantity be marked off in periods of three digits each, there will be one digit in the first power for each period in the third power. The left hand period may contain only one digit.

From the mode of finding the third power from the first, we can deduce, by the converse process, a rule for finding the first power from the third. We know by the rule of involution that the third power of 25 is 15625. If we resolve 25 into

20+5, and perform the multiplication in that form,
we have 20+5

400+100
100+25

400+200+25=$(20+5)^2$
20+5

8000+4000+500
2000+1000+125

8000+6000+1500+125=$(20+5)^3$=15625

Now, 8000 is the third power of 20, and 125 is the third power of 5; also, 6000 is three times the product of 5, and the second power of 20, and 1500 is three times the product of 20, and the second power of 5. Let a represent 20 and b represent 5, then

$$
\begin{aligned}
a^3 &= 20^3 &&= 8000\\
3a^2 b &= 3\times20^2\times5 &&= 6000\\
3ab^2 &= 3\times20\times5^2 &&= 1500\\
b^3 &= 5^3 &&= 125\\
&&& \overline{15625}
\end{aligned}
$$

By using these symbols we obtain the simplest possible method of extracting the third root of any quantity, as exhibited by the subjoined scheme:

Given quantity..........	15625
$a^3=20^3=20\times20\times20$..........=	8000
Remainder	7625
$3a^2b=3\times20^2\times5$ ....=	6000
Remainder	1625
$3ab^2=3\times20\times5^2$...............=	1500
Remainder	125
$b^3=5^3=5\times5\times5$.................=	125

From this and similar examples we see that a number denoted by more than one digit may be resolved into tens and units. Thus, 25 is 2 tens and 5 units, 123 is 12 tens and 3 units, and so of all numbers.

www.ingramcontent.com/pod-product-compliance
Lightning Source LLC
LaVergne TN
LVHW010229110826
845151LV00004B/1236

* 9 7 8 1 4 2 5 5 3 7 0 0 5 *